THE OFFICIAL
MAJOR
LEAGUE
BASEBALL
SCOREBOOK
1991

MAJOR LEAGUE BASEBALL

MAJOR LEAGUE BASEBALL PROPERTIES, INC.

Collier Books

Macmillan Publishing Company ◆ New York

PROJECT STAFF:

Cynthia A. McManus, Supervisor, Publishing, Major League Baseball Properties, Inc.
Craig Barberino, Research, Baseball Office of the Commissioner
Fred Coseglia, Research, Major League Baseball Properties, Inc.
Jeanine Bucek, Editor, Macmillan Publishing
Created and Produced by Michael Cader

Collier Books
Macmillan Publishing Company
866 Third Avenue, New York, NY 10022

Collier Macmillan Canada, Inc.
1200 Eglinton Avenue East, Suite 200
Don Mills, Ontario M3C 3N1

ISBN: 0-02-063384-X

Macmillan books are available at special discounts for bulk purchases for sales promotions, premiums, fund-raising, or educational use. For details, contact:

    Special Sales Director
    Macmillan Publishing Company
    866 Third Avenue
    New York, NY 10022

First Collier Books Edition 1991

10 9 8 7 6 5 4 3 2 1

Printed in the United States of America

◆ CONTENTS ◆

This book is specially designed to assist you in keeping a complete, personalized record of the 1991 baseball season. Starting with Spring Training and continuing on through the World Series, you will find complete schedules, listings of nationally televised games, recaps of last year's major results, and places to record your favorite team's up and downs every day of the season. It requires no special expertise, and the book has been designed so that you may record your information on a number of different levels of detail. The following sections explain exactly how to use each of the book's features.

The Daily Box Score

For every day of both spring training and the regular season, there is a box like the one shown below in which to record information. Enter the team names and final score at the top of the box. Within the box, you may either enter significant information by hand, or simply clip the box score from your newspaper and place it over the fill-in area.

Enter team names and final score here

Winning Pitcher:

Losing Pitcher:

Home Runs:

Highlights:

Score by innings:

MONDAY 8

Paste box score in here, or enter key information as listed by hand

The Schedule

The complete schedule for the week is found at the lower right-hand corner of each weekly spread. The visiting team is always listed first, and Cactus League and National League games are italicized. Please check local listings for confirmation of game times. Nationally televised CBS games are noted on the daily boxes, as are nationally televised ESPN games. In all cases, primary games (the ones you are most likely to see) are listed first. Once again, please check local listings for confirmation of this information.

The Weekly Statistics

At the end of every week, there are two pages for statistical data. The left-hand page shows the standings and the leaders in seven different statistical categories as of the corresponding Sunday in the 1990 season (except for information from Memorial Day and Labor Day weekends, which is taken as of that Monday). The top of the page notes the exact date of the statistics listed. The right-hand page provides blank spaces in which you can enter by hand, or clip from your newspaper, the same standings and statistics for the 1991 season. This way, you can tell on a week-by-week basis exactly how your team and your favorite players are doing in relationship to last year's performance. You may also use the blank spaces to follow statistical categories other than the ones listed which may be of greater interest to you.

The Blank Scorecards

At the end of the regular season listings, there are 30 blank scorecards. You can use these for scoring games on television or radio, or you can take the book to the ballpark with you. If you need more scorecards before the season is over, photocopy a blank scorecard and insert it into the book along with your other completed scorecards.

The following page tells you how to use all of the scoring symbols. There is also a scoring key on each of the scorecard pages, to remind you of the basic signs and symbols. An additional feature, Balance Your Box Score, lets you check to make sure that you have scored the game correctly.

The Post-Season

Special scorecards are provided to cover each of the League Championship Series, World Series, and All-Star games. On each of these scorecards, you will also find the box score from the corresponding game from the 1990 season for reference.

If you don't want to score the entire game, there is space in which you can note the highlights and clip the box score, as you do for regular season games.

We've also listed complete historical results for LCS, World Series and All-Star games.

Awards

The final page of the book recaps recent winners of baseball's premier annual awards and lets you complete your record of the 1991 season with places to record the coming year's winners.

Please note that all of the information in this book is current as of January 1, 1991 and is subject to change. Please check with your local team or refer to local listings for confirmation of any details.

The best part about scoring a game is that it's easy. All you need is a basic knowledge of baseball's rules. Experts use a simple code, which is based on numbering players by their positions, listed to the right.

Scoring Hits

Record the result of each player's at bat by using the symbols from the scoring key, shown at the bottom of the page. Each corner of the box represents a base, starting with the lower right-hand corner, which is first base, and moving counterclockwise around the box. For example, a walk would be denoted as W in the lower right corner of the box.

Hits are noted by drawing a diagonal line and then writing a dot next to the based reached (for a double, you draw two connected lines and place two dots in the upper right hand corner). For a home run, draw all four lines and then write HR in the middle. As the runners advance to other bases, you mark the appropriate symbols in the proper corner. Each time a runner advances safely to another base, draw a diagonal line to represent the base taken.

Runs Scored

When a runner scores, in the lower left corner write the number that represents the spot in the batting order of the player that drove him in. For instance, if the leadoff hitter doubles and scores on a single by the seond hitter, record a "2" in the lower left corner and circle it. This makes it easier to spot runs scored.

Scoring Outs

When a batter makes an out, use the number that corresponds to the defensive players involved to record the out. For instance, if a batter grounds out shortstop to first, record a "6–3" in the box. If he flies out, record a "9".

There are special symbols for strikeouts, and strikeouts by a called third strike.

Sacrifices, sacrifice flies, foul outs and double plays are also scored by special symbols. shown in the list to the right.

Special Circumstances

You will also find scoring symbols listed for stolen bases, being caught stealing, wild pitches, passed balls, being hit by the pitch, and intentional walks.

If you are ever confused about how to score a play the scoring key shown here is also reproduced on each scorecard spread.

Balancing Your Box Score

Once you are finished scoring the game, you can check all of your totals to make sure that you scored properly. Total up the left column of the balance your box score box (at-bats, bases-on-balls, hit-by-pitches, scarifice flys and interference calls that result in a run scored). Then total up the right column (runs, outs, men left on base). The two totals should be the same if you are scoring correctly.

NUMBER PLAYERS AS FOLLOWS

1—Pitcher
2—Catcher
3—First Baseman
4—Second Baseman
5—Third Baseman
6—Shortstop
7—Left Fielder
8—Center Fielder
9—Right Fielder
DH—Designated Hitter

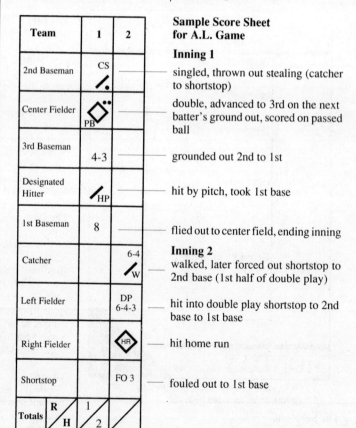

Team	1	2
2nd Baseman	CS	
Center Fielder	PB	
3rd Baseman	4-3	
Designated Hitter	HP	
1st Baseman	8	
Catcher		6-4 W
Left Fielder		DP 6-4-3
Right Fielder		HR
Shortstop		FO 3
Totals	R — H	1 — 2

Sample Score Sheet for A.L. Game

Inning 1

singled, thrown out stealing (catcher to shortstop)

double, advanced to 3rd on the next batter's ground out, scored on passed ball

grounded out 2nd to 1st

hit by pitch, took 1st base

flied out to center field, ending inning

Inning 2

walked, later forced out shortstop to 2nd base (1st half of double play)

hit into double play shortstop to 2nd base to 1st base

hit home run

fouled out to 1st base

SPRING TRAINING

GRAPEFRUIT LEAGUE—FLORIDA

Addresses are for stadiums only (team office mailing addresses will differ). Phone numbers are subject to change. Please consult local directories.

ATLANTA
Municipal Stadium
W. Palm Beach, FL 33401
(407) 683-6100

BALTIMORE
Twin Lakes Park
6700 Clark Road
Sarasota, FL 34241
(813) 923-1996

BOSTON
Chain O' Lakes Park
Winter Haven, FL 33880
(813) 293-3900

CHICAGO WHITE SOX
Ed Smith Stadium
12th and Tutle Sts.
Sarasota, FL 34237
(831) 954-5722

CINCINNATI
Plant City Stadium
1900 South Park Road
Plant City, FL 33566
(813) 752-1878

DETROIT
Marchant Stadium
1901 Lake Avenue
Lakeland, FL 33802
(813) 686-8075

HOUSTON
Osceola Stadium
1000 Osceola Blvd.
Kissimmee, FL 32743
(407) 933-6500

KANSAS CITY
Baseball City Stadium
Interstate 4 and US 27
Baseball City, FL 33844
(305) 424-7211

LOS ANGELES
Holman Stadium
4001 26th Street
Vero Beach, FL 32961
(407) 569-4900

MINNESOTA
Lee County Sports Complex
Ft. Myers, FL 33905
phone # to be determined

MONTREAL
Municipal Stadium
W. Palm Beach, FL 33401
(407) 684-6801

NEW YORK METS
St. Lucie County Stadium
Port St. Lucie, FL 34986
(407) 340-0440

NEW YORK YANKEES
Ft. Lauderdale Stadium
Ft. Lauderdale, FL 33309
(305) 776-1921

PHILADELPHIA
Jack Russell Stadium
800 Phillies Drive
Clearwater, FL 33515
(813) 441-9941

PITTSBURGH
McKechnie Field
17th Ave. W. & 9th St. W.
Bradenton, FL 34208
(813) 748-4610

ST. LOUIS
Al Lang Stadium
St. Petersburg, FL 33701
(813) 896-4641

TEXAS
Charlotte County Stadium
2300 El Jobean Road
Port Charlotte, FL 33948
(813) 625-6500

TORONTO
Grant Field
311 Douglas Ave.
at Beltrees
Dunedin, FL 34697
(813) 733-9302

CACTUS LEAGUE—ARIZONA

Addresses are for stadiums only (team office mailing addresses will differ). Phone numbers are subject to change. Please consult local directories.

CALIFORNIA
Gene Autry Park
Mesa, AZ 85206
(602) 830-4137
 (as of 3/15)
Angels Stadium
Sunrise Way &
 Barristo Road
Palm Springs, CA 92263
(619) 327-1266

CHICAGO CUBS
Ho Ho Kam Park
1235 North Center St.
Mesa, AZ 85201
(602) 461-0061

CLEVELAND
Hi Corbett Field
Randolph Park
Tucson, AZ 85726
(602) 881-5710

MILWAUKEE
Compadre Stadium
1425 W. Ocotillo Road
Chandler, AZ 85245
(602) 821-2100

OAKLAND
Phoenix Stadium
Phoenix, AZ 85008
(602) 275-8314

SAN DIEGO
Desert Sun Stadium
Avenue A at 35th Avenue
Yuma, AZ 85364
(602) 726-6040

SAN FRANCISCO
Scottsdale Stadium
Scottsdale, AZ 85251
(602) 990-7972

SEATTLE
Tempe Diablo Stadium
2200 West Alameda
Tempe, AZ 85282
(602) 438-8803

Winning Pitcher:

Losing Pitcher:

Home Runs:

Highlights:

Score by innings:

THURSDAY

7

M · A · R · C · H

FRIDAY 8

_____

Winning Pitcher:

Losing Pitcher:

Home Runs:

Highlights:

Score by innings:

SATURDAY 9

_____

Winning Pitcher:

Losing Pitcher:

Home Runs:

Highlights:

Score by innings:

SUNDAY 10

_____

Winning Pitcher:

Losing Pitcher:

Home Runs:

Highlights:

Score by innings:

SCHEDULE

THURSDAY	Edison College vs. Min	
U. of Georgia vs. Atl		
Det vs. LA		
Pitt vs. Bos		
Bal vs. White Sox		
FRIDAY	Mon vs. Yankees	*SF vs. Cubs*
Atl vs. Hou	Pitt vs. Min	*Cal vs. SD*
LA vs. Mets	StL vs. Tor	*Sea vs. Mil*
KC vs. Cin	Bal vs. Tex	*Cleve vs. Oak*
Bos vs. Phil	Det vs. White Sox	
SATURDAY	Phil vs. Tor	*Mil vs. Cubs*
Mon vs. Atl	Bal vs. Yankees	*Cal vs. SD*
Hou vs. Cin	Bos vs. Det	*Cleve vs. SF*
LA vs. Mets	White Sox vs. KC	*Oak vs. Sea*
Pitt vs. StL	Tex vs. Min	
SUNDAY	KC vs. Hou	*Cal vs. SD*
Mets vs. LA	Tor vs. Phil	*SF vs. Cleve*
Atl vs. Mon	Det vs. Bos	*Cubs vs. Mil*
StL vs. Pitt	Bal vs. Yankees	*Sea vs. Oak*
White Sox vs. Cin	Min vs. Tex	

MONDAY 11

Winning Pitcher:

Losing Pitcher:

Home Runs:

Highlights:

Score by innings:

TUESDAY 12

Winning Pitcher:

Losing Pitcher:

Home Runs:

Highlights:

Score by innings:

WEDNESDAY 13

Winning Pitcher:

Losing Pitcher:

Home Runs:

Highlights:

Score by innings:

THURSDAY 14

Winning Pitcher:

Losing Pitcher:

Home Runs:

Highlights:

Score by innings:

M • A • R • C • H

FRIDAY 15

Winning Pitcher:

Losing Pitcher:

Home Runs:

Highlights:

Score by innings:

SATURDAY 16

Winning Pitcher:

Losing Pitcher:

Home Runs:

Highlights:

Score by innings:

SUNDAY 17

Winning Pitcher:

Losing Pitcher:

Home Runs:

Highlights:

Score by innings:

*ESPN: Oakland vs. San Francisco
California vs. Cubs*

SCHEDULE

MONDAY	Atl vs. Yankees	*Cleve vs. Cubs*
LA vs. Mon	Cin vs. Tex	*SF(ss) vs. Mil(ss)*
Hou vs. Mets	Bos vs. Bal	*SF(ss) vs. Sea*
Phil vs. StL	Det vs. KC	*SD vs. Cal*
Pitt vs. White Sox	Tor vs. Min	*Mil(ss) vs. Oak*
TUESDAY	Hou vs. Det	*KC vs. Tor*
Mets vs. Atl	Pitt vs. Tex(ss)	*SD vs. SF*
Mon vs. LA	Tex(ss) vs. Bal	*Cubs vs. Mil*
Cin vs. Phil	White Sox vs. Bos	*Cal vs. Oak*
Min(ss) vs. StL	Yankees vs. Min(ss)	*Cleve vs. Sea*
WEDNESDAY	Min vs. Pitt	*Cubs vs. SF*
Mets vs. Hou	LA vs. Yankees	*SD vs. Cleve*
Atl vs. Mon	StL vs. Tex	*Cal vs. Mil*
KC vs. Cin	Bal vs. Bos	*Oak vs. Sea*
Tor vs. Phil	Det vs. White Sox	
THURSDAY	Tex vs. StL	*White Sox(ss) vs. Min*
LA vs. Atl	Hou vs. KC(ss)	*Bos(ss) vs. Tor*
Cin vs. Mets	Mon vs. Yankees	*SD vs. Cubs*
Phil vs. Pitt	Bal vs. White Sox(ss)	*Mil vs. SF*
Det vs. Hou	KC(ss) vs. Bos(ss)	*Cleve vs. Oak*
		Cal vs. Sea
FRIDAY	Yankees vs. Phil	*Mil(ss) vs. Cubs(ss)*
StL vs. Cin	Tex vs. White Sox	*Cubs(ss) vs. SF*
Pitt vs. Hou	KC vs. Det	*SD vs. Oak*
Atl vs. LA	Bal vs. Min	*Cal vs. Cleve*
Bos vs. Mon	Mets vs. Tor	*Sea vs. Mil(ss)*
SATURDAY	Cin vs. KC	*SD vs. Mil*
Atl vs. Hou	Yankees vs. White Sox	*SF vs. Oak*
LA vs. Mon	Bos vs. Min	*Cubs vs. Sea*
Pitt vs. Phil	Bal vs. Tex	*Cal vs. Cleve*
Det vs. StL	Mets vs. Tor	
SUNDAY	Min(ss) vs. Phil	Bal vs. Tor
Mon vs. Atl	Cin vs. Bos	*Cal vs. Cubs*
Hou vs. LA	Yankees vs. White Sox	*Oak vs. SF*
StL vs. Pitt	Tex(ss) vs. Det	*SD vs. Sea*
KC vs. Mets	Min(ss) vs. Tex(ss)	*Cleve vs. Mil*

MONDAY 18

Winning Pitcher:

Losing Pitcher:

Home Runs:

Highlights:

Score by innings:

TUESDAY 19

Winning Pitcher:

Losing Pitcher:

Home Runs:

Highlights:

Score by innings:

WEDNESDAY 20

Winning Pitcher:

Losing Pitcher:

Home Runs:

Highlights:

Score by innings:

THURSDAY 21

Winning Pitcher:

Losing Pitcher:

Home Runs:

Highlights:

Score by innings:

FRIDAY 22

_____ ___
_____ ___

Winning Pitcher:

Losing Pitcher:

Home Runs:

Highlights:

Score by innings:

SATURDAY 23

_____ ___
_____ ___

Winning Pitcher:

Losing Pitcher:

Home Runs:

Highlights:

Score by innings:

SUNDAY 24

_____ ___
_____ ___

Winning Pitcher:

Losing Pitcher:

Home Runs:

Highlights:

Score by innings:

ESPN: *Cincinnati vs. Mets*
Detroit vs. Minnesota

SCHEDULE

MONDAY	Pitt vs. Min	*SD vs Cubs*
Mets vs. Atl	Mon vs. Yankees	*Cal vs. SF*
LA vs. Cin	Tex vs. Bos(ss)	*Sea(ss) vs. Cleve(ss)*
StL vs. Phil	Tor vs. White Sox	*Mil vs. Oak*
Hou vs. Det	Bos(ss) vs. KC	*Cleve(ss) vs. Sea(ss)*
TUESDAY	Hou vs. KC	White Sox vs. Tex
LA vs. Atl	StL vs. Tor	*SD vs. SF*
Mon vs. Cin	Det vs. Bal(ss)	*Oak vs. Cubs*
Phil vs. Mets	Bos vs. Det	*Cal vs. Sea*
Min vs. Pitt	Bal(ss) vs. Yankees	
WEDNESDAY	StL vs. White Sox(ss)	*Sea vs. Cubs*
Phil vs. LA	Cin vs. KC	*SD vs. Cleve*
Bos(ss) vs. Hou	White Sox(ss) vs. Bos(ss)	*Cal vs. Mil*
Yankees vs. Mon	Tex vs. Min	*Mil vs. Sea*
Bal vs. Mets	Det vs. Tor	
THURSDAY	Cin vs. White Sox	*SD(ss) vs. SF(ss)*
Mets vs. Hou	Phil vs. Yankees	*Mil vs. Cubs*
Atl vs. Mon	KC vs. Det	*SF(ss) vs. Cleve*
LA vs. StL	Min vs. Tex	*SD(ss) vs. Sea*
Bos vs. Pitt	Bal vs. Tor	*Cal vs. Oak*
FRIDAY	Tex vs. Pitt	White Sox vs. Yankees
Mon vs. Atl	Tor vs. StL	*LA vs. Oak*
Hou vs. Mets	Cin(ss) vs. KC(ss)	*Cubs vs. Cleve*
LA(ss) vs. Phil	Min vs. Bal	*SF vs. Sea*
Det vs. Cin(ss)	KC(ss) vs. Bos	*Oak(ss) vs. Mil*
SATURDAY	StL vs. Det	Min vs. Tex
Phil vs. Cin	Pitt vs. Tor	*LA vs. Oak*
LA(ss) vs. Mon	Bos(ss) vs. White Sox(ss)	*Mil vs. SD*
Atl vs. Mets	Bal vs. KC	*Cleve vs. SF*
Hou vs. Bos(ss)	White Sox(ss) vs. Yankees	*Cubs vs. Oak(ss)*
		Sea vs. Cal
SUNDAY	Yankees vs. Mon	*SF vs. Cubs*
Atl vs. LA	Tor vs. StL	*Mil vs. SD*
Cin vs. Mets	Bal vs. White Sox	*Sea vs. Cal*
Phil vs. Pitt	Det vs. Min	*Oak vs. Cleve*
KC vs. Hou	Bos vs. Tex	

M • A • R • C • H

MONDAY 25

_____ ___
_____ ___

Winning Pitcher:

Losing Pitcher:

Home Runs:

Highlights:

Score by innings:

TUESDAY 26

_____ ___
_____ ___

Winning Pitcher:

Losing Pitcher:

Home Runs:

Highlights:

Score by innings:

WEDNESDAY 27

_____ ___
_____ ___

Winning Pitcher:

Losing Pitcher:

Home Runs:

Highlights:

Score by innings:

THURSDAY 28

_____ ___
_____ ___

Winning Pitcher:

Losing Pitcher:

Home Runs:

Highlights:

Score by innings:

**ESPN: Kansas City vs. Los Angeles
Minnesota vs. White Sox**

FRIDAY 29

Winning Pitcher:

Losing Pitcher:

Home Runs:

Highlights:

Score by innings:

SATURDAY 30

Winning Pitcher:

Losing Pitcher:

Home Runs:

Highlights:

Score by innings:

ESPN: Texas vs. Pittsburgh
Toronto vs. Boston

SUNDAY 31

Winning Pitcher:

Losing Pitcher:

Home Runs:

Highlights:

Score by innings:

SCHEDULE

MONDAY	Bos vs. White Sox	Oak vs. SF
LA vs. Atl	Det vs. Tex	Mil vs. Cal
Mon vs. Mets	Min vs. Tor	
Bal vs. Pitt	Cleve vs. Cubs	
KC vs. StL	Sea vs. SD	
TUESDAY	White Sox vs. Pitt	Cubs vs. Cal
Hou vs. Atl	Mets vs. Min	Cleve vs. Oak
Bos vs. Cin	Det vs. KC	
Yankees vs. LA	Tex vs. Tor	
Bal vs. Phil	SF vs. SD	
WEDNESDAY	Cin vs. Bos	Cubs vs. Cal
StL vs. Hou	Phil vs. Min	Sea vs. Cleve
Mon vs. Mets	Pitt vs. Tex	Oak vs. Mil
Yankees vs. Atl	Tor vs. Det	
Bal vs. LA	SF vs. SD	
THURSDAY	Bal vs. Mon	Cubs vs. SD
Mets vs. Cin	Atl vs. Yankees	Sea(ss) vs. SF(ss)
Hou vs. Pitt	Det vs. Bos	SF(ss) vs. Cal
Phil vs. StL	Min vs. White Sox	Mil vs. Cleve
KC vs. LA	Tor vs. Tex	Sea(ss) vs. Oak
FRIDAY	LA vs. Det	Mil vs. Cubs
Phil vs. Cin	Min vs. Bos	Oak vs. SD
Atl vs. Hou	Tex vs. KC	Sea vs. SF
Mets vs. Mon	Bal vs. Yankees	Cleve vs. Cal
Pitt vs. StL	White Sox vs. Tor	
SATURDAY	Tex vs. Pitt	Oak(ss) vs. SD
LA vs. Atl	Yankees vs. Bal	Mil(ss) vs. SF
Cin vs. Hou	Tor vs. Bos	Cubs(ss) vs. Mil(ss)
Mon vs. Mets	KC vs. White Sox	Cleve vs. Cal
StL vs. Phil	Min vs. Det	Sea(ss) vs. Oak(ss)
		Cubs(ss) vs. Sea(ss)
SUNDAY	Hou vs. White Sox	SF vs. Cubs
Mets vs. Atl	Pitt vs. Min	Cleve vs. SD
Mon vs. LA	Phil vs. Tor	Oak vs. Cal
Det vs. Cin	Yankees vs. Bal	Sea vs. Mil
Tex vs. StL	Bos vs. KC	

A · P · R · I · L

MONDAY 1

Winning Pitcher:

Losing Pitcher:

Home Runs:

Highlights:

Score by innings:

TUESDAY 2

Winning Pitcher:

Losing Pitcher:

Home Runs:

Highlights:

Score by innings:

ESPN: Boston vs. Cincinnati
Toronto vs. Philadelphia

WEDNESDAY 3

Winning Pitcher:

Losing Pitcher:

Home Runs:

Highlights:

Score by innings:

THURSDAY 4

Winning Pitcher:

Losing Pitcher:

Home Runs:

Highlights:

Score by innings:

ESPN: Baltimore vs. Yankees
White Sox vs. St. Louis

FRIDAY 5

_____ ___
_____ ___

Winning Pitcher:

Losing Pitcher:

Home Runs:

Highlights:

Score by innings:

SATURDAY 6

_____ ___
_____ ___

Winning Pitcher:

Losing Pitcher:

Home Runs:

Highlights:

Score by innings:

SUNDAY 7

_____ ___
_____ ___

Winning Pitcher:

Losing Pitcher:

Home Runs:

Highlights:

Score by innings:

SCHEDULE

MONDAY	Hou vs. Bos	_SD vs. Cal_
Cin vs. LA	Phil vs. Det	_Cubs vs. Cleve_
Atl vs. Mets	StL vs. KC	_SF vs. Oak_
Bal vs. Mon	Min vs. Yankees	_Mil vs. Sea_
Tor vs. Pitt	White Sox vs. Tex	
TUESDAY	Det vs. Pitt	_SD vs. Cal_
LA vs. Hou	Mets vs. KC	_SF vs. Mil_
Bal vs. Atl	StL vs. Min	_Cubs vs. Sea_
Bos vs. Cin	Mon vs. Yankees	_Oak vs. Cleve_
Tor vs. Phil	Tex vs. White Sox	
WEDNESDAY	Pitt vs. Bos	_Mil vs. SF_
Mets vs. LA	Cin vs. Det	_SD vs. Cal_
StL vs. Phil	Hou vs. KC	_Cubs vs. Oak_
Yankees vs. Atl	Min vs. Tex	_Sea vs. Cleve_
Bal vs. Mon	White Sox vs. Tor	
THURSDAY	White Sox vs. StL	_Cleve vs. Mil_
Hou vs. Cin	Tor vs. KC	
Mets vs. Mon	Tex vs. Min	
Det vs. Phil	Bal vs. Yankees	
Bos vs. Pitt	_Sea vs. Cubs_	
FRIDAY	Cin vs. SD	_Cubs vs. Mil_
Mon vs. Atl	Pitt vs. Tex	_SF vs. Oak_
KC vs. Hou	Min vs. White Sox	
Tor vs. StL	LA vs. _Cal_	
Phil vs. Bos	_Sea vs. SD_	
SATURDAY	StL vs. Atl	_Sea vs. SD_
Hou vs. Phil	Tor vs. Mets	_SF vs. Oak_
Pitt vs. Det	LA vs. _Cal_	
Mon vs. Yankees	Bos vs. Bal	
Tex vs. Min	_Mil vs. Cubs_	
SUNDAY	Atl vs. StL	_Cin vs. Cleve_
Phil vs. Hou	Cal vs. LA	
Yankees vs. Mon	Bos vs. Bal	
Portland vs. Min	_Sea vs. SD_	
Atl vs. StL	Oak vs. SF	

FINAL SPRING STANDINGS

GRAPEFRUIT LEAGUE	Won	Lost	Tie	Pct.

CACTUS LEAGUE	Won	Lost	Tie	Pct.

INDIVIDUAL LEADERS

GRAPEFRUIT LEAGUE

BATTING

HOME RUNS   **WINS**

RBI   **E.R.A.**

SLUGGING   **SAVES**

CACTUS LEAGUE

BATTING

HOME RUNS   **WINS**

RBI   **E.R.A.**

SLUGGING   **SAVES**

REGULAR SEASON

A · P · R · I · L

MONDAY 8

Winning Pitcher:

Losing Pitcher:

Home Runs:

Highlights:

Score by innings:

CBS: *Hou vs. Cin*; Bos vs. Tor (day)
Mil vs. Tex; *Mon vs. Pitt* (night)

TUESDAY 9

Winning Pitcher:

Losing Pitcher:

Home Runs:

Highlights:

Score by innings:

WEDNESDAY 10

Winning Pitcher:

Losing Pitcher:

Home Runs:

Highlights:

Score by innings:

THURSDAY 11

Winning Pitcher:

Losing Pitcher:

Home Runs:

Highlights:

Score by innings:

A · P · R · I · L

_____ ____

FRIDAY 12

Winning Pitcher:

Losing Pitcher:

Home Runs:

Highlights: WATCHED
BUCS BEAT
WENT
TO CUBS 3-1 SMILEY
TWINS OPENER UNHITABLE

Score by innings:
PUCKETT 3-4
LEIUS LOOKS GOOD
TAPANI BRILLIANT
6-0 OVER RANGERS

_____ ____

SATURDAY 13

Winning Pitcher:

Losing Pitcher:

Home Runs:

Highlights:

Score by innings:

_____

SUNDAY 14

Winning Pitcher:

Losing Pitcher:

Home Runs:

Highlights:

Score by innings:

ESPN: Seattle vs. Oakland

SCHEDULE

MONDAY	Chi vs. Bal	
Mil. vs. Tex	Phil vs. NY	
Cleve vs. KC	Mon vs. Pitt	
NY vs. Det	Hou vs. Cin	
Bos vs. Tor		
TUESDAY	Phil vs. NY	
Cal vs. Sea	Mon vs. Pitt	
Min vs. Oak	StL vs. Chi	
Cleve vs. KC	LA vs. Atl	
Bos vs. Tor	SF vs. SD	
WEDNESDAY	NY vs. Det	StL vs. Chi
Cal vs. Sea	Bos vs. Tor	LA vs. Atl
Min vs. Oak	Chi vs. Bal	Hou vs. Cin
Mil. vs. Tex	Phil vs. NY	SF vs. SD
Cleve vs. KC	Mon vs. Pitt	
THURSDAY	Cleve vs. Bos	SF vs. SD
Cal vs. Sea	Mon vs. NY	
Min vs. Oak	StL vs. Chi	
NY vs. Det	LA vs. Atl	
Mil vs. Tor	Hou vs. Cin	
FRIDAY	Chi vs. Det	Atl vs. Cin
Sea vs. Oak	Mil. vs. Tor	SF vs. Hou
Bal vs. Tex	Mon vs. NY	SD vs. LA
NY vs. KC	StL vs. Phil	
Cal vs. Min	Pitt vs. Chi	
SATURDAY	Chi vs. Det	Atl vs. Cin
Sea vs. Oak	Mil. vs. Tor	Pitt vs. Chi
Bal vs. Tex	Cleve vs. Bos	SF vs. Hou
NY vs. KC	Mon vs. NY	SD vs. LA
Cal vs. Min	StL vs. Phil	
SUNDAY	Chi vs. Det	Atl vs. Cin
Sea vs. Oak	Mil. vs. Tor	Pitt vs. Chi
Bal vs. Tex	Cleve vs. Bos	SF vs. Hou
NY vs. KC	Mon vs. NY	SD vs. LA
Cal vs. Min	StL vs. Phil	

1990 STANDINGS

AMERICAN LEAGUE — Through April 15 — NATIONAL LEAGUE

East	Won	Lost	Pct.	GB	East	Won	Lost	Pct.	GB
New York	3	1	.750	–	Chicago	4	2	.667	–
Boston	4	2	.667	–	St. Louis	3	3	.500	1
Toronto	4	3	.571	½	Pittsburgh	3	3	.500	1
Detroit	3	4	.429	1½	Philadelphia	3	3	.500	1
Baltimore	2	3	.400	1½	Montreal	3	3	.500	1
Milwaukee	1	3	.250	2	New York	2	4	.333	2
Cleveland	1	3	.250	2					

West	Won	Lost	Pct.	GB	West	Won	Lost	Pct.	GB
Oakland	5	1	.833	–	Cincinnati	5	0	1.000	–
Chicago	4	1	.800	½	San Diego	5	2	.714	1
California	5	2	.714	½	Los Angeles	4	3	.571	2
Texas	3	4	.429	2½	San Francisco	2	4	.333	3½
Kansas City	2	3	.400	2½	Atlanta	1	4	.200	4
Minnesota	2	5	.286	3½	Houston	1	5	.167	4½
Seattle	1	5	.167	4					

INDIVIDUAL LEADERS

AMERICAN LEAGUE — NATIONAL LEAGUE

BATTING

Based on 3.1 plate appearances per game

	G	AB	R	H	Pct.		G	AB	R	H	Pct.
Diaz,E Mil	4	13	4	6	.462	Larkin,B Cin	5	23	5	12	.522
Fisk,C Chi	5	20	3	9	.450	Sandberg,R Chi	5	22	5	10	.455
Maldonado,C Cleve	4	14	2	6	.429	McGee,W StL	6	25	5	11	.440
Evans,D Bos	6	26	4	11	.423	Santiago,B SD	7	23	2	9	.391
Jackson,B KC	5	19	5	8	.421	Duncan,M Cin	5	18	4	7	.389
Lansford,C Oak	6	27	3	11	.407	Deshields,D Mon	6	27	4	10	.370
Mattingly,D NY	4	15	1	6	.400	Thompson,R SF	6	22	4	8	.364
Palmeiro,R Tex	7	23	6	9	.391	Strawberry,D NY	6	22	0	8	.364
Boggs,W Bos	6	26	5	10	.385	Biggio,C Hou	6	25	3	9	.360
						Clark,W SF	6	25	4	9	.360

HOME RUNS | WINS — HOME RUNS | WINS

HOME RUNS		WINS		HOME RUNS		WINS	
Bichette,D Cal	2	Finley,C Cal	2	Sabo,C Cin	3	Harris,G SD	2
McGwire,M Oak	2	Plunk,E NY	2	Lyons,B NY	2		
Buechele,S Tex	2	Ryan,N Tex	2	Scioscia,M LA	2		
Horn,S Bal	2	Stieb,D Tor	2	Van Slyke,A Pitt	2		
McGriff,F Tor	2	Stewart,D Oak	2	Bonilla,B Pitt	2		
Bell,G Tor	2	Clemens,R Bos	2	Johnson,H NY	2		
Hrbek,K Min	2	Welch,B Oak	2	Lynn,F SD	2		
Parrish,L Cal	2						
Henderson,D Oak	2						

RBI | E.R.A. — RBI | E.R.A.

RBI		E.R.A.		RBI		E.R.A.	
Johnson,L Chi	7	Gordon,T KC	0.00	Clark,W SF	8	Armstrong,J Cin	0.00
Incaviglia,P Tex	7	Finley,C	0.00	Sabo,C Cin	6	Harris,G SD	0.00
Evans,D Bos	7	Crim,C Mil	0.00	Larkin,B Cin	6	Dibble,R Cin	0.00
Bichette,D Cal	6	Guetterman,L NY	0.00	Santiago,B SD	6	Maddux,G Chi	0.00
Horn,S Bal	6	Higuera,T	0.00	McDowell,O Atl	6	Tewksbury,B StL	0.00
Maldonado,C Cleve	6	Langston,M Cal	0.00	Davis,E Cin	6	Andersen,L Hou	0.00
Bell,G Tor	6	Perez,M NY	0.00	Bonilla,B Pitt	6	Viola,F NY	0.00
Trammell,A Det	6	Petry,D Det	0.00	McGee,W StL	6	Tudor,J StL	0.00
		Welch,B Oak	0.77			Cook,D Phil	0.79
		Bosio,C Mil	0.90			Morgan,M LA	1.08

SLUGGING | SAVES — SLUGGING | SAVES

SLUGGING		SAVES		SLUGGING		SAVES	
Robidoux,B Bos	.786	Thigpen,B Chi	3	Sabo,C Cin	.727	Williams,M Chi	4
Felix,J Tor	.773	Smith,L Bos	3	Larkin,B Cin	.696	Myers,R Cin	2
Maldonado,C Cleve	.714	Eckersley,D Oak	3	Sandberg,R Chi	.682	Burke,T Mon	2
Palmeiro,R Tex	.696	Olson,G Bal	2	Duncan,M Cin	.667	McDowell,R Phil	2
Horn,S Bal	.667	Wells,D Tor	2	Brunansky,T StL	.667	Lefferts,C SD	2
Henderson,D Oak	.636	Aguilera,R Min	2	Butler,B SF	.650	Franco,J NY	2
Gagne,G Min	.583	Davis,M KC	2	McGee,W StL	.640		
Jackson,B KC	.579	Eichhorn,M Cal	2	Bonilla,B Pitt	.615		
Hrbek,K Min	.579	Righetti,D NY	2	Thompson,R SF	.591		
Evans,D Bos	.577			Gwynn,T SD	.586		

1991 STANDINGS

AMERICAN LEAGUE

East	Won	Lost	Pct.	GB

West	Won	Lost	Pct.	GB

NATIONAL LEAGUE

East	Won	Lost	Pct.	GB

West	Won	Lost	Pct.	GB

INDIVIDUAL LEADERS

AMERICAN LEAGUE

BATTING

HOME RUNS

WINS

RBI

E.R.A.

SLUGGING

SAVES

NATIONAL LEAGUE

BATTING

HOME RUNS

WINS

RBI

E.R.A.

SLUGGING

SAVES

A · P · R · I · L

_____ ___

Winning Pitcher:

Losing Pitcher:

Home Runs:

Highlights:

Score by innings:

MONDAY 15

_____ ___

Winning Pitcher:

Losing Pitcher:

Home Runs:

Highlights:

Score by innings:

TUESDAY 16

_____ ___

Winning Pitcher:

Losing Pitcher:

Home Runs:

Highlights:

Score by innings:

WEDNESDAY 17

_____ ___

Winning Pitcher:

Losing Pitcher:

Home Runs:

Highlights:

Score by innings:

THURSDAY 18

A ◆ P ◆ R ◆ I ◆ L

FRIDAY 19

_____ _____ _____
_____ _____

Winning Pitcher:

Losing Pitcher:

Home Runs:

Highlights:

Score by innings:

SATURDAY 20

_____ _____ _____
_____ _____

Winning Pitcher:

Losing Pitcher:

Home Runs:

Highlights:

Score by innings:

CBS: *Mets vs. Montreal*
Detroit vs. White Sox

SUNDAY 21

_____ _____ _____
_____ _____

Winning Pitcher:

Losing Pitcher:

Home Runs:

Highlights:

Score by innings:

ESPN: *Mets vs. Montreal*

SCHEDULE

MONDAY	Chi vs. NY	*Hou vs. Atl*
Min vs. Sea	Cleve vs. Bos	*Cin vs. SD*
Oak vs. Cal	*StL vs. Mon*	*LA vs. SF*
Bal vs. Mil	*NY vs. Pitt*	
Tor vs. Det	*Phil vs. Chi*	
TUESDAY	Chi vs. NY	*Hou vs. Atl*
Min vs. Sea	KC vs. Bos	*Cin vs. SD*
Oak vs. Cal	*StL vs. Mon*	*LA vs. SF*
Tor vs. Det	*NY vs. Pitt*	
Tex vs. Cleve	*Phil vs. Chi*	
WEDNESDAY	Chi vs. NY	*Hou vs. Atl*
Min vs. Sea	KC vs. Bos	*Chi vs. SD*
Oak vs. Cal	*StL vs. Mon*	*LA vs. SF*
Bal vs. Mil	*NY vs. Pitt*	
Tor vs. Det	*Phil vs. Chi*	
THURSDAY	KC vs. Bos	
Oak vs. Cal	*Chi vs. Pitt*	
Det vs. Chi	*Phil vs. StL*	
Bal vs. Mil	*LA vs. SD*	
Tex vs. Cleve		
FRIDAY	Tex vs. Bal	*Cin vs. Atl*
Oak vs. Sea	KC vs. NY	*LA vs. SD*
Min vs. Cal	*NY vs. Mon*	*Hou vs. SF*
Tor vs. Mil	*Chi vs. Pitt*	
Bos vs. Cleve	*Phil vs. StL*	
SATURDAY	Bos vs. Cleve	*Phil vs. StL*
Oak vs. Sea	Tex vs. Bal	*Cin vs. Atl*
Min vs. Cal	KC vs. NY	*LA vs. SD*
Det vs. Chi	*NY vs. Mon*	*Hou vs. SF*
Tor vs. Mil	*Chi vs. Pitt*	
SUNDAY	Bos vs. Cleve	*Phil vs. StL*
Oak vs. Sea	Tex vs. Bal	*Cin vs. Atl*
Min vs. Cal	KC vs. NY	*LA vs. SD*
Det vs. Chi	*NY vs. Mon*	*Hou vs. SF*
Tor vs. Mil	*Chi vs. Pitt*	

1990 STANDINGS

Through April 22

AMERICAN LEAGUE

East	Won	Lost	Pct.	GB
Toronto	8	5	.615	—
Milwaukee	6	5	.545	1
Cleveland	5	5	.500	1½
Boston	6	6	.500	1½
Baltimore	6	6	.500	1½
New York	4	6	.400	2½
Detroit	5	8	.385	3

West	Won	Lost	Pct.	GB
Oakland	9	3	.750	—
Chicago	5	4	.556	2½
Texas	7	6	.538	2½
California	6	6	.500	3
Minnesota	6	7	.462	3½
Kansas City	5	6	.455	3½
Seattle	4	9	.308	5½

NATIONAL LEAGUE

East	Won	Lost	Pct.	GB
Pittsburgh	8	5	.615	—
Philadelphia	7	6	.538	1
Montreal	7	6	.538	1
New York	6	7	.462	2
Chicago	6	7	.462	2
St. Louis	5	8	.385	3

West	Won	Lost	Pct.	GB
Cincinnati	9	1	.900	—
Los Angeles	8	6	.571	3
San Diego	6	6	.500	4
San Francisco	5	7	.417	5
Houston	5	7	.417	5
Atlanta	2	8	.200	7

INDIVIDUAL LEADERS

AMERICAN LEAGUE

BATTING

Based on 3.1 plate appearances per game

	G	AB	R	H	Pct.
Wilson,W KC	9	30	7	13	.433
Palmeiro,R Tex	13	45	12	18	.400
Pena,T Bos	12	43	4	17	.395
Mattingly,D NY	10	39	5	15	.385
Griffey,K Sea	13	53	6	20	.377
Snyder,C Cleve	10	39	5	14	.359
Diaz,E Mil	11	39	9	14	.359
Felix,J Tor	13	42	7	15	.357
Canseco,J Oak	12	42	11	15	.357
Parker,D Mil	11	42	6	15	.357

HOME RUNS

Bell,G Tor	4

WINS

Brown,K Tex	3
Finley,C Cal	3
Ryan,N Tex	3
Stieb,D Tor	3
Stewart,D Oak	3
Clemens,R Bos	3

RBI

Griffey,K Sea	13
Bell,G Tor	12
Felix,J Tor	11
Incaviglia,P Tex	11
Palmeiro,R Tex	10
Gruber,K Tor	10

E.R.A.

Dopson,J Bos	0.00
Higuera,T Mil	0.00
Perez,P NY	0.00
Bosio,C Mil	0.47
Gordon,T KC	0.75
McCaskill,K Cal	0.75
Finley,C Cal	0.87
Tapani,K Min	0.95
Leary,T NY	1.32
Eichhorn,M Cal	1.35

SLUGGING

Palmeiro,R Tex	.733
Felix,J Tor	.667
Winfield,D NY	.630
Snyder,C Cleve	.615
Wilson,W KC	.600
Hrbek,K Min	.583
Vaughn,G Mil	.581
Canseco,J Oak	.571
Griffey,K Sea	.566
Bichette,D Cal	.542

SAVES

Olson,G Bal	4
Jones,D Cleve	4
Aguilera,R Min	4
Russell,J Tex	4
Smith,L Bos	4
Eckersley,D Oak	4

NATIONAL LEAGUE

BATTING

	G	AB	R	H	Pct.
Larkin,B Cin	10	43	10	22	.512
Duncan,M Cin	9	32	8	14	.438
Santiago,B SD	12	41	5	17	.415
Daniels,K LA	12	33	6	13	.394
Butler,B SF	12	48	10	18	.375
Griffin,A LA	14	46	9	17	.370
Deshields,D Mon	12	52	6	19	.365
Sabo,C Cin	10	44	10	16	.364
Biggio,C Hou	12	47	6	17	.362
McGee,W StL	13	54	9	19	.352

HOME RUNS

Bonilla,B Pitt	5
Sabo,C Cin	4
Brooks,H LA	4
Santiago,B SD	3
Davis,G Hou	3
Scioscia,M LA	3
Van Slyke,A Pitt	3
Clark,J SD	3
Johnson,H NY	3
Murray,E LA	3

WINS

Armstrong,J Cin	3
Lacoss,M SF	3
Heaton,N Pitt	3
Viola,F NY	3

RBI

Bonilla,B Pitt	16
Clark,W SF	12
Santiago,B SD	11
Brooks,H LA	11
Guerrero,P StL	11
Larkin,B Cin	10
O'Neill,P Cin	10
Dawson,A Chi	10
Johnson,H NY	10
Murray,E LA	10

E.R.A.

Tudor,J StL	0.00
Cook,D Phil	0.44
Assenmacher,P Chi	0.63
Armstrong,J Cin	0.95
Harris,G SD	1.38
Viola,F NY	1.61
Hammaker,A SF	1.69
Smith,Z Mon	1.71
Maddux,G Chi	1.84
Morgan,M LA	1.84

SLUGGING

Duncan,M Cin	.781
Sabo,C Cin	.705
Santiago,B SD	.659
Bonilla,B Pitt	.648
Daniels,K LA	.606
Larkin,B Cin	.605
Clark,W SF	.592
Owen,S Mon	.578
Davis,G Hou	.558
Brooks,H LA	.544

SAVES

Williams,M Chi	4
McDowell,R Phil	4
Franco,J NY	4
Smith,D Hou	4
Frey,S Mon	3
Myers,R Cin	3
Burke,T Mon	3

1991 STANDINGS

AMERICAN LEAGUE

East	Won	Lost	Pct.	GB

West	Won	Lost	Pct.	GB

NATIONAL LEAGUE

East	Won	Lost	Pct.	GB

West	Won	Lost	Pct.	GB

INDIVIDUAL LEADERS

AMERICAN LEAGUE

BATTING

HOME RUNS

WINS

RBI

E.R.A.

SLUGGING

SAVES

NATIONAL LEAGUE

BATTING

HOME RUNS

WINS

RBI

E.R.A.

SLUGGING

SAVES

Winning Pitcher:

Losing Pitcher:

Home Runs:

Highlights:

Score by innings:

MONDAY 22

Winning Pitcher:

Losing Pitcher:

Home Runs:

Highlights:

Score by innings:

TUESDAY 23

Winning Pitcher:

Losing Pitcher:

Home Runs:

Highlights:

Score by innings:

WEDNESDAY 24

Winning Pitcher:

Losing Pitcher:

Home Runs:

Highlights:

Score by innings:

THURSDAY 25

FRIDAY 26

_____ ___

Winning Pitcher:

Losing Pitcher:

Home Runs:

Highlights:

Score by innings:

SATURDAY 27

_____ ___

Winning Pitcher:

Losing Pitcher:

Home Runs:

Highlights:

Score by innings:

CBS: *Cubs vs. Cincinnati*
Seattle vs. Minnesota

SUNDAY 28

_____ ___

Winning Pitcher:

Losing Pitcher:

Home Runs:

Highlights:

Score by innings:

ESPN: Boston vs. Kansas City

SCHEDULE

MONDAY	Det vs. NY	*SD vs. SF*
Sea vs. Cal	Tor vs. Bos	
Oak vs. Min	*Cin vs. Hou*	
Bal vs. Chi	*Chi vs. StL*	
KC vs. Cleve	*Atl vs. LA*	
TUESDAY	KC vs. Cleve	*Chi vs. StL*
Sea vs. Cal	Det vs. NY	*Cin vs. Hou*
Oak vs. Min	Tor vs. Bos	*Atl vs. LA*
Bal vs. Chi	*Pitt vs. Mon*	*SD vs. SF*
Tex vs. Mil	*NY vs. Phil*	
WEDNESDAY	KC vs. Cleve	*Chi vs. StL*
Sea vs. Cal	Det vs. NY	*Cin vs. Hou*
Oak vs. Min	Tor vs. Bos	*Atl vs. LA*
Bal vs. Chi	*Pitt vs. Mon*	*SD vs. SF*
Tex vs. Mil	*NY vs. Phil*	
THURSDAY	*NY vs. Phil*	
Sea vs. Min	*Chi vs. Cin*	
Tex vs. Mil	*SF vs. LA*	
Det vs. Tor		
Pitt vs. Mon		
FRIDAY	NY vs. Chi	*Mon vs. StL*
Cal vs. Oak	Det vs. Tor	*Chi vs. Cin*
Cleve vs. Tex	Mil vs. Bal	*Atl vs. Hou*
Bos vs. KC	*Pitt vs. NY*	*SF vs. LA*
Sea vs. Min	*SD vs. Phil*	
SATURDAY	NY vs. Chi	*Mon vs. StL*
Cal vs. Oak	Det vs. Tor	*Chi vs. Cin*
Cleve vs. Tex	Mil vs. Bal	*Atl vs. Hou*
Bos vs. KC	*Pitt vs. NY*	*SF vs. LA*
Sea vs. Min	*SD vs. Phil*	
SUNDAY	NY vs. Chi	*Mon vs. StL*
Cal vs. Oak	Det vs. Tor	*Chi vs. Cin*
Cleve vs. Tex	Mil vs. Bal	*Atl vs. Hou*
Bos vs. KC	*Pitt vs. NY*	*SF vs. LA*
Sea vs. Min	*SD vs. Phil*	

1990 STANDINGS

AMERICAN LEAGUE Through April 29 **NATIONAL LEAGUE**

East	Won	Lost	Pct.	GB
Milwaukee	11	6	.647	–
Boston	10	8	.556	1½
Toronto	11	9	.550	1½
Cleveland	9	8	.529	2
New York	7	9	.438	3½
Detroit	8	11	.421	4
Baltimore	8	11	.421	4

East	Won	Lost	Pct.	GB
Pittsburgh	14	6	.700	–
Philadelphia	10	8	.556	3
Montreal	10	8	.556	3
New York	9	9	.500	4
St. Louis	9	11	.450	5
Chicago	8	11	.421	5½

West	Won	Lost	Pct.	GB
Oakland	13	5	.722	–
Chicago	9	6	.600	2½
Texas	11	8	.579	2½
California	8	10	.444	5
Seattle	8	11	.421	5½
Minnesota	7	12	.368	6½
Kansas City	6	12	.333	7

West	Won	Lost	Pct.	GB
Cincinnati	12	3	.800	–
Los Angeles	11	9	.550	3½
San Diego	9	10	.474	5
Houston	8	10	.444	5½
San Francisco	7	12	.368	7
Atlanta	3	13	.188	9½

INDIVIDUAL LEADERS

AMERICAN LEAGUE **NATIONAL LEAGUE**

BATTING

AMERICAN LEAGUE

Based on 3.1 plate appearances per game

	G	AB	R	H	Pct.
Griffey,K Sea	19	76	10	30	.395
Pena,T Bos	18	67	6	26	.388
Stillwell,K KC	17	57	10	22	.386
Wilson,W KC	16	55	9	19	.345
Larkin,G Min	17	64	10	22	.344
Jackson,B KC	14	53	11	18	.340
Reed,J Bos	17	59	7	20	.339
Felix,J Tor	19	62	8	21	.339
Moseby,L Det	17	62	10	21	.339
Maldonado,C Cleve	17	65	9	22	.338

NATIONAL LEAGUE

	G	AB	R	H	Pct.
Duncan,M Cin	14	46	12	19	.413
Larkin,B Cin	15	63	11	25	.397
Santiago,B SD	18	63	9	25	.397
Sabo,C Cin	15	64	16	25	.391
Butler,B SF	19	78	15	30	.385
Benzinger,T Cin	15	55	8	20	.364
McGee,W StL	20	83	15	30	.361
Owen,S Mon	18	60	6	21	.350
Daniels,K LA	17	49	7	17	.347
Dawson,A Chi	17	59	7	20	.339

HOME RUNS (AL)

Gruber,K Tor	7
McGwire,M Oak	6
Fielder,C Det	6
Griffey,K Sea	5
Bell,G Tor	5
Sierra,R Tex	4
Incaviglia,P Tex	4
Canseco,J Oak	4
Maldonado,C Cleve	4
McGriff,F Tor	4

WINS (AL)

Stewart,D Oak	5
Brown,K Tex	4
Ryan,N Tex	4
Clemens,R Bos	4
Finley,C Cal	3
Holman,B Sea	3
Bosio,C Mil	3
Candiotti,T Cleve	3
Stieb,D Tor	3

HOME RUNS (NL)

Bonilla,B Pitt	7
Sabo,C Cin	5
Guerrero,P StL	5

WINS (NL)

Armstrong,J Cin	4
Drabek,D Pitt	4
Heaton,N Pitt	4
Viola,F NY	4
Tudor,J StL	4
Cook,D Phil	3
Maddux,G Chi	3
Morgan,M LA	3
Lacoss,M SD	3

RBI (AL)

Gruber,K Tor	19
Fielder,C Det	18
Griffey,K Sea	17
McGwire,M Oak	17
Felix,J Tor	16
Sierra,R Tex	16
Incaviglia,P Tex	14
Bell,G Tor	14

E.R.A. (AL)

Higuera,T Mil	0.00
Finley,C Cal	0.96
Stewart,D Oak	1.32
Bosio,C Mil	1.39
Welch,B Oak	1.44
Langston,M Cal	2.16
Ryan,N Tex	2.25
Holman,B Sea	2.33
Stieb,D Tor	2.35
Black,B Cleve	2.73

RBI (NL)

Bonilla,B Pitt	21
Guerrero,P StL	20
Carter,J SD	17
Clark,W SD	15
Dawson,A Chi	15
Duncan,M Cin	14
Bonds,B Pitt	13
Kruk,J Phil	13
Santiago,B SD	13
O'Neill, P Cin	13

E.R.A. (NL)

Cook,D Phil	0.66
Tudor,J StL	0.96
Viola,F NY	1.32
Armstrong,J Cin	1.40
Whitson,E SD	1.50
Smith,Z Mon	1.61
Martinez,De Mon	1.67
Deshaies,J Hou	1.73
Morgan,M LA	1.82
Smith,P Atl	1.91

SLUGGING (AL)

Gruber,K Tor	.658
Griffey,K Sea	.645
Palmeiro,R Tex	.603
Felix,J Tor	.597
Stillwell,K KC	.596
Maldonado,C Cleve	.585
Snyder,C Cleve	.552
Sierra,R Tex	.547
Barfield,J NY	.543
McGwire,M Oak	.536

SAVES (AL)

Eckersley,D Oak	7
Jones,D Cleve	6
Schooler,M Sea	5
Henneman,M Det	5
Thigpen,B Chi	5
Righetti,D NY	5

SLUGGING (NL)

Duncan,M Cin	.804
Sabo,C Cin	.719
Santiago,B SD	.667
Bonds,B Pitt	.617
Dawson,A Chi	.610
Davis,G Hou	.600
Owen,S Mon	.583
Bonilla,B Pitt	.570
Van Slyke,A Pitt	.536

SAVES (NL)

Burke,T Mon	6
McDowell,R Phil	6
Franco,J NY	6
Smith,D Hou	6
Williams,M Chi	5
Myers,R Cin	4
Frey,S Mon	3
Landrum,B Pitt	3
Bedrosian,S SF	3

1991 STANDINGS

AMERICAN LEAGUE					NATIONAL LEAGUE				
East	**Won**	**Lost**	**Pct.**	**GB**	**East**	**Won**	**Lost**	**Pct.**	**GB**
West	**Won**	**Lost**	**Pct.**	**GB**	**West**	**Won**	**Lost**	**Pct.**	**GB**

INDIVIDUAL LEADERS

AMERICAN LEAGUE

BATTING

HOME RUNS

WINS

RBI

E.R.A.

SLUGGING

SAVES

NATIONAL LEAGUE

BATTING

HOME RUNS

WINS

RBI

E.R.A.

SLUGGING

SAVES

A · P · R · I · L

MONDAY 29

_____ ____ _

Winning Pitcher:

Losing Pitcher:

Home Runs:

Highlights:

Score by innings:

TUESDAY 30

_____ ____ _

Winning Pitcher:

Losing Pitcher:

Home Runs:

Highlights:

Score by innings:

WEDNESDAY 1

_____ ____ _

Winning Pitcher:

Losing Pitcher:

Home Runs:

Highlights:

Score by innings:

The first day clubs may re-sign free agents who refused arbitration and were unsigned after January 8.

THURSDAY 2

_____ ____ _

Winning Pitcher:

Losing Pitcher:

Home Runs:

Highlights:

Score by innings:

M · A · Y

FRIDAY 3

_____ ___

Winning Pitcher:

Losing Pitcher:

Home Runs:

Highlights:

Score by innings:

SATURDAY 4

_____ ___

Winning Pitcher:

Losing Pitcher:

Home Runs:

Highlights:

Score by innings:

SUNDAY 5

_____ ___

Winning Pitcher:

Losing Pitcher:

Home Runs:

Highlights:

Score by innings:

CBS: Bos vs. White Sox; Cleve vs. Oak
ESPN: Yankees vs. Seattle

SCHEDULE

MONDAY		
Det vs. KC		
Sea vs. Bal		
SD vs. Phil		
Atl vs. StL		
TUESDAY	Bos vs. Min	*SF vs. Phil*
NY vs. Oak	Chi vs. Mil	*Hou vs. Chi*
Cleve vs. Cal	Sea vs. Bal	*Atl vs. StL*
Tor vs. Tex	*LA vs. Mon*	*Pitt vs. Cin*
Det vs. KC	*SD vs. NY*	
WEDNESDAY	Bos vs. Min	*SF vs. Phil*
NY vs. Oak	Chi vs. Mil	*Hou vs. Chi*
Cleve vs. Cal	Sea vs. Bal	*Atl vs. StL*
Tor vs. Tex	*LA vs. Mon*	*Pitt vs. Cin*
Det vs. KC	*SD vs. NY*	
THURSDAY		
Tor vs. KC		
Min vs. Mil		
FRIDAY	Bos vs. Chi	*LA vs. Phil*
NY vs. Sea	Min vs. Mil	*Hou vs. Pitt*
Cleve vs. Oak	Tex vs. Det	*Chi vs. Atl*
Bal vs. Cal	*SD vs. Mon*	*StL vs. Cin*
Tor vs. KC	*SF vs. NY*	
SATURDAY	Bos vs. Chi	*LA vs. Phil*
NY vs. Sea	Min vs. Mil	*Hou vs. Pitt*
Cleve vs. Oak	Tex vs. Det	*Chi vs. Atl*
Bal vs. Cal	*SD vs. Mon*	*StL vs. Cin*
Tor vs. KC	*SF vs. NY*	
SUNDAY	Bos vs. Chi	*LA vs. Phil*
NY vs. Sea	Min vs. Mil	*Hou vs. Pitt*
Cleve vs. Oak	Tex vs. Det	*Chi vs. Atl*
Bal vs. Cal	*SD vs. Mon*	*StL vs. Cin*
Tor vs. KC	*SF vs. NY*	

1990 STANDINGS

East	Won	Lost	Pct.	GB	East	Won	Lost	Pct.	GB
Milwaukee	14	8	.636	–	Pittsburgh	16	8	.667	–
Toronto	15	11	.577	1	Philadelphia	14	11	.560	2½
Cleveland	13	11	.542	2	Montreal	13	12	.520	3½
Boston	13	11	.542	2	New York	12	13	.480	4½
New York	10	13	.435	4½	Chicago	11	13	.458	5
Baltimore	10	15	.400	5½	St. Louis	10	15	.400	6½
Detroit	9	17	.346	7					

West	Won	Lost	Pct.	GB	West	Won	Lost	Pct.	GB
Oakland	18	6	.750	–	Cincinnati	17	5	.773	–
Chicago	13	8	.619	3½	Los Angeles	14	12	.538	5
Texas	13	12	.520	5½	San Diego	12	12	.500	6
Minnesota	12	12	.500	6	Houston	11	14	.440	7½
Seattle	12	14	.462	7	San Francisco	9	16	.360	9½
California	10	15	.400	8½	Atlanta	7	15	.318	10
Kansas City	7	16	.304	10½					

INDIVIDUAL LEADERS

AMERICAN LEAGUE

BATTING

Based on 3.1 plate appearances per game

	G	AB	R	H	Pct.
Griffey,K Sea	26	104	15	40	.385
Henderson,R Oak	22	84	20	32	.381
Stillwell,K KC	22	75	12	27	.360
Jacoby,B Cleve	21	75	16	27	.360
Guillen,O Chi	21	73	12	25	.342
Maldonado,C Cleve	23	86	14	29	.337
Brock,G Mil	21	66	11	22	.333
Gruber,K Tor	25	99	15	33	.333
Pena,T Bos	24	91	10	30	.330
Hrbek,K Min	22	68	14	22	.324

HOME RUNS

Fielder,C Det	10
Gruber,K Tor	9
McGwire,M Oak	7
Maldonado,C Cleve	7
Canseco,J Oak	6
Bell,G Tor	6

WINS

Stewart,D Oak	6
Brown,K Tex	5
Stottlemeyer,T Tor	4
Holman,B Sea	4
Ryan,N Tex	4
Candiotti,T Cleve	4
Stieb,D Tor	4
Clemens,R Bos	4

RBI

Fielder,C Det	25
Gruber,K Tor	23
Leonard,J Sea	21
Griffey,K Sea	20
Maldonado,C Cleve	20
Felix,J Tor	18
McGwire, M Oak	18
Sierra, R Tex	18
Bell, G Tor	17
Evans, D Bos	17

E.R.A.

Stewart,D Oak	1.54
Gordon,T KC	1.57
Higuera,T Mil	1.62
Welch,B Oak	1.71
Finley,C Cal	2.03
Black,B Cleve	2.08
Bosio,C Mil	2.09
King,E Chi	2.17
Hanson,E Sea	2.40
Stieb,D Tor	2.40

SLUGGING

Gruber, K Tor	.677
Fielder, C Det	.656
Henderson, R Oak	.655
Maldonado, C Cleve	.640
Jacoby, B Cleve	.613
Griffey, K Sea	.596
Felix, J Tor	.576
McGriff, F Tor	.563
Hrbek, K Min	.559
Palmeiro, R Tex	.553

SAVES

Jones,D Cleve	9
Eckersley,D Oak	9
Schooler,M Sea	8
Henneman,M Det	6
Thigpen,B Chi	6
Righetti,D NY	6
Olson,G Bal	5
Aguilera,R Min	5
Eichhorn,M Cal	5

NATIONAL LEAGUE

BATTING

	G	AB	R	H	Pct.
Duncan,M Cin	21	70	18	29	.414
Santiago,B SD	22	79	12	30	.380
Dykstra,L Phil	20	82	17	30	.366
Sabo,C Cin	21	90	22	32	.356
Daniels,K LA	22	68	9	24	.353
Butler,B SD	25	102	17	36	.353
McGee,W StL	25	102	18	36	.353
Larkin,B Cin	22	91	15	32	.352
Benzinger,T Cin	22	84	11	29	.345
Hatcher,B Cin	21	85	13	29	.341

HOME RUNS

Davis,G Hou	7
Bonilla,B Pitt	7
Johnson,H NY	7
Mitchell,K SF	6
Brooks,H LA	6
Guerrero,P StL	6

WINS

Armstrong,J Cin	5
Drabek,D Pitt	5
Heaton,N Pitt	5
Viola,F NY	5
Cook,D Phil	4
Maddux,G Chi	4
Morgan,M LA	4
Tudor,J StL	4

RBI

Carter,J SD	22
Bonilla,B Pitt	22
Guerrero,P StL	21
Dawson,A Chi	20
Williams,M SF	19
Clark,W SF	19
Brooks,H LA	19
Davis,G Hou	19
O'Neill,P Cin	18

E.R.A.

Viola,F NY	0.99
Armstrong,J Cin	1.08
Gardner,M Mon	1.32
Morgan,M LA	1.40
Cook,D Phil	1.57
Tudor,J StL	1.89
Smith,P Atl	1.91
Maddux,G Chi	1.96
Whitson,E SD	1.98
Drabek,D Pitt	2.17

SLUGGING

Duncan,M Cin	.729
Santiago,B SD	.658
Sabo,C Cin	.611
Davis,G Hou	.602
Dawson,A Chi	.584
Mitchell,K SF	.565
Daniels,K LA	.559
Bonds,B Pitt	.557
Bonilla,B Pitt	.545
Johnson,H NY	.537

SAVES

Smith,D Hou	8
Burke,T Mon	7
McDowell,R Phil	7
Myers,R Cin	6
Williams,M Chi	6
Franco,J NY	6
Dibble,R Cin	4

1991 STANDINGS

AMERICAN LEAGUE

East	Won	Lost	Pct.	GB

West	Won	Lost	Pct.	GB

NATIONAL LEAGUE

East	Won	Lost	Pct.	GB

West	Won	Lost	Pct.	GB

INDIVIDUAL LEADERS

AMERICAN LEAGUE

BATTING

HOME RUNS

WINS

RBI

E.R.A.

SLUGGING

SAVES

NATIONAL LEAGUE

BATTING

HOME RUNS

WINS

RBI

E.R.A.

SLUGGING

SAVES

M • A • Y

MONDAY 6

_____ ____

Winning Pitcher:

Losing Pitcher:

Home Runs:

Highlights:

Score by innings:

TUESDAY 7

_____ ____

Winning Pitcher:

Losing Pitcher:

Home Runs:

Highlights:

Score by innings:

WEDNESDAY 8

_____ ____

Winning Pitcher:

Losing Pitcher:

Home Runs:

Highlights:

Score by innings:

THURSDAY 9

_____ ____

Winning Pitcher:

Losing Pitcher:

Home Runs:

Highlights:

Score by innings:

M • A • Y

FRIDAY 10

_____
_____

Winning Pitcher:

Losing Pitcher:

Home Runs:

Highlights:

Score by innings:

SATURDAY 11

_____
_____

Winning Pitcher:

Losing Pitcher:

Home Runs:

Highlights:

Score by innings:

SUNDAY 12

_____
_____

Winning Pitcher:

Losing Pitcher:

Home Runs:

Highlights:

Score by innings:

ESPN: St. Louis vs. Houston

SCHEDULE

MONDAY	*Chi vs. Hou*	
NY vs. Sea		
Bal vs. Cal		
SF vs. Mon		
Cin vs. Pitt		
TUESDAY	KC vs. Det	*Cin vs. Pitt*
Cleve vs. Sea	Tex vs. Tor	*StL vs. Atl*
Bal vs. Oak	Min vs. Bos	*Chi vs. Hou*
NY vs. Cal	*SF vs. Mon*	*Phil vs. SD*
Mil vs. Chi	*LA vs. NY*	
WEDNESDAY	KC vs. Det	*Cin vs. Pitt*
Cleve vs. Sea	Tex vs. Tor	*StL vs. Atl*
Bal vs. Oak	Min vs. Bos	*Chi vs. Hou*
NY vs. Cal	*SF vs. Mon*	*Phil vs. SD*
Mil vs. Chi	*LA vs. NY*	
THURSDAY		
Det vs. Min		
Chi vs. Tor		
Tex vs. Bos		
Phil vs. SD		
FRIDAY	Chi vs. Tor	*StL vs. Hou*
Bal vs. Sea	Oak vs. NY	*Phil vs. LA*
Det vs. Min	Tex vs. Bos	*Mon vs. SD*
KC vs. Mil	*Atl vs. Pitt*	*NY vs. SF*
Cal vs. Cleve	*Cin vs. Chi*	
SATURDAY	Chi vs. Tor	*StL vs. Hou*
Bal vs. Sea	Oak vs. NY	*Phil vs. LA*
Det vs. Min	Tex vs. Bos	*Mon vs. SD*
KC vs. Mil	*Atl vs. Pitt*	*NY vs. SF*
Cal vs. Cleve	*Cin vs. Chi*	
SUNDAY	Chi vs. Tor	*StL vs. Hou*
Bal vs. Sea	Oak vs. NY	*Phil vs. LA*
Det vs. Min	Tex vs. Bos	*Mon vs. SD*
KC vs. Mil	*Atl vs. Pitt*	*NY vs. SF*
Cal vs. Cleve	*Cin vs. Chi*	

1990 STANDINGS

AMERICAN LEAGUE **Through May 13** NATIONAL LEAGUE

East	Won	Lost	Pct.	GB
Milwaukee	17	11	.607	–
Toronto	19	13	.594	–
Boston	17	13	.567	1
Cleveland	16	15	.516	2½
Baltimore	14	17	.452	4½
New York	12	17	.414	5½
Detroit	11	21	.344	8

East	Won	Lost	Pct.	GB
Pittsburgh	22	9	.710	–
Philadelphia	17	13	.567	4½
Montreal	18	14	.563	4½
New York	16	14	.533	5½
Chicago	14	16	.467	7½
St. Louis	13	18	.419	9

West	Won	Lost	Pct.	GB
Oakland	22	8	.733	–
Chicago	17	10	.630	3½
Minnesota	16	14	.533	6
Texas	15	16	.484	7½
Seattle	15	18	.455	8½
California	12	20	.375	11
Kansas City	10	20	.333	12

West	Won	Lost	Pct.	GB
Cincinnati	21	7	.750	–
San Diego	15	16	.484	7½
Los Angeles	14	17	.452	8½
Houston	12	19	.387	10½
San Francisco	11	20	.355	11½
Atlanta	9	19	.321	12

INDIVIDUAL LEADERS

AMERICAN LEAGUE NATIONAL LEAGUE

BATTING

Based on 3.1 plate appearances per game

	G	AB	R	H	Pct.
Griffey,K Sea	33	127	23	47	.370
Henderson,R Oak	28	106	24	37	.349
Parker,D Mil	26	99	12	34	.343
Gladden,D Min	28	114	17	38	.333
Jacoby,B Cleve	28	102	17	34	.333
Stillwell,K KC	29	101	17	33	.327
Kelly,R NY	29	111	15	36	.324
Guillen,O Chi	27	93	16	30	.323
Gruber,K Tor	31	124	18	40	.323
Larkin,G Min	28	101	16	32	.317

BATTING

	G	AB	R	H	Pct.
Dykstra,L Phil	25	103	23	41	.398
Duncan,M Cin	26	89	21	34	.382
Alomar,R Cin	30	120	16	44	.367
Larkin,B Cin	28	115	21	42	.365
Santiago,B SD	28	99	13	35	.354
Sabo,C Cin	26	109	24	38	.349
Hatcher,B Cin	27	109	17	38	.349
Bonds,B Pitt	28	96	25	32	.333
Van Slyke,A Pitt	28	99	17	33	.333
Treadway,J Atl	23	88	8	29	.330

HOME RUNS
Fielder,C Det	13
Gruber,K Tor	10
McGwire,M Oak	9
Canseco,J Oak	9
Griffey,K Sea	7
Maldonado,C Cleve	7
Deer,R Mil	7
Bell,G Tor	7

WINS
Stewart,D Oak	6
Brown,K Tex	5
Finley,C Cal	5
Holman,B Sea	5
Stieb,D Tor	5
Clemens,R Bos	5

HOME RUNS
Bonilla,B Pitt	8
Dawson,A Chi	8
Mitchell,K SF	7
Davis,G Hou	7
Johnson,H NY	7

WINS
Viola,F NY	7
Drabek,D Pitt	6
Heaton,N Pitt	6
Armstrong,J Cin	5
Cook,D Phil	5
Maddux,G Chi	4
Morgan,M LA	4
Gross,K Mon	4
Smith,B StL	4
Tudor,J StL	4

RBI
Fielder,C Det	32
Gruber,K Tor	28
Leonard,J Sea	24
Canseco,J Oak	23
Maldonado,C Cleve	23
Griffey,K Sea	22
McGwire,M Oak	22
Sierra,R Tex	22
Felix,J Tor	21

E.R.A.
Welch,B Oak	1.41
Stewart,D Oak	1.46
Higuera,T Mil	1.62
Finley,C Cal	2.09
Bosio,C Mil	2.12
Black,B Cleve	2.16
King,E Chi	2.31
Stieb,D Tor	2.47
Petry,D Det	2.48
Sanderson,S Oak	2.50

RBI
Carter,J SD	26
Dawson,A Chi	26
Bonilla,B Pitt	25
Williams,M SF	24
O'Neill,P Cin	24
Clark,W SF	23
Guerrero,P StL	23
Wallach,T Mon	22
Bonds,B Pitt	21
Davis,G Hou	20

E.R.A.
Viola,F NY	0.87
Cook,D Phil	1.46
Armstrong,J Cin	1.88
Gardner,M Mon	1.89
Whitson,E SD	2.06
Heaton,N Pitt	2.11
Drabek,D Pitt	2.36
Martinez,De Mon	2.42
Smith,B StL	2.54
Maddux,G Chi	2.66

SLUGGING
Fielder,C Det	.694
Gruber,K Tor	.637
Henderson,R Oak	.604
Griffey,K Sea	.591
Maldonado,C Cleve	.561
Canseco,J Oak	.551
Felix,J Tor	.524
Jacoby,B Cleve	.520
McGriff,F Tor	.519
Sierra,R Tex	.517

SAVES
Jones,D Cleve	12
Schooler,M Sea	9
Aguilera,R Min	9
Eckersley,D Oak	9
Olson,G Bal	8
Thigpen,B Chi	8
Henneman,M Det	7
Plesac,D Mil	7
Righetti,D NY	7

SLUGGING
Duncan,M Cin	.629
Dawson,A Chi	.624
Sabo,C Cin	.606
Bonds,B Pitt	.604
Mitchell,K SF	.577
Santiago,B SD	.576
Davis,G Hou	.548
Bonilla,B Pitt	.535
Van Slyke,A Pitt	.535
Dunston,S Chi	.527

SAVES
Burke,T Mon	8
Smith,D Hou	8
Williams,M Chi	7
McDowell,R Phil	7
Franco,J NY	7
Landrum,B Pitt	6
Myers,R Cin	6
Dibble,R Cin	5
Boever,J Atl	4
Bedrosian,S SF	4

1991 STANDINGS

AMERICAN LEAGUE					NATIONAL LEAGUE				
East	**Won**	**Lost**	**Pct.**	**GB**	**East**	**Won**	**Lost**	**Pct.**	**GB**
West	**Won**	**Lost**	**Pct.**	**GB**	**West**	**Won**	**Lost**	**Pct.**	**GB**

INDIVIDUAL LEADERS

AMERICAN LEAGUE

NATIONAL LEAGUE

BATTING

HOME RUNS

WINS

RBI

E.R.A.

SLUGGING

SAVES

BATTING

HOME RUNS

WINS

RBI

E.R.A.

SLUGGING

SAVES

_____ ____

Winning Pitcher:

Losing Pitcher:

Home Runs:

Highlights:

Score by innings:

MONDAY 13

_____ ____

Winning Pitcher:

Losing Pitcher:

Home Runs:

Highlights:

Score by innings:

TUESDAY 14

_____ ____

Winning Pitcher:

Losing Pitcher:

Home Runs:

Highlights:

Score by innings:

WEDNESDAY 15

_____ ____

Winning Pitcher:

Losing Pitcher:

Home Runs:

Highlights:

Score by innings:

THURSDAY 16

M · A · Y

FRIDAY 17

_____ _____

Winning Pitcher:

Losing Pitcher:

Home Runs:

Highlights:

Score by innings:

SATURDAY 18

_____ _____

Winning Pitcher:

Losing Pitcher:

Home Runs:

Highlights:

Score by innings:

CBS: Mets vs. Los Angeles

SUNDAY 19

_____ _____

Winning Pitcher:

Losing Pitcher:

Home Runs:

Highlights:

Score by innings:

ESPN: Cubs vs. Philadelphia

SCHEDULE

MONDAY	Chi vs. Bos	NY vs. SD
Det vs. Tex	Atl vs. Chi	Phil vs. SF
Cal vs. Cleve	Cin vs. StL	
KC vs. Tor	Pitt vs. Hou	
Oak vs. NY	Mon vs. LA	
TUESDAY	Oak vs. Bal	Pitt vs. Hou
Det vs. Tex	Cal vs. NY	Mon vs. LA
Mil vs. Min	Chi vs. Bos	NY vs. SD
Sea vs. Cleve	Atl vs. Chi	Phil vs. SF
KC vs. Tor	Cin vs. StL	
WEDNESDAY	Oak vs. Bal	Pitt vs. Hou
Det vs. Tex	Cal vs. NY	Mon vs. LA
Mil vs. Min	Chi vs. Bos	NY vs. SD
Sea vs. Cleve	Atl vs. Chi	Phil vs. SF
KC vs. Tor	Cin vs. StL	
THURSDAY	Mon vs. SF	
Mil vs. Min		
Sea vs. Cleve		
Oak vs. Bal		
Cal vs. NY		
FRIDAY	Oak vs. Cleve	Pitt vs. Atl
Bos vs. Tex	Cal vs. Bal	SD vs. Cin
Mil vs. KC	Sea vs. NY	NY vs. LA
Tor vs. Chi	Chi vs. Phil	Mon vs. SF
Min vs. Det	Hou vs. StL	
SATURDAY	Oak vs. Cleve	Pitt vs. Atl
Bos vs. Tex	Cal vs. Bal	SD vs. Cin
Mil vs. KC	Sea vs. NY	NY vs. LA
Tor vs. Chi	Chi vs. Phil	Mon vs. SF
Min vs. Det	Hou vs. StL	
SUNDAY	Oak vs. Cleve	Pitt vs. Atl
Bos vs. Tex	Cal vs. Bal	SD vs. Cin
Mil vs. KC	Sea vs. NY	NY vs. LA
Tor vs. Chi	Chi vs. Phil	Mon vs. SF
Min vs. Det	Hou vs. StL	

1 9 9 0 S T A N D I N G S

AMERICAN LEAGUE　　　Through May 20　　　NATIONAL LEAGUE

East	Won	Lost	Pct.	GB	East	Won	Lost	Pct.	GB
Milwaukee	21	13	.618	–	Pittsburgh	23	14	.622	–
Boston	19	16	.543	2½	Philadelphia	20	16	.556	2½
Toronto	21	18	.538	2½	Montreal	20	18	.526	3½
Cleveland	19	17	.528	3	Chicago	18	19	.486	5
Detroit	17	22	.436	6½	New York	17	19	.472	5½
Baltimore	16	21	.432	6½	St. Louis	17	20	.459	6
New York	14	20	.412	7					

West	Won	Lost	Pct.	GB	West	Won	Lost	Pct.	GB
Oakland	24	12	.667	–	Cincinnati	25	9	.735	–
Chicago	20	13	.606	2½	Los Angeles	19	18	.514	7½
Minnesota	20	16	.556	4	San Diego	18	19	.486	8½
Seattle	19	20	.487	6½	San Francisco	15	22	.405	11½
Texas	16	21	.432	8½	Atlanta	14	21	.400	11½
California	15	23	.395	10	Houston	13	24	.351	13½
Kansas City	13	22	.371	10½					

I N D I V I D U A L L E A D E R S

AMERICAN LEAGUE　　　NATIONAL LEAGUE

BATTING　　　BATTING

Based on 3.1 plate appearances per game

	G	AB	R	H	Pct.		G	AB	R	H	Pct.
Griffey,K Sea	39	152	29	57	.375	Dykstra,L Phil	31	126	30	50	.397
Martinez,E Sea	34	120	22	43	.358	Alomar,R SD	36	143	18	51	.357
Guillen,O Chi	33	114	17	40	.351	Dawson,A Chi	35	129	25	45	.349
Parker,D Mil	31	117	14	40	.342	Sabo,C Cin	32	132	29	46	.348
Davis,A Sea	36	131	20	44	.336	Larkin,B Cin	34	134	22	46	.343
Sheffield,G Mil	27	102	17	34	.333	Hatcher,B Cin	33	132	20	44	.333
Gladden,D Min	34	141	21	47	.333	Gwynn,T SD	37	148	23	49	.331
Stillwell,K KC	34	122	18	40	.328	McGee,W StL	37	149	28	49	.329
Fielder,C Det	38	135	26	44	.326	Santiago,B SD	34	119	15	39	.328
Kelly,R NY	34	123	17	43	.326	Van Slyke,A Pitt	34	123	20	40	.325

HOME RUNS　　WINS　　HOME RUNS　　WINS

HOME RUNS		WINS		HOME RUNS		WINS	
Fielder,C Det	16	Stewart,D Oak	7	Dawson,A Chi	13	Armstrong,J Cin	7
Canseco,J Oak	13	Jones,B Chi	6	Bonilla,B Pitt	11	Viola,F NY	7
McGwire,M Oak	11	Holman,B Sea	6	Mitchell,K SF	8	Drabek,D Pitt	6
Gruber,K Tor	10	Clemens,R Bos	6	Wallach,T Mon	8	Heaton,N Pitt	6
Griffey,K Sea	9	Tapani,K Min	5	Johnson,H NY	8	Cook,D Phil	5
Maldonado,C Cleve	9	Brown,K Tex	5	Williams,M SF	7	Morgan,M LA	5
Deer,R Mil	7	Finley,C Cal	5	Sabo,C Cin	7	Gross,K Mon	5
Kittle, R Chi	7	Stieb,D Tor	5	Daniels,K LA	7	Smith,B StL	5
Bell,G Tor	7	Boddicker,M Bos	5	Brooks,H LA	7		
Hrbek,K Min	7			Davis,G Hou	7		

RBI　　E.R.A.　　RBI　　E.R.A.

RBI		E.R.A.		RBI		E.R.A.	
Fielder,C Det	37	Welch,B Oak	1.71	Dawson,A Chi	41	Viola,F NY	1.66
Gruber,K Tor	32	Black,B Cleve	1.83	Bonilla,B Pitt	34	Armstrong,J Cin	1.86
Canseco,J Oak	31	Finley,C Cal	2.09	Carter,J SD	31	Gardner,M Mon	2.01
Maldonado,C Cleve	29	Stewart,D Oak	2.12	Clark,W SF	29	Drabek,D Pitt	2.36
Leonard,J Sea	29	Bosio,C Mil	2.13	Williams,M SF	27	Cook,D Phil	2.38
Felix,J Tor	26	Higuera,T Mil	2.23	Guerrero,P StL	27	Heaton,N Pitt	2.44
McGwire,M Oak	26	Gordon,T KC	2.29	O'Neill,P Cin	26	Walk,B Pitt	2.45
Hrbek,K Min	25	Petry,D Det	2.56	Bonds,B Pitt	25	Whitson,E SD	2.50
Griffey,K Sea	24	King,E Chi	2.63	Wallach,T Mon	25	Glavine,T Atl	2.56
Bell,G Tor	24	Tapani,K Min	2.79			Morgan,M LA	2.66

SLUGGING　　SAVES　　SLUGGING　　SAVES

SLUGGING		SAVES		SLUGGING		SAVES	
Fielder,C Det	.756	Jones,D Cleve	14	Dawson,A Chi	.721	Burke,T Mon	10
Canseco,J Oak	.606	Schooler,M Sea	11	Bonilla,B Pitt	.605	McDowell,R Phil	9
Griffey,K Sea	.605	Aguilera,R Min	11	Sabo,C Cin	.591	Williams,M Chi	8
Maldonado,C Cleve	.584	Henneman,M Det	10	Daniels,K LA	.559	Franco,J NY	8
Gruber,K Tor	.583	Thigpen,B Chi	10	Bonds,B Pitt	.550	Smith,D Hou	8
Kittle,R Chi	.558	Olson,G Bal	9	Mitchell,K SF	.545	Myers,R Cin	7
Henderson,R Oak	.556	Eckersley,D Oak	9	Wallach,T Mon	.540	Landrum,B Pitt	6
Martinez,E Sea	.542	Plesac,D Mil	8	Dykstra,L Phil	.540	Bedrosian,S SF	6
Hrbek,K Min	.535	Eichhorn,M Cal	7	Santiago,B SD	.513		
Felix,J Tor	.525	Righetti,D NY	7	Van Slyke,A Pitt	.496		

1991 STANDINGS

AMERICAN LEAGUE

East	Won	Lost	Pct.	GB

West	Won	Lost	Pct.	GB

NATIONAL LEAGUE

East	Won	Lost	Pct.	GB

West	Won	Lost	Pct.	GB

INDIVIDUAL LEADERS

AMERICAN LEAGUE

BATTING

HOME RUNS

WINS

RBI

E.R.A.

SLUGGING

SAVES

NATIONAL LEAGUE

BATTING

HOME RUNS

WINS

RBI

E.R.A.

SLUGGING

SAVES

MONDAY 20

_____ ____

Winning Pitcher:

Losing Pitcher:

Home Runs:

Highlights:

Score by innings:

TUESDAY 21

_____ ____

Winning Pitcher:

Losing Pitcher:

Home Runs:

Highlights:

Score by innings:

WEDNESDAY 22

_____ ____

Winning Pitcher:

Losing Pitcher:

Home Runs:

Highlights:

Score by innings:

THURSDAY 23

_____ ____

Winning Pitcher:

Losing Pitcher:

Home Runs:

Highlights:

Score by innings:

M · A · Y

FRIDAY 24

_____
_____

Winning Pitcher:

Losing Pitcher:

Home Runs:

Highlights:

Score by innings:

SATURDAY 25

_____
_____

Winning Pitcher:

Losing Pitcher:

Home Runs:

Highlights:

Score by innings:

CBS: _Los Angeles vs. Cincinnati_
Cleveland vs. Milwaukee

SUNDAY 26

_____
_____

Winning Pitcher:

Losing Pitcher:

Home Runs:

Highlights:

Score by innings:

ESPN: **Cleveland vs. Milwaukee**
Texas vs. Seattle

SCHEDULE

MONDAY	NY vs. Cleve	
Tor vs. Oak	Mil vs. Bos	
Chi vs. Cal	_SD vs. Atl_	
Sea vs. KC	_LA vs. Hou_	
Bal vs. Det		
TUESDAY	Bal vs. Det	_StL vs. Pitt_
Tor vs. Oak	NY vs. Cleve	_SD vs. Atl_
Chi vs. Cal	Mil vs. Bos	_SF vs. Cin_
Sea vs. KC	_Phil vs. Mon_	_LA vs. Hou_
Tex vs. Min	_Chi vs. NY_	
WEDNESDAY	Bal vs. Det	_StL vs. Pitt_
Tor vs. Oak	NY vs. Cleve	_SD vs. Atl_
Chi vs. Cal	Mil vs. Bos	_SF vs. Cin_
Sea vs. KC	_Phil vs. Mon_	_LA vs. Hou_
Tex vs. Min	_Chi vs. NY_	
THURSDAY	_Phil vs. Mon_	_LA vs. Hou_
Chi vs. Oak	_Chi vs. NY_	
Tex vs. Min	_StL vs. Pitt_	
Cleve vs. Mil	_SD vs. Atl_	
Bos vs. Det	_SF vs. Cin_	
FRIDAY	Cleve vs. Mil	_Mon vs. Chi_
Tex vs. Sea	Bos vs. Det	_SF vs. Atl_
Chi vs. Oak	NY vs. Bal	_LA vs. Cin_
Tor vs. Cal	_StL vs. NY_	_SD vs. Hou_
KC vs. Min	_Phil vs. Pitt_	
SATURDAY	Cleve vs. Mil	_Mon vs. Chi_
Tex vs. Sea	Bos vs. Det	_SF vs. Atl_
Chi vs. Oak	NY vs. Bal	_LA vs. Cin_
Tor vs. Cal	_StL vs. NY_	_SD vs. Hou_
KC vs. Min	_Phil vs. Pitt_	
SUNDAY	Cleve vs. Mil	_Mon vs. Chi_
Tex vs. Sea	Bos vs. Det	_SF vs. Atl_
Chi vs. Oak	NY vs. Bal	_LA vs. Cin_
Tor vs. Cal	_StL vs. NY_	_SD vs. Hou_
KC vs. Min	_Phil vs. Pitt_	

1990 STANDINGS

AMERICAN LEAGUE   Through May 27   **NATIONAL LEAGUE**

East	Won	Lost	Pct.	GB	East	Won	Lost	Pct.	GB
Milwaukee	22	19	.537	—	Pittsburgh	26	17	.605	—
Toronto	24	22	.522	½	Philadelphia	24	18	.571	1½
Boston	21	21	.500	1½	Montreal	23	21	.523	3½
Cleveland	20	22	.476	2½	New York	20	22	.476	5½
Baltimore	20	24	.455	3½	Chicago	20	24	.455	6½
Detroit	20	26	.435	4½	St. Louis	19	25	.432	7½
New York	17	24	.415	5					

West	Won	Lost	Pct.	GB	West	Won	Lost	Pct.	GB
Oakland	30	12	.714	—	Cincinnati	29	11	.725	—
Chicago	25	15	.625	4	Los Angeles	24	20	.545	7
Minnesota	25	18	.581	5½	San Diego	21	22	.488	9½
California	22	23	.489	9½	Atlanta	17	24	.415	12½
Seattle	21	25	.457	11	Houston	17	26	.395	13½
Texas	18	26	.409	13	San Francisco	17	27	.386	14
Kansas City	17	25	.405	13					

INDIVIDUAL LEADERS

AMERICAN LEAGUE   **NATIONAL LEAGUE**

BATTING

Based on 3.1 plate appearances per game

	G	AB	R	H	Pct.		G	AB	R	H	Pct.
Guillen,O Chi	40	138	19	49	.355	Dykstra,L Phil	37	151	35	61	.404
Griffey,K Sea	46	180	32	63	.350	Larkin,B Cin	40	155	25	55	.355
Martinez,E Sea	41	146	25	50	.342	Dawson,A Chi	42	149	26	51	.342
Canseco,J Oak	42	156	38	53	.340	Van Slyke,A Pitt	39	144	22	48	.333
Henderson,R Oak	39	143	36	48	.336	Hatcher,B Cin	38	154	23	51	.331
Orsulak,J Bal	37	125	20	41	.328	Alomar,R SD	42	167	18	55	.329
Parker,D Oak	38	144	15	47	.326	Sabo,C Cin	38	157	34	51	.325
Gruber,K Tor	44	173	28	56	.324	Treadway,J Atl	34	127	16	41	.323
Gladden,D Min	41	165	29	53	.321	Santiago,B SD	39	138	16	44	.319
Fielder,C Det	45	162	30	52	.321	Mitchell,K, SF	40	151	29	48	.318

HOME RUNS / WINS

HOME RUNS		WINS		HOME RUNS		WINS	
Fielder,C Det	18	Stewart,D Oak	8	Dawson,A Chi	13	Armstrong,J Cin	8
Canseco,J Oak	18	Finley,C Cal	7	Mitchell,K SF	12	Heaton,N Pitt	8
Gruber,K Tor	13	Clemens,R Bos	7	Bonilla,B Pitt	12	Drabek,D Pitt	7
McGwire,M Oak	12	Tapani,K Min	6	Wallach,T Mon	10	Viola,F NY	7
Griffey,K Sea	10	Jones,B Chi	6	Davis,G Hou	10	Morgan,M LA	6
Maldonado,C Cleve	10	Holman,B Sea	6	Sabo,C Cin	9	Martinez,R LA	5
Felix,J Tor	8	Boddicker,M Bos	6	Bonds,B Pitt	9	Cook,D Phil	5
Kittle,R Chi	8	Welch,B Oak	6	Clark,W SF	9	Howell,K Phil	5
Bell,G Tor	8			Sandberg,R Chi	9	Gross,K Mon	5
Hrbek,K Min	8					Smith,B StL	5

RBI / E.R.A.

RBI		E.R.A.		RBI		E.R.A.	
Canseco,J Oak	47	Welch,B Oak	1.86	Dawson,A Chi	42	Armstrong,J Cin	1.61
Fielder,C Det	41	Stewart,D Oak	1.90	Bonilla,B Pitt	38	Viola,F NY	2.14
Gruber,K Tor	40	Higuera,T Mil	1.94	Carter,J SD	36	Gardner,M Mon	2.28
Maldonado,C Cleve	32	Black,B Cleve	2.17	Bonds,B Pitt	34	Walk,B Pitt	2.36
Leonard,J Sea	32	Finley,C Cal	2.31	Clark,W SF	33	Glavine,T Atl	2.45
Griffey,K Sea	30	Hibbard,G Chi	2.42	Davis,G Hou	32	Martinez,De Mon	2.59
Bell,G Tor	30	Petry,D Det	2.44	Guerrero,P StL	31	Cook,D Phil	2.61
		Bosio,C Mil	2.49	Wallach,T Mon	30	Drabek,D Pitt	2.66
		Leary,T NY	2.56	Williams,M SF	29	Browning,T Cin	2.67
		Stieb,D Tor	2.83	Hayes,V Phil	28	Fernandez,S NY	2.72

SLUGGING / SAVES

SLUGGING		SAVES		SLUGGING		SAVES	
Fielder,C Det	.716	Jones,D Cleve	15	Dawson,A Chi	.685	McDowell,R Phil	12
Canseco,J Oak	.699	Thigpen,B Chi	14	Mitchell,K SF	.616	Burke,T Mon	11
Gruber,K Tor	.624	Aguilera,R Min	13	Bonds,B Pitt	.610	Myers,R Cin	9
Felix,J Tor	.582	Eckersley,D Oak	13	Bonilla,B Pitt	.599	Williams,M Chi	8
Maldonado,C Cleve	.578	Schooler,M Sea	12	Wallach,T Mon	.582	Lefferts,C SD	8
Henderson,R Oak	.573	Henneman,M Det	11	Sabo,C Cin	.573	Franco,J NY	8
Griffey,K Sea	.572	Olson,G Bal	9	Dykstra,L Phil	.550	Smith,D Hou	8
Orsulak,J Bal	.560	Righetti,D NY	9	Daniels,K LA	.543	Landrum,B Pitt	6
Kittle,R Chi	.559			Davis, G Hou	.538	Bedrosian,S SF	6
Martinez,E Sea	.548			Sandberg,R Chi	.530		

1991 STANDINGS

AMERICAN LEAGUE

East	Won	Lost	Pct.	GB

West	Won	Lost	Pct.	GB

NATIONAL LEAGUE

East	Won	Lost	Pct.	GB

West	Won	Lost	Pct.	GB

INDIVIDUAL LEADERS

AMERICAN LEAGUE

BATTING

HOME RUNS

WINS

RBI

E.R.A.

SLUGGING

SAVES

NATIONAL LEAGUE

BATTING

HOME RUNS

WINS

RBI

E.R.A.

SLUGGING

SAVES

M · A · Y

MONDAY 27

_____
_____ __

Winning Pitcher:

Losing Pitcher:

Home Runs:

Highlights:

Score by innings:

CBS: Bos vs. NY; Det vs. Mil (day); *Mon vs. Phil*;
Min vs. Tex (night); *Cin vs. SF*; *Hou vs. LA* (late)

TUESDAY 28

_____
_____ __

Winning Pitcher:

Losing Pitcher:

Home Runs:

Highlights:

Score by innings:

WEDNESDAY 29

_____
_____ __

Winning Pitcher:

Losing Pitcher:

Home Runs:

Highlights:

Score by innings:

THURSDAY 30

_____
_____ __

Winning Pitcher:

Losing Pitcher:

Home Runs:

Highlights:

Score by innings:

J • U • N • E

FRIDAY 31

____ __

Winning Pitcher:

Losing Pitcher:

Home Runs:

Highlights:

Score by innings:

SATURDAY 1

____ __

Winning Pitcher:

Losing Pitcher:

Home Runs:

Highlights:

Score by innings:

SUNDAY 2

____ __

Winning Pitcher:

Losing Pitcher:

Home Runs:

Highlights:

Score by innings:

**ESPN: Oakland vs. White Sox
Seattle vs. Texas**

SCHEDULE

MONDAY	Bos vs. NY	Atl vs. SD
KC vs. Sea	Mon vs. Phil	Cin vs. SF
Min vs. Tex	NY vs. Chi	
Det vs. Mil	Pitt vs. StL	
Cleve vs. Bal	Hou vs. LA	
TUESDAY	Oak vs. Tor	Pitt vs. StL
KC vs. Sea	Cleve vs. Bal	Hou vs. LA
Min vs. Tex	Bos vs. NY	Atl vs. SD
Cal vs. Chi	Mon vs. Phil	Cin vs. SF
Det vs. Mil	NY vs. Chi	
WEDNESDAY	Oak vs. Tor	Pitt vs. StL
KC vs. Sea	Cleve vs. Bal	Hou vs. LA
Min vs. Tex	Bos vs. NY	Atl vs. SD
Cal vs. Chi	Mon vs. Phil	Cin vs. SF
Det vs. Mil	NY vs. Chi	
THURSDAY	Bal vs. Bos	
Sea vs. Tex	Cin vs. LA	
Min vs. KC	Hou vs. SD	
Cal vs. Chi	Atl vs. SF	
Oak vs. Tor		
FRIDAY	Cal vs. Tor	NY vs. StL
Sea vs. Tex	Mil vs. NY	Cin vs. LA
Min vs. KC	Bal vs. Bos	Hou vs. SD
Oak vs. Chi	Chi vs. Mon	Atl vs. SF
Det vs. Cleve	Pitt vs. Phil	
SATURDAY	Cal vs. Tor	NY vs. StL
Sea vs. Tex	Mil vs. NY	Cin vs. LA
Min vs. KC	Bal vs. Bos	Hou vs. SD
Oak vs. Chi	Chi vs. Mon	Atl vs. SF
Det vs. Cleve	Pitt vs. Phil	
SUNDAY	Cal vs. Tor	NY vs. StL
Sea vs. Tex	Mil vs. NY	Cin vs. LA
Min vs. KC	Bal vs. Bos	Hou vs. SD
Oak vs. Chi	Chi vs. Mon	Atl vs. SF
Det vs. Cleve	Pitt vs. Phil	

1990 STANDINGS

AMERICAN LEAGUE   Through June 3   NATIONAL LEAGUE

East	Won	Lost	Pct.	GB
Milwaukee	25	22	.532	–
Boston	25	23	.521	$\frac{1}{2}$
Toronto	27	25	.519	$\frac{1}{2}$
Cleveland	23	25	.479	$2\frac{1}{2}$
Baltimore	23	27	.460	$3\frac{1}{2}$
Detroit	22	30	.423	$5\frac{1}{2}$
New York	18	29	.383	7

East	Won	Lost	Pct.	GB
Pittsburgh	30	19	.612	–
Philadelphia	26	21	.553	3
Montreal	27	22	.551	3
New York	21	25	.457	$7\frac{1}{2}$
St. Louis	22	28	.440	$8\frac{1}{2}$
Chicago	22	28	.440	$8\frac{1}{2}$

West	Won	Lost	Pct.	GB
Oakland	33	16	.673	–
Chicago	30	17	.638	2
Minnesota	29	21	.580	$4\frac{1}{2}$
California	25	26	.490	9
Seattle	24	28	.462	$10\frac{1}{2}$
Kansas City	22	27	.449	11
Texas	20	30	.400	$13\frac{1}{2}$

West	Won	Lost	Pct.	GB
Cincinnati	33	12	.733	–
San Diego	25	24	.510	10
Los Angeles	25	26	.490	11
San Francisco	22	29	.431	14
Atlanta	19	28	.404	15
Houston	20	30	.400	$15\frac{1}{2}$

INDIVIDUAL LEADERS

AMERICAN LEAGUE   NATIONAL LEAGUE

BATTING

Based on 3.1 plate appearances per game

	G	AB	R	H	Pct.
Guillen,O Chi	46	154	20	54	.351
Parker,D Mil	44	168	21	58	.345
Henderson,R Oak	45	167	38	57	.341
Griffey,K Sea	52	200	35	68	.340
Martinez,E Sea	47	164	26	55	.335
Puckett,K Min	50	188	37	62	.330
Canseco,J Oak	49	184	40	60	.326
Gladden,D Min	48	194	32	61	.314
Maldonado,C Cleve	46	172	26	54	.314
Fielder,C Det	51	182	33	57	.313

BATTING

	G	AB	R	H	Pct.
Dykstra,L Phil	42	172	39	71	.413
Larkin,B Cin	45	174	28	62	.356
Dawson,A Chi	48	171	26	59	.345
Alomar,R SD	48	193	23	64	.332
Lind,J Pitt	48	172	16	57	.331
Van Slyke,A Pitt	44	160	23	53	.331
Gwynn,T SD	49	194	32	64	.330
Hatcher,B Cin	43	173	25	57	.329
Dunston,S Chi	48	185	25	60	.324
Santiago,B SD	45	158	21	51	.323

HOME RUNS

Fielder,C Det	19
Canseco,J Oak	19
Gruber,K Tor	14
McGwire,M Oak	13
Griffey,K Sea	10
Maldonado,C Cleve	10
Barfield,J NY	10
Felix,J Tor	9
Puckett,K Min	9
Bell,G Tor	9

WINS

Clemens,R Bos	9
Stewart,D Oak	8
Jones,B Chi	7
Finley,C Cal	7
Stieb,D Tor	7
Welch,B Oak	7

HOME RUNS

Davis,G Hou	15
Mitchell,K SF	14
Dawson,A Chi	13
Bonilla,B Pitt	12
Wallach,T Mon	11
Sandberg,R Chi	11
Sabo,C Cin	10
Bonds,B Pitt	10
Daniels,K LA	10

WINS

Armstrong,J Cin	8
Heaton,N Pitt	8
Viola,F NY	8
Drabek,D Pitt	7
Gross,K Mon	7
Howell,K Phil	6
Morgan,M LA	6
Smith,B StL	6

RBI

Canseco,K Oak	49
Fielder,C Det	47
Gruber,K Tor	43
Leonard,J Sea	36
Maldonado,C Cleve	35
McGwire,M Oak	34
Puckett,K Min	34
Griffey,K Sea	31
Bell,G Tor	31
Gaetti,G Min	31

E.R.A.

Higuera,T Mil	1.89
Welch,B Oak	2.07
Hibbard,G Chi	2.43
King,E Chi	2.44
Stewart,D Oak	2.45
Black,B Cleve	2.45
Bosio,C Mil	2.46
Stieb,D Tor	2.61
Petry,D Det	2.72
Leary,T NY	2.72

RBI

Dawson,A Chi	44
Carter,J SD	43
Davis,G Hou	41
Bonilla,B Pitt	40
Bonds,B Pitt	37
Clark,W SF	37
Williams,M SF	35
Wallach,T Mon	35
Guerrero,P StL	35
Hayes,V Phil	34

E.R.A.

Armstrong,J Cin	1.55
Viola,F NY	1.90
Gardner,M Mon	2.28
Browning,T Cin	2.30
Martinez,De Mon	2.59
Whitson,E SD	2.68
Drabek,D Pitt	2.78
Tudor,J StL	2.78
Walk,B Pitt	2.83
Heaton,N Pitt	2.84

SLUGGING

Fielder,C Det	.687
Canseco,J Oak	.652
Gruber,K Tor	.595
Henderson,R Oak	.593
Puckett,K Min	.585
Felix,J Tor	.571
Griffey,K Sea	.555
Maldonado,C Cleve	.552
Barfield,J NY	.531
Martinez,E Sea	.524

SAVES

Jones,D Cleve	18
Thigpen,B Chi	17
Eckersley,D Oak	16
Aguilera,R Min	15
Schooler,M Sea	14
Henneman,M Det	13
Olson,G Bal	11
Plesac,D Mil	10
Eichhorn,M Cal	10
Righetti,D NY	10

SLUGGING

Dawson,A Chi	.649
Bonds,B Pitt	.599
Mitchell,K SF	.589
Wallach,T Mon	.587
Davis,G Hou	.583
Bonilla,B Pitt	.567
Daniels,K LA	.567
Dykstra,L Phil	.552
Sabo,C Cin	.552
Sandberg,R Chi	.547

SAVES

McDowell,R Phil	13
Myers,R Cin	11
Burke,T Mon	11
Smith,D Hou	10
Williams,M Chi	9
Lefferts,C SD	8
Franco,J NY	8
Landrum,B Pitt	7
Bedrosian,S SF	7

1991 STANDINGS

AMERICAN LEAGUE

East	Won	Lost	Pct.	GB

West	Won	Lost	Pct.	GB

NATIONAL LEAGUE

East	Won	Lost	Pct.	GB

West	Won	Lost	Pct.	GB

INDIVIDUAL LEADERS

AMERICAN LEAGUE

BATTING

HOME RUNS

WINS

RBI

E.R.A.

SLUGGING

SAVES

NATIONAL LEAGUE

BATTING

HOME RUNS

WINS

RBI

E.R.A.

SLUGGING

SAVES

J · U · N · E

MONDAY 3

_____ ____

Winning Pitcher:

Losing Pitcher:

Home Runs:

Highlights:

Score by innings:

Summer free agent draft begins

TUESDAY 4

_____ ____

Winning Pitcher:

Losing Pitcher:

Home Runs:

Highlights:

Score by innings:

WEDNESDAY 5

_____ ____

Winning Pitcher:

Losing Pitcher:

Home Runs:

Highlights:

Score by innings:

Summer free agent draft ends

THURSDAY 6

_____ ____

Winning Pitcher:

Losing Pitcher:

Home Runs:

Highlights:

Score by innings:

J • U • N • E

FRIDAY 7

Winning Pitcher:

Losing Pitcher:

Home Runs:

Highlights:

Score by innings:

SATURDAY 8

Winning Pitcher:

Losing Pitcher:

Home Runs:

Highlights:

Score by innings:

SUNDAY 9

Winning Pitcher:

Losing Pitcher:

Home Runs:

Highlights:

Score by innings:

ESPN: Toronto vs. Baltimore

SCHEDULE

MONDAY	*SF vs. Pitt*	*Mon vs. Hou*
Bal vs. Min	*SD vs. Chi*	
Oak vs. Chi	*LA vs. StL*	
Det vs. Cleve	*Phil vs. Atl*	
Tor vs. NY	*NY vs. Cin*	
TUESDAY	Sea vs. Det	*LA vs. StL*
Mil vs. Oak	Chi vs. Cleve	*Phil vs. Atl*
Bos vs. Cal	Tor vs. NY	*NY vs. Cin*
Tex vs. KC	SF vs. Pitt	*Mon vs. Hou*
Bal vs. Min	*SD vs. Chi*	
WEDNESDAY	Sea vs. Det	*LA vs. StL*
Mil vs. Oak	Chi vs. Cleve	*Phil vs. Atl*
Bos vs. Cal	Tor vs. NY	*NY vs. Cin*
Tex vs. KC	SF vs. Pitt	*Mon vs. Hou*
Bal vs. Min	*SD vs. Chi*	
THURSDAY	Chi vs. Cleve	*Mon vs. Atl*
Mil vs. Oak	Tor vs. Bal	*Phil vs. Cin*
Bos vs. Cal	SD vs. Pitt	*NY vs. Hou*
Tex vs. KC	LA vs. Chi	
Sea vs. Det	*SF vs. StL*	
FRIDAY	Cleve vs. Min	*SF vs. StL*
Mil vs. Sea	Tor vs. Bal	*Mon vs. Atl*
Bos vs. Oak	Tex vs. NY	*Phil vs. Cin*
Det vs. Cal	SD vs. Pitt	*NY vs. Hou*
Chi vs. KC	*LA vs. Chi*	
SATURDAY	Cleve vs. Min	*SF vs. StL*
Mil vs. Sea	Tor vs. Bal	*Mon vs. Atl*
Bos vs. Oak	Tex vs. NY	*Phil vs. Cin*
Det vs. Cal	SD vs. Pitt	*NY vs. Hou*
Chi vs. KC	*LA vs. Chi*	
SUNDAY	Cleve vs. Min	*SF vs. StL*
Mil vs. Sea	Tor vs. Bal	*Mon vs. Atl*
Bos vs. Oak	Tex vs. NY	*Phil vs. Cin*
Det vs. Cal	SD vs. Pitt	*NY vs. Hou*
Chi vs. KC	*LA vs. Chi*	

1990 STANDINGS

East	Won	Lost	Pct.	GB	East	Won	Lost	Pct.	GB
Boston	31	24	.564	–	Pittsburgh	34	22	.607	–
Toronto	32	36	.552	½	Montreal	31	25	.554	3
Baltimore	28	29	.491	4	Philadelphia	28	26	.519	5
Milwaukee	26	28	.481	4½	New York	26	27	.491	6½
Detroit	27	32	.458	6	St. Louis	25	32	.439	9½
Cleveland	24	30	.444	6½	Chicago	25	32	.439	9½
New York	19	35	.352	11½					

West	Won	Lost	Pct.	GB	West	Won	Lost	Pct.	GB
Oakland	38	17	.691	–	Cincinnati	34	18	.654	–
Chicago	34	19	.642	3	San Diego	30	25	.545	5½
Minnesota	30	26	.536	8½	Los Angeles	28	29	.491	8½
California	29	29	.500	10½	San Francisco	27	30	.474	9½
Seattle	28	31	.475	12	Houston	23	34	.404	13½
Texas	24	33	.421	15	Atlanta	21	32	.396	13½
Kansas City	22	33	.400	16					

INDIVIDUAL LEADERS

AMERICAN LEAGUE   NATIONAL LEAGUE

BATTING

Based on 3.1 plate appearances per game

	G	AB	R	H	Pct.		G	AB	R	H	Pct.
Guillen,O Chi	52	176	22	62	.352	Dykstra,L Phil	49	204	42	83	.407
Griffey,K Sea	59	227	39	79	.348	Larkin,B Cin	52	201	30	70	.348
Henderson,R Oak	51	190	42	66	.347	Gwynn,T SD	55	218	39	75	.344
Puckett,K Min	56	210	40	70	.333	Alomar,R SD	54	220	28	74	.336
Parker,D Mil	51	195	23	64	.328	Dawson,A Chi	55	194	32	65	.335
Fielder,C Det	58	206	39	66	.320	Sandberg,R Chi	56	226	41	75	.332
Canseco,J Oak	52	194	43	62	.320	Gant,R Atl	45	152	35	50	.329
Martinez,E Sea	54	189	29	60	.317	Lind,J Pitt	55	195	17	64	.328
Sheffield,G Mil	41	156	26	49	.314	Wallach,T Mon	56	217	29	71	.327
Gruber,K Tor	56	220	39	69	.314	Uribe,J SF	55	181	20	59	.326

HOME RUNS / WINS / HOME RUNS / WINS

HOME RUNS		WINS		HOME RUNS		WINS	
Fielder,C Det	22	Clemens,R Bos	10	Davis,G Hou	18	Viola,F NY	9
Canseco,J Oak	20	Stewart,D Oak	9	Dawson,A Chi	16	Armstrong,J Cin	8
Gruber,K Tor	17	Welch,B Oak	9	Mitchell,K SF	15	Drabek,D Pitt	8
McGwire,M Oak	16	Finley,C Cal	8	Bonilla,B Pitt	14	Heaton,N Pitt	8
Bell,G Tor	12	Stieb,D Tor	8	Sandberg,R Chi	14	Howell,K Phil	7
Barfield,J NY	11			Clark,W SF	13	Gross,K Mon	7
Griffey,K Sea	10			Strawberry,D NY	12		
Incaviglia,P Tex	10						
Maldonado,C Cleve	10						
McGriff,F Tor	10						

RBI / E.R.A. / RBI / E.R.A.

RBI		E.R.A.		RBI		E.R.A.	
Fielder,C Det	56	Higuera,T Mil	1.79	Carter,J SD	49	Viola,F NY	1.85
Canseco,J Oak	50	Stewart,D Oak	2.21	Dawson,A Chi	47	Armstrong,J Cin	1.85
Gruber,K Tor	50	Welch,B Oak	2.32	Clark,W SF	46	Browning,T Cin	2.07
Bell,G Tor	42	King,E Chi	2.48	Davis,G Hou	45	Gardner,M Mon	2.22
McGwire,M Oak	41	Stieb,D Tor	2.57	Bonilla,B Pitt	45	Tudor,J StL	2.48
Leonard,J Sea	40	Saberhagen,B KC	2.67	Williams,M SF	43	Martinez,De Mon	2.62
Maldonado,C Cleve	36	Finley,C Cal	2.71	Bonds,B Pitt	41	Drabek,D Pitt	2.64
Burks,E Bos	35	Clemens,R Bos	2.72	Wallach,T Mon	41	Heaton,N Pitt	2.77
Puckett,K Min	35	Petry,D Det	2.75	Guerrero,P StL	39	Morgan,M LA	2.78
Gaetti,G Min	35	Black,B Cleve	2.79	Hayes,V Phil	36	Whitson,E SD	2.95

SLUGGING / SAVES / SLUGGING / SAVES

SLUGGING		SAVES		SLUGGING		SAVES	
Fielder,C Det	.694	Thigpen,B Chi	20	Dawson,A Chi	.649	McDowell,R Phil	13
Canseco,J Oak	.644	Eckersley,D Oak	20	Wallach,T Mon	.590	Myers,R Cin	11
Gruber,K Tor	.609	Jones,D Cleve	19	Bonds,B Pitt	.584	Burke,T Mon	11
Henderson,R Oak	.579	Henneman,M Det	15	Bonilla,B Pitt	.583	Smith,D Hou	11
Puckett,K Min	.567	Aguilera,R Min	15	Davis,G Hou	.583	Williams,M Chi	9
Felix,J Tor	.552	Olson,G Bal	14	Sandberg,R Chi	.580	Lefferts,C SD	9
Griffey,K Sea	.551	Schooler,M Sea	14	Mitchell,K SF	.577	Franco,J NY	9
McGwire,M Oak	.532	Eichhorn,M Cal	12	Gant,R Atl	.572	Landrum,B Pitt	8
Barfield,J NY	.527	Righetti,D NY	11	Sabo,C Cin	.552	Brantley,J SF	7
Burks,E Bos	.510	Plesac,D Mil	10	Daniels,K LA	.533	Bedrosian,S SF	7

1991 STANDINGS

AMERICAN LEAGUE

East	Won	Lost	Pct.	GB

West	Won	Lost	Pct.	GB

NATIONAL LEAGUE

East	Won	Lost	Pct.	GB

West	Won	Lost	Pct.	GB

INDIVIDUAL LEADERS

AMERICAN LEAGUE

BATTING

HOME RUNS	WINS

RBI	E.R.A.

SLUGGING	SAVES

NATIONAL LEAGUE

BATTING

HOME RUNS	WINS

RBI	E.R.A.

SLUGGING	SAVES

J • U • N • E

Winning Pitcher:

Losing Pitcher:

Home Runs:

Highlights:

Score by innings:

MONDAY 10

Winning Pitcher:

Losing Pitcher:

Home Runs:

Highlights:

Score by innings:

TUESDAY 11

Winning Pitcher:

Losing Pitcher:

Home Runs:

Highlights:

Score by innings:

WEDNESDAY 12

Winning Pitcher:

Losing Pitcher:

Home Runs:

Highlights:

Score by innings:

THURSDAY 13

FRIDAY 14

_____ __

_____ ___

Winning Pitcher:

Losing Pitcher:

Home Runs:

Highlights:

Score by innings:

SATURDAY 15

_____ __

_____ ___

Winning Pitcher:

Losing Pitcher:

Home Runs:

Highlights:

Score by innings:

CBS: *Cubs vs. San Diego*

SUNDAY 16

_____ __

_____ ___

Winning Pitcher:

Losing Pitcher:

Home Runs:

Highlights:

Score by innings:

ESPN: *Pittsburgh vs. San Francisco*
Yankees vs. Texas

SCHEDULE

MONDAY	Cleve vs. Min	*Phil vs. Cin*
Bos vs. Sea	*SD vs. Pitt*	*NY vs. Hou*
Det vs. Oak	*LA vs. Chi*	
Mil vs. Cal	*SF vs. StL*	
Chi vs. Tex	*Mon vs. Atl*	
TUESDAY	NY vs. Min	*LA vs. Pitt*
Bos vs. Sea	Tor vs. Cleve	*SF vs. Chi*
Det vs. Oak	KC vs. Bal	*Phil vs. Hou*
Mil vs. Cal	*Cin vs. Mon*	*StL vs. SD*
Chi vs. Tex	*Atl vs. NY*	
WEDNESDAY	NY vs. Min	*LA vs. Pitt*
Bos vs. Sea	Tor vs. Cleve	*SF vs. Chi*
Det vs. Oak	KC vs. Bal	*Phil vs. Hou*
Mil vs. Cal	*Cin vs. Mon*	*StL vs. SD*
Chi vs. Tex	*Atl vs. NY*	
THURSDAY	KC vs. Bal	*Phil vs. Hou*
Det vs. Sea	*Cin vs. Mon*	*StL vs. SD*
Chi vs. Tex	*Atl vs. NY*	
NY vs. Min	*LA vs. Pitt*	
Tor vs. Cleve	*SF vs. Chi*	
FRIDAY	Min vs. Cleve	*Cin vs. Phil*
Det vs. Sea	Bal vs. Tor	*StL vs. LA*
NY vs. Tex	Cal vs. Bos	*Chi vs. SD*
KC vs. Chi	*Atl vs. Mon*	*Pitt vs. SF*
Oak vs. Mil	*Hou vs. NY*	
SATURDAY	Min vs. Cleve	*Cin vs. Phil*
Det vs. Sea	Bal vs. Tor	*StL vs. LA*
NY vs. Tex	Cal vs. Bos	*Chi vs. SD*
KC vs. Chi	*Atl vs. Mon*	*Pitt vs. SF*
Oak vs. Mil	*Hou vs. NY*	
SUNDAY	Min vs. Cleve	*Cin vs. Phil*
Det vs. Sea	Bal vs. Tor	*StL vs. LA*
NY vs. Tex	Cal vs. Bos	*Chi vs. SD*
KC vs. Chi	*Atl vs. Mon*	*Pitt vs. SF*
Oak vs. Mil	*Hou vs. NY*	

1990 STANDINGS

AMERICAN LEAGUE — Through June 17 — NATIONAL LEAGUE

East	Won	Lost	Pct.	GB	East	Won	Lost	Pct.	GB
Toronto	38	27	.585	–	Pittsburgh	38	24	.613	–
Boston	35	27	.565	1½	Montreal	36	28	.563	3
Detroit	31	34	.477	7	New York	31	29	.517	6
Milwaukee	29	32	.475	7	Philadelphia	32	30	.516	6
Cleveland	29	32	.475	7	St. Louis	27	37	.422	12
Baltimore	29	34	.460	8	Chicago	27	38	.415	12½
New York	21	39	.350	14½					

West	Won	Lost	Pct.	GB	West	Won	Lost	Pct.	GB
Oakland	42	20	.677	–	Cincinnati	39	20	.661	–
Chicago	37	23	.617	4	San Francisco	34	30	.531	7½
Minnesota	31	31	.500	11	San Diego	31	30	.508	9
California	32	32	.500	11	Los Angeles	30	33	.476	11
Seattle	32	34	.485	12	Houston	26	37	.413	15
Texas	27	37	.422	16	Atlanta	23	38	.377	17
Kansas City	25	36	.410	16½					

INDIVIDUAL LEADERS

AMERICAN LEAGUE — NATIONAL LEAGUE

BATTING

Based on 3.1 plate appearances per game

	G	AB	R	H	Pct.		G	AB	R	H	Pct.
Henderson,R Oak	58	213	47	71	.333	Dykstra,L Phil	56	230	46	89	.387
Guillen,O Chi	59	195	23	64	.328	Larkin,B Cin	59	228	37	79	.346
Griffey,K Sea	66	253	41	83	.328	Dawson,A Chi	61	218	37	75	.344
Harper,B Min	54	181	26	59	.326	Hatcher,B Cin	55	221	29	74	.335
Puckett,K Min	62	223	42	75	.322	Sandberg,R Chi	64	263	48	88	.335
Fielder,C Det	64	227	44	73	.322	Gwynn,T SD	61	240	41	79	.329
Canseco,J Oak	52	194	43	62	.320	Mitchell,K SF	59	229	47	74	.323
Parker,D Mil	58	224	25	71	.317	Gant,R Atl	53	186	40	60	.323
Sheffield,G Mil	47	180	29	57	.317	Bonds,B Pitt	55	199	44	64	.322
Martinez,E Sea	60	210	32	66	.314	Sabo,C Cin	56	227	49	73	.322

HOME RUNS — WINS — HOME RUNS — WINS

HOME RUNS		WINS		HOME RUNS		WINS	
Fielder,C Det	25	Clemens,R Bos	11	Davis,G Hou	19	Armstrong,J Cin	9
Canseco,J Oak	20	Finley,C Cal	10	Sandberg,R Chi	18	Heaton,N Pitt	9
McGwire,M Oak	17	Welch,B Oak	10	Mitchell,K SF	17	Viola,F NY	9
Gruber,K Tor	17	Stieb,D Tor	9	Dawson,A Chi	17	Drabek,D Pitt	8
McGriff,F Tor	13	Stewart,D Oak	9	Bonilla,B Pitt	15	Howell,K Phil	8
Bell,G Tor	12	Brown,K Tex	8	Strawberry,D NY	14	Gross,K Mon	8
Parrish,L Cal	12	Sanderson,S Oak	8	Williams,M SF	13	Martinez,R LA	7
Maldonado,C Cleve	11	Boddicker,M Bos	8	Sabo,C Cin	13	Burkett,J SF	7
Barfield,J NY	11			Clark,W SF	13	Morgan,M LA	7

RBI — E.R.A. — RBI — E.R.A.

RBI		E.R.A.		RBI		E.R.A.	
Fielder,C, Det	61	Stewart,D Oak	2.30	Williams,M SF	55	Armstrong,J Cin	1.99
Gruber,K Tor	56	King,E Chi	2.41	Carter,J SD	54	Browning,T Cin	2.24
Canseco,J Oak	50	Stieb,D Tor	2.46	Clark,W SF	51	Gardner,M Mon	2.28
Leonard,J Sea	45	Welch,B Oak	2.52	Bonilla,B Pitt	49	Tudor,J StL	2.51
Bell,G Tor	45	Finley,C Cal	2.59	Bonds,B Pitt	48	Viola,F NY	2.62
McGwire,M Oak	43	Clemens,R Bos	2.60	Davis,G Hou	48	Martinez,De Mon	2.64
Felix,J Tor	40	Petry,D Det	2.61	Dawson,A Chi	48	Martinez,R LA	2.78
Maldonado,C Cleve	40	Black,B Cleve	2.82	Guerrero,P StL	44	Whitson,E SD	2.89
Parker,D Mil	39	Saberhagen,B KC	2.82	Wallach,T Mon	43	Rijo,J Cin	2.96
		Leary,T NY	2.86	Sandberg,R Chi	43	Heaton,N Pitt	2.99

SLUGGING — SAVES — SLUGGING — SAVES

SLUGGING		SAVES		SLUGGING		SAVES	
Fielder,C Det	.705	Eckersley,D Oak	22	Dawson,A Chi	.661	McDowell,R Phil	13
Canseco,J Oak	.644	Jones,D Cleve	21	Mitchell,K SF	.607	Smith,D Hou	13
Gruber,K Tor	.588	Thigpen,B Chi	21	Gant,R Atl	.602	Myers,R Cin	12
Henderson,R Oak	.559	Aguilera,R Min	16	Bonds,B Pitt	.598	Burke,T Mon	11
Puckett,K Min	.541	Schooler,M Sea	15	Sandberg,R Chi	.593	Franco,J NY	11
Felix,J Tor	.531	Henneman,M Det	15	Sabo,C Cin	.577	Landrum,B Pitt	10
McGwire,M Oak	.529	Olson,G Bal	14	Bonilla,B Pitt	.569	Williams,M Chi	8
Parrish,L Cal	.525	Righetti,D NY	13	Davis,G Hou	.568	Lefferts,C SD	9
Griffey,K Sea	.514	Plesac,D Mil	12	Wallach,T Mon	.560		
Maldonado,C Cleve	.507	Eichhorn,M Cal	12	Williams,M SF	.526		

1991 STANDINGS

AMERICAN LEAGUE

East	Won	Lost	Pct.	GB

West	Won	Lost	Pct.	GB

NATIONAL LEAGUE

East	Won	Lost	Pct.	GB

West	Won	Lost	Pct.	GB

INDIVIDUAL LEADERS

AMERICAN LEAGUE

BATTING

HOME RUNS

WINS

RBI

E.R.A.

SLUGGING

SAVES

NATIONAL LEAGUE

BATTING

HOME RUNS

WINS

RBI

E.R.A.

SLUGGING

SAVES

Winning Pitcher:

Losing Pitcher:

Home Runs:

Highlights:

Score by innings:

MONDAY | **17**

Winning Pitcher:

Losing Pitcher:

Home Runs:

Highlights:

Score by innings:

TUESDAY | **18**

Winning Pitcher:

Losing Pitcher:

Home Runs:

Highlights:

Score by innings:

WEDNESDAY | **19**

Winning Pitcher:

Losing Pitcher:

Home Runs:

Highlights:

Score by innings:

THURSDAY | **20**

J · U · N · E

FRIDAY 21

Winning Pitcher:

Losing Pitcher:

Home Runs:

Highlights:

Score by innings:

SATURDAY 22

Winning Pitcher:

Losing Pitcher:

Home Runs:

Highlights:

Score by innings:

CBS: *Pittsburgh vs. Los Angeles*

SUNDAY 23

Winning Pitcher:

Losing Pitcher:

Home Runs:

Highlights:

Score by innings:

ESPN: **California vs. Detroit**

SCHEDULE

MONDAY	*Hou vs. Mon*	*StL vs. SF*
KC vs. Tex	*Cin vs. NY*	
Oak vs. Mil	*Atl vs. Phil*	
Min vs. Bal	*Chi vs. LA*	
Cal vs. Bos	*Pitt vs. SD*	
TUESDAY	NY vs. Tor	*Atl vs. Phil*
KC vs. Tex	Min vs. Bal	*Chi vs. LA*
Cleve vs. Chi	Sea vs. Bos	*Pitt vs. SD*
Cal vs. Mil	*Hou vs. Mon*	*StL vs. SF*
Oak vs. Det	*Cin vs. NY*	
WEDNESDAY	NY vs. Tor	*Atl vs. Phil*
KC vs. Tex	Min vs. Bal	*Chi vs. LA*
Cleve vs. Chi	Sea vs. Bos	*Pitt vs. SD*
Cal vs. Mil	*Hou vs. Mon*	*StL vs. SF*
Oak vs. Det	*Cin vs. NY*	
THURSDAY	NY vs. Tor	*Pitt vs. LA*
Bal vs. KC	Oak vs. Bos	*Chi vs. SF*
Tex vs. Chi	*Hou vs. Phil*	
Sea vs. Mil	*NY vs. Atl*	
Cal vs. Det	*Mon vs. Cin*	
FRIDAY	Cleve vs. Tor	*NY vs. Atl*
Bal vs. KC	Min vs. NY	*Mon vs. Cin*
Tex vs. Chi	Oak vs. Bos	*Pitt vs. LA*
Sea vs. Mil	*Hou vs. Phil*	*Chi vs. SF*
Cal vs. Det	*SD vs. StL*	
SATURDAY	Cleve vs. Tor	*NY vs. Atl*
Bal vs. KC	Min vs. NY	*Mon vs. Cin*
Tex vs. Chi	Oak vs. Bos	*Pitt vs. LA*
Sea vs. Mil	*Hou vs. Phil*	*Chi vs. SF*
Cal vs. Det	*SD vs. StL*	
SUNDAY	Cleve vs. Tor	*NY vs. Atl*
Bal vs. KC	Min vs. NY	*Mon vs. Cin*
Tex vs. Chi	Oak vs. Bos	*Pitt vs. LA*
Sea vs. Mil	*Hou vs. Phil*	*Chi vs. SF*
Cal vs. Det	*SD vs. StL*	

1 9 9 0 S T A N D I N G S

AMERICAN LEAGUE — Through June 24 — **NATIONAL LEAGUE**

East	Won	Lost	Pct.	GB	East	Won	Lost	Pct.	GB
Toronto	41	30	.577	–	Pittsburgh	39	28	.582	–
Boston	39	29	.574	$\frac{1}{2}$	Montreal	40	30	.571	$\frac{1}{2}$
Milwaukee	32	35	.478	7	New York	36	29	.554	2
Cleveland	32	35	.478	7	Philadelphia	34	33	.507	5
Detroit	34	38	.472	$7\frac{1}{2}$	St. Louis	29	40	.420	11
Baltimore	31	39	.443	$9\frac{1}{2}$	Chicago	29	42	.408	12
New York	25	42	.373	14					

West	Won	Lost	Pct.	GB	West	Won	Lost	Pct.	GB
Oakland	43	25	.632	–	Cincinnati	43	23	.652	–
Chicago	41	25	.621	1	San Diego	34	32	.515	9
California	37	34	.521	$7\frac{1}{2}$	San Francisco	36	34	.514	9
Seattle	35	37	.486	10	Los Angeles	34	35	.493	$10\frac{1}{2}$
Minnesota	33	36	.478	$10\frac{1}{2}$	Houston	28	41	.406	$16\frac{1}{2}$
Texas	31	39	.443	13	Atlanta	26	41	.388	$17\frac{1}{2}$
Kansas City	29	39	.426	14					

I N D I V I D U A L L E A D E R S

AMERICAN LEAGUE — **NATIONAL LEAGUE**

BATTING

AMERICAN LEAGUE — BATTING
Based on 3.1 plate appearances per game

	G	AB	R	H	Pct.
Guillen,O Chi	65	215	27	72	.335
Griffey,K Sea	72	275	46	91	.331
Henderson,R Oak	63	230	51	76	.330
Parker,D Mil	64	249	30	80	.321
Puckett,K Min	68	253	45	80	.316
Canseco,J Oak	53	198	43	62	.313
Sheffield,G Mil	53	203	33	63	.310
Martinez,E Sea	66	232	36	72	.310
Gruber,K Tor	69	274	53	85	.310
Palmeiro,R Tex	64	246	32	76	.309

NATIONAL LEAGUE — BATTING

	G	AB	R	H	Pct.
Dykstra,L Phil	61	248	51	92	.371
Sandberg,R Chi	70	284	55	98	.345
Bonds,B Pitt	59	214	48	73	.341
Dawson,A Chi	66	236	38	78	.331
Larkin,B Cin	66	258	39	85	.329
Gwynn,T SD	66	263	43	86	.327
Alomar,R SD	65	268	34	86	.321
McGee,W StL	69	275	49	88	.320
Gant,R Atl	59	210	42	67	.319
Hatcher,B Cin	62	248	32	79	.319

HOME RUNS (AL)
Fielder,C Det	25
Canseco,J Oak	20
McGwire,M Oak	19
Gruber,K Tor	18
Bell,G Tor	17
Parrish,L Cal	14
McGriff,F Tor	13

WINS (AL)
Clemens,R Bos	11
Welch,B Oak	11
Finley,C Cal	10
Stieb,D Tor	10
Brown,K Tex	9
Stewart,D Oak	9
Boddicker,M Bos	9

HOME RUNS (NL)
Sandberg,R Chi	21
Davis,G Hou	19
Mitchell,K SF	17
Dawson,A Chi	17
Sabo,C Cin	16
Bonilla,B Pitt	16
Strawberry,D NY	15
Williams,M SF	14
Gant,R Atl	14

WINS (NL)
Heaton,N Pitt	10
Viola,F NY	10
Armstrong,J Cin	9
Martinez,R LA	8
Drabek,D Pitt	8
Howell,K Phil	8
Gross,K Mon	8
Burkett,J SF	7
Browning,T Cin	7
Morgan,M LA	7

RBI (AL)
Fielder,C Det	63
Gruber,K Tor	60
Bell,G Tor	56
Canseco,J Oak	50
McGwire,M Oak	47
Parker,D Mil	47
Trammell,A Det	46
Leonard,J Sea	45
Maldonado,C Cleve	43

E.R.A. (AL)
King,E Chi	2.15
Stieb,D Tor	2.26
Finley,C Cal	2.36
Welch,B Oak	2.46
Clemens,R Bos	2.59
Stewart,D Oak	2.75
Hibbard,G Chi	2.85
Saberhagen,B KC	2.89
Brown,K Tex	3.04
Harris,G Bos	3.17

RBI (NL)
Williams,M SF	57
Carter,J SD	57
Clark,W SF	55
Bonds,B Pitt	52
Bonilla,B Pitt	51
Dawson,A Chi	49
Sandberg,R Chi	49
Davis,G Hou	48
Guerrero,P StL	46
Wallach,T Mon	45

E.R.A. (NL)
Armstrong,J Cin	2.11
Gardner,M Mon	2.19
Viola,F NY	2.50
Martinez,De Mon	2.50
Browning,T Cin	2.57
Martinez,R LA	2.78
Tudor,J StL	2.84
Heaton,N Pitt	2.89
Whitson,E SD	2.96
Drabek,D Pitt	3.04

SLUGGING (AL)
Fielder,C Det	.651
Canseco,J Oak	.631
Gruber,K Tor	.588
Henderson,R Oak	.565
Parrish,L Cal	.530
Bell,G Tor	.530
Puckett,K Min	.530
Griffey,K Sea	.527
McGwire,M Oak	.523
Burks,E Bos	.512

SAVES (AL)
Thigpen,B Chi	23
Eckersley,D Oak	22
Jones,D Cleve	21
Schooler,M Sea	17
Aguilera,R Min	17
Henneman,M Det	16
Olson,G Bal	15
Righetti,D NY	15
Plesac,D Mil	13
Eichhorn,M Cal	13

SLUGGING (NL)
Dawson,A Chi	.631
Bonds,B Pitt	.631
Sandberg,R Chi	.623
Gant,R Atl	.600
Sabo,C Cin	.580
Mitchell,K SF	.567
Bonilla,B Pitt	.556
Davis,G Hou	.556
Wallach,T Mon	.531
Daniels,K LA	.525

SAVES (NL)
Smith,D Hou	14
Myers,R Cin	13
McDowell,R Phil	13
Franco,J NY	12
Burke,T Mon	11
Lefferts,C SD	11
Landrum,B Pitt	10
Brantley,J SF	9
Williams,M Chi	9
Schmidt,D Mon	9

1991 STANDINGS

AMERICAN LEAGUE

East	Won	Lost	Pct.	GB

West	Won	Lost	Pct.	GB

NATIONAL LEAGUE

East	Won	Lost	Pct.	GB

West	Won	Lost	Pct.	GB

INDIVIDUAL LEADERS

AMERICAN LEAGUE

BATTING

HOME RUNS

WINS

RBI

E.R.A.

SLUGGING

SAVES

NATIONAL LEAGUE

BATTING

HOME RUNS

WINS

RBI

E.R.A.

SLUGGING

SAVES

J · U · N · E

MONDAY 24

_____ ___

Winning Pitcher:

Losing Pitcher:

Home Runs:

Highlights:

Score by innings:

TUESDAY 25

_____ ___

Winning Pitcher:

Losing Pitcher:

Home Runs:

Highlights:

Score by innings:

WEDNESDAY 26

_____ ___

Winning Pitcher:

Losing Pitcher:

Home Runs:

Highlights:

Score by innings:

THURSDAY 27

_____ ___

Winning Pitcher:

Losing Pitcher:

Home Runs:

Highlights:

Score by innings:

J • U • N • E

FRIDAY 28

Winning Pitcher:

Losing Pitcher:

Home Runs:

Highlights:

Score by innings:

SATURDAY 29

Winning Pitcher:

Losing Pitcher:

Home Runs:

Highlights:

Score by innings:

CBS: *St. Louis vs. Cubs*
Boston vs. Baltimore

SUNDAY 30

Winning Pitcher:

Losing Pitcher:

Home Runs:

Highlights:

Score by innings:

ESPN: *Los Angeles vs. Atlanta*

SCHEDULE

MONDAY	*SD vs. StL*	
Cal vs. KC		
Sea vs. Chi		
Cleve vs. Tor		
Min vs. NY		
TUESDAY	Mil vs. Det	*Phil vs. StL*
Tex vs. Oak	Bal vs. Cleve	*SD vs. Cin*
Cal vs. KC	NY vs. Bos	*Atl vs. Hou*
Tor vs. Min	*Mon vs. NY*	*SF vs. LA*
Sea vs. Chi	*Chi vs. Pitt*	
WEDNESDAY	Mil vs. Det	*Phil vs. StL*
Tex vs. Oak	Bal vs. Cleve	*SD vs. Cin*
Cal vs. KC	NY vs. Bos	*Atl vs. Hou*
Tor vs. Min	*Mon vs. NY*	*SF vs. LA*
Sea vs. Chi	*Chi vs. Pitt*	
THURSDAY	Bal vs. Cleve	*SD vs. Cin*
Tex vs. Oak	NY vs. Bos	*Atl vs. Hou*
Tor vs. Min	*Mon vs. NY*	
Sea vs. Chi	*Chi vs. Pitt*	
Mil vs. Det	*Phil vs. StL*	
FRIDAY	Cleve vs. Det	*StL vs. Chi*
KC vs. Oak	Sea vs. Tor	*LA vs. Atl*
Tex vs. Cal	Bos vs. Bal	*Hou vs. Cin*
Chi vs. Min	*Pitt vs. Mon*	*SF vs. SD*
NY vs. Mil	*Phil vs. NY*	
SATURDAY	Cleve vs. Det	*StL vs. Chi*
KC vs. Oak	Sea vs. Tor	*LA vs. Atl*
Tex vs. Cal	Bos vs. Bal	*Hou vs. Cin*
Chi vs. Min	*Pitt vs. Mon*	*SF vs. SD*
NY vs. Mil	*Phil vs. NY*	
SUNDAY	Cleve vs. Det	*StL vs. Chi*
KC vs. Oak	Sea vs. Tor	*LA vs. Atl*
Tex vs. Cal	Bos vs. Bal	*Hou vs. Cin*
Chi vs. Min	*Pitt vs. Mon*	*SF vs. SD*
NY vs. Mil	*Phil vs. NY*	

1990 STANDINGS

AMERICAN LEAGUE — Through June 30 — **NATIONAL LEAGUE**

East	Won	Lost	Pct.	GB		East	Won	Lost	Pct.	GB
Boston	43	31	.581	–		Pittsburgh	43	30	.589	–
Toronto	41	36	.532	3½		New York	41	30	.577	1
Cleveland	36	37	.493	6½		Montreal	42	34	.553	2½
Detroit	36	41	.468	8½		Philadelphia	35	37	.486	7½
Baltimore	34	41	.453	9½		Chicago	33	44	.429	12
Milwaukee	33	40	.452	9½		St. Louis	31	44	.413	13
New York	28	44	.389	14						

West	Won	Lost	Pct.	GB		West	Won	Lost	Pct.	GB
Oakland	47	26	.644	–		Cincinnati	46	26	.639	–
Chicago	45	26	.634	1		San Francisco	38	37	.507	9½
Seattle	39	38	.506	10		Los Angeles	36	38	.486	11
California	38	38	.500	10½		San Diego	35	37	.486	11
Minnesota	35	40	.467	13		Houston	32	43	.427	15½
Texas	35	41	.461	13½		Atlanta	30	42	.417	16
Kansas City	31	42	.425	16						

INDIVIDUAL LEADERS

AMERICAN LEAGUE

BATTING

Based on 3.1 plate appearances per game

	G	AB	R	H	Pct.
Henderson,R Oak	68	244	58	82	.336
Griffey,K Sea	77	295	48	98	.332
Guillen,O Chi	70	230	28	74	.322
Palmeiro,R Tex	70	271	33	87	.321
Parker,D Mil	70	271	34	87	.321
Jacoby,B Cleve	69	251	40	80	.319
Martinez,E Sea	71	246	41	77	.313
Gruber,K Tor	75	299	57	92	.308
Canseco,J Oak	55	203	43	62	.305
Trammell,A Det	74	288	33	87	.302

HOME RUNS

Fielder,C Det	26
McGwire,M Oak	20
Canseco,J Oak	20
Gruber,K Tor	20
Bell,G Tor	17
McGriff,F Tor	16
Kittle,R Chi	14
Parrish,L Cal	14
Henderson,D Oak	14

WINS

Welch,B Oak	13
Clemens,R Bos	12
Finley,C Cal	10
Stieb,D Tor	10
Stewart,D Oak	10
Boddicker,M Bos	10
Brown,K Tex	9
Jones,B Chi	9
Sanderson,S Oak	9
Candiotti,T Cleve	9

RBI

Fielder,C Det	65
Gruber,K Tor	64
Bell,G Tor	56
McGwire,M Oak	50
Canseco,J Oak	50
Parker,D Mil	50
Leonard,J Sea	49
Trammell,A Det	46
Maldonado,C Cleve	44

E.R.A.

King,E Chi	2.18
Stewart,D Oak	2.55
Hibbard,G Chi	2.59
Finley,C Cal	2.62
Clemens,R Bos	2.64
Welch,B Oak	2.69
Saberhagen,B KC	2.96
Brown,K Tex	3.06
Harris,G Bos	3.09
Langston,M Cal	3.13

SLUGGING

Fielder,C Det	.629
Canseco,J Oak	.616
Gruber,K Tor	.592
Henderson,R Oak	.590
Parrish,L Cal	.526
Griffey,K Sea	.519
Puckett,K Min	.513
McGwire,M Oak	.509
Burks,E Bos	.507
Jacoby,B Cleve	.506

SAVES

Thigpen,B Chi	26
Eckersley,D Oak	24
Jones,D Cleve	22
Schooler,M Sea	20
Aguilera,R Min	18
Henneman,M Det	17
Righetti,D NY	16
Olson,G Bal	15

NATIONAL LEAGUE

BATTING

	G	AB	R	H	Pct.
Dykstra,L Phil	66	269	53	100	.372
Sandberg,R Chi	76	308	62	106	.344
Bonds,B Pitt	65	232	50	77	.332
Alomar,R SD	71	292	37	94	.322
Dawson,A Chi	72	258	40	83	.322
Larkin,B Cin	72	281	40	89	.317
Gwynn,T SD	72	288	43	91	.316
McGee,W StL	75	302	50	95	.315
Gant,R Atl	63	226	44	71	.314
Sabo,C Cin	68	278	59	87	.313

HOME RUNS

Sandberg,R Chi	24
Mitchell,K SF	19
Davis,G Hou	19
Dawson,A Chi	18
Strawberry,D NY	17
Bonilla,B Pitt	17
Williams,M SF	16
Sabo,C Cin	16
Gant,R Atl	15
Clark,W SF	14

WINS

Viola,F NY	11
Armstrong,J Cin	10
Heaton,N Pitt	10
Martinez,R LA	9
Drabek,D Pitt	8
Howell,K Phil	8
Gross,K Mon	8

RBI

Williams,M SF	62
Clark,W SF	58
Carter,J SD	58
Bonilla,B Pitt	54
Bonds,B Pitt	53
Sandberg,R Chi	53
Dawson,A Chi	52
Wallach,T Mon	49
Davis,G Hou	48
Guerrero,P StL	48

E.R.A.

Armstrong,J Cin	2.34
Viola,F NY	2.45
Martinez,De Mon	2.66
Gardner,M Mon	2.80
Martinez,R LA	2.83
Whitson,E SD	2.88
Tudor,J StL	2.93
Browning,T Cin	2.94
Gullickson,B Hou	3.23
Morgan,M LA	3.24

SLUGGING

Sandberg,R Chi	.636
Dawson,A Chi	.612
Bonds,B Pitt	.612
Mitchell,K SF	.589
Gant,R Atl	.588
Sabo,C Cin	.565
Davis,G Hou	.556
Bonilla,B Pitt	.539
Strawberry,D NY	.535
Wallach,T Mon	.526

SAVES

Myers,R Cin	15
Smith,D Hou	15
Franco,J NY	14
McDowell,R Phil	13
Landrum,B Pitt	11
Burke,T Mon	11
Lefferts,C SD	11
Brantley,J SF	10

1991 STANDINGS

AMERICAN LEAGUE					NATIONAL LEAGUE				
East	Won	Lost	Pct.	GB	East	Won	Lost	Pct.	GB
West	Won	Lost	Pct.	GB	West	Won	Lost	Pct.	GB

INDIVIDUAL LEADERS

AMERICAN LEAGUE	NATIONAL LEAGUE
BATTING	BATTING

HOME RUNS	WINS	HOME RUNS	WINS

RBI	E.R.A.	RBI	E.R.A.

SLUGGING	SAVES	SLUGGING	SAVES

J • U • L • Y

MONDAY 1

_____ __

Winning Pitcher:

Losing Pitcher:

Home Runs:

Highlights:

Score by innings:

TUESDAY 2

_____ __

Winning Pitcher:

Losing Pitcher:

Home Runs:

Highlights:

Score by innings:

WEDNESDAY 3

_____ __

Winning Pitcher:

Losing Pitcher:

Home Runs:

Highlights:

Score by innings:

THURSDAY 4

_____ __

Winning Pitcher:

Losing Pitcher:

Home Runs:

Highlights:

Score by innings:

CBS: Bal vs. NY; *Pitt vs. Chi* (day); *NY vs. Mon*; *StL vs. Phil* (night); *LA vs. SD*; *Hou vs. SF* (late)

J · U · L · Y

FRIDAY 5

_____ ____

Winning Pitcher:

Losing Pitcher:

Home Runs:

Highlights:

Score by innings:

SATURDAY 6

_____ ____

Winning Pitcher:

Losing Pitcher:

Home Runs:

Highlights:

Score by innings:

SUNDAY 7

_____

Winning Pitcher:

Losing Pitcher:

Home Runs:

Highlights:

Score by innings:

ESPN: Cubs vs. St. Louis
California vs. Texas

SCHEDULE

MONDAY	Sea vs. Tor	*Pitt vs. Chi*
KC vs. Oak	Det vs. Bal	
Tex vs. Cal	Cleve vs. NY	
Chi vs. Min	*NY vs. Mon*	
Bos vs. Mil	*StL vs. Phil*	
TUESDAY	Min vs. Tor	*Pitt vs. Chi*
Chi vs. Sea	Det vs. Bal	*Cin vs. Atl*
KC vs. Cal	Cleve vs. NY	*LA vs. SD*
Oak vs. Tex	*NY vs. Mon*	*Hou vs. SF*
Bos vs. Mil	*StL vs. Phil*	
WEDNESDAY	Min vs. Tor	*Pitt vs. Chi*
Chi vs. Sea	Det vs. Bal	*Cin vs. Atl*
KC vs. Cal	Cleve vs. NY	*LA vs. SD*
Oak vs. Tex	*NY vs. Mon*	*Hou vs. SF*
Bos vs. Mil	*StL vs. Phil*	
THURSDAY	Min vs. Tor	*Pitt vs. Chi*
Chi vs. Sea	Bal vs. NY	*Cin vs. Atl*
KC vs. Cal	Det vs. Bos	*LA vs. SD*
Oak vs. Tex	*NY vs. Mon*	*Hou vs. SF*
Mil vs. Cleve	*StL vs. Phil*	
FRIDAY	Mil vs. Cleve	*Chi vs. StL*
Tor vs. Sea	Bal vs. NY	*Cin vs. Hou*
Cal vs. Tex	Det vs. Bos	*Atl vs. LA*
Oak vs. KC	*NY vs. Phil*	*SD vs. SF*
Min vs. Chi	*Mon vs. Pitt*	
SATURDAY	Mil vs. Cleve	*Chi vs. StL*
Tor vs. Sea	Bal vs. NY	*Cin vs. Hou*
Cal vs. Tex	Det vs. Bos	*Atl vs. LA*
Oak vs. KC	*NY vs. Phil*	*SD vs. SF*
Min vs. Chi	*Mon vs. Pitt*	
SUNDAY	Mil vs. Cleve	*Chi vs. StL*
Tor vs. Sea	Bal vs. NY	*Cin vs. Hou*
Cal vs. Tex	Det vs. Bos	*Atl vs. LA*
Oak vs. KC	*NY vs. Phil*	*SD vs. SF*
Min vs. Chi	*Mon vs. Pitt*	

1990 STANDINGS

AMERICAN LEAGUE — Through July 8 — NATIONAL LEAGUE

East	Won	Lost	Pct.	GB	East	Won	Lost	Pct.	GB
Boston	46	36	.561	—	Pittsburgh	49	32	.605	—
Toronto	47	38	.553	$\frac{1}{2}$	New York	47	31	.603	$\frac{1}{2}$
Cleveland	40	42	.488	6	Montreal	47	37	.560	$3\frac{1}{2}$
Detroit	41	44	.482	$6\frac{1}{2}$	Philadelphia	39	41	.488	$9\frac{1}{2}$
Baltimore	37	45	.451	9	Chicago	36	49	.424	15
Milwaukee	36	44	.450	9	St. Louis	35	48	.422	15
New York	30	50	.375	15					

West	Won	Lost	Pct.	GB	West	Won	Lost	Pct.	GB
Oakland	51	31	.622	—	Cincinnati	50	29	.633	—
Chicago	48	30	.615	1	San Francisco	44	39	.530	8
Seattle	43	41	.512	9	Los Angeles	39	43	.476	$12\frac{1}{2}$
California	41	43	.488	11	San Diego	37	43	.463	$13\frac{1}{2}$
Minnesota	40	43	.482	$11\frac{1}{2}$	Atlanta	33	47	.413	$17\frac{1}{2}$
Texas	40	44	.476	12	Houston	33	50	.398	19
Kansas City	36	45	.444	$14\frac{1}{2}$					

INDIVIDUAL LEADERS

AMERICAN LEAGUE — NATIONAL LEAGUE

BATTING

Based on 3.1 plate appearances per game

	G	AB	R	H	Pct.		G	AB	R	H	Pct.
Henderson,R Oak	77	278	66	93	.335	Dykstra,L Phil	74	289	57	104	.360
Griffey,K Sea	84	323	54	107	.331	Bonds,B Pitt	73	262	55	89	.340
Guillen,O Chi	77	254	32	81	.319	Sandberg,R Chi	83	334	67	112	.335
Parker,D Mil	77	302	37	95	.315	Dawson,A Chi	78	281	45	91	.324
Jacoby,B Cleve	78	280	42	88	.314	McGee,W StL	83	331	53	106	.320
Palmeiro,R Tex	78	298	36	93	.312	Gant,R Atl	71	258	50	82	.318
Sheffield,G Mil	66	263	38	82	.312	Mitchell,K SF	73	276	55	86	.312
Harper,B Min	72	246	31	76	.309	Gwynn,T SD	79	318	47	99	.311
Boggs,W Bos	78	307	50	94	.306	Alomar,R SD	79	322	40	100	.311
Puckett,K Min	81	303	53	92	.304	Larkin,B Cin	79	309	45	95	.307

HOME RUNS — WINS — HOME RUNS — WINS

HOME RUNS		WINS		HOME RUNS		WINS	
Fielder,C Det	28	Welch,B Oak	13	Sandberg,R Chi	24	Viola,F NY	13
McGwire,M Oak	22	Clemens,R Bos	12	Mitchell,K SF	21	Armstrong,J Cin	11
Canseco,J Oak	22	Finley,C Cal	11	Strawberry,D NY	21	Heaton,N Pitt	10
Gruber,K Tor	20	Stieb,D Tor	11	Davis,G Hou	19	Martinez,R LA	9
McGriff,F Tor	18	Stewart,D Oak	11	Bonilla,B Pitt	19	Burkett,J SF	9
Bell,G Tor	17	Boddicker,M Bos	11	Dawson,A Chi	19	Drabek,D Pitt	9
Henderson,R Oak	17	Brown,K Tex	10	Williams,M SF	17	Browning,T Cin	8
Jackson,B KC	16	Jones,B Chi	10	Gant,R Atl	17	Howell,K Phil	8
Kittle,R Chi	16			Sabo,C Cin	16	Gross,K Mon	8
Parrish,L Cal	16			Bonds,B Pitt	15	Gooden,D NY	8

RBI — E.R.A. — RBI — E.R.A.

RBI		E.R.A.		RBI		E.R.A.	
Fielder,C Det	75	Finley,C Cal	2.54	Williams,M SF	69	Viola,F NY	2.20
Gruber,K Tor	66	Hibbard,G Chi	2.58	Bonds,B Pitt	62	Armstrong,J Cin	2.28
Bell,G Tor	60	Clemens,R Bos	2.59	Clark,W SF	61	Gardner,M Mon	2.54
McGwire,M Oak	56	Stewart,D Oak	2.91	Bonilla,B Pitt	61	Martinez,De Mon	2.84
Parker,D Mil	56	Welch,B Oak	2.91	Carter,J SD	59	Browning,T Cin	2.85
Leonard,J Sea	55	Saberhagen,B KC	2.98	Dawson,A Chi	57	Whitson,E SD	2.89
Canseco,J Oak	54	King,E Chi	2.99	Sandberg,R Chi	57	Smith,Z Mon	2.93
Jackson,B KC	49	Black,B Cleve	3.11	Strawberry,D NY	56	Tudor,J StL	2.93
Incaviglia,P Tex	48	Harris,G Bos	3.12	Wallach,T Mon	54	Boyd,D Mon	3.17
		Stieb,D Tor	3.15	Guerrero,P StL	51	Martinez,R LA	3.20

SLUGGING — SAVES — SLUGGING — SAVES

SLUGGING		SAVES		SLUGGING		SAVES	
Fielder,C Det	.611	Thigpen,B Chi	27	Bonds,B Pitt	.615	Myers,R Cin	17
Henderson,R Oak	.601	Eckersley,D Oak	25	Sandberg,R Chi	.608	Franco,J NY	17
Canseco,J Oak	.599	Jones,D Cleve	23	Dawson,A Chi	.605	Smith,D Hou	16
Gruber,K Tor	.561	Schooler,M Sea	22	Mitchell,K SF	.598	Brantley,J SF	13
Parrish,L Cal	.519	Aguilera,R Min	21	Gant,R Atl	.597	McDowell,R Phil	13
Parker,D Mil	.510	Olson,G Bal	17	Strawberry,D NY	.572	Landrum,B Pitt	12
Puckett,K Min	.508	Henneman,M Det	17	Davis,G Hou	.556	Schmidt,D Mon	12
Griffey,K Sea	.508	Righetti,D NY	17	Bonilla,B Pitt	.546	Burke,T Mon	11
Burks,E Bos	.503	Henke,T Tor	16	Sabo,C Cin	.534	Lefferts,C SD	11
McGwire,M Oak	.500			Wallach,T Mon	.525	Smith,L StL	11

1991 STANDINGS

AMERICAN LEAGUE					NATIONAL LEAGUE				
East	**Won**	**Lost**	**Pct.**	**GB**	**East**	**Won**	**Lost**	**Pct.**	**GB**
West	**Won**	**Lost**	**Pct.**	**GB**	**West**	**Won**	**Lost**	**Pct.**	**GB**

INDIVIDUAL LEADERS

AMERICAN LEAGUE

BATTING

HOME RUNS

WINS

RBI

E.R.A.

SLUGGING

SAVES

NATIONAL LEAGUE

BATTING

HOME RUNS

WINS

RBI

E.R.A.

SLUGGING

SAVES

J · U · L · Y

All-Star Break

MONDAY 8

All-Star Game

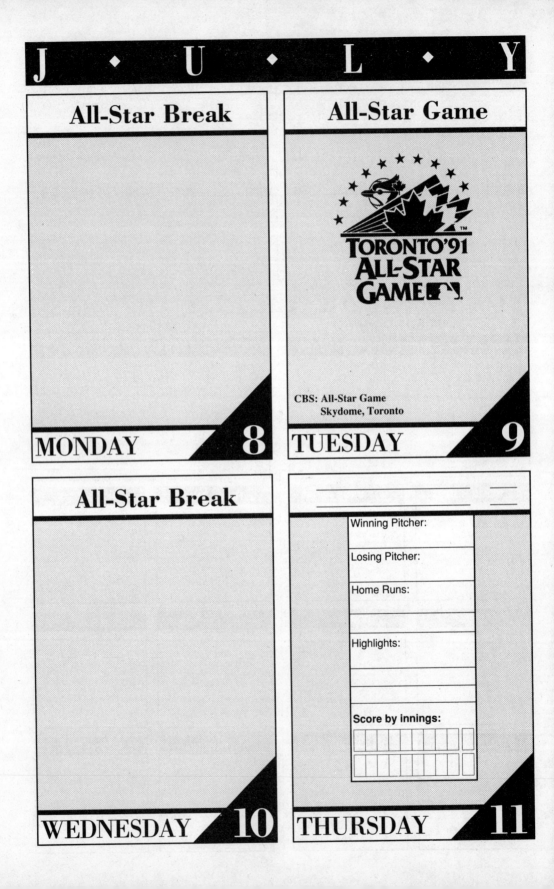

TORONTO '91
ALL-STAR
GAME

CBS: All-Star Game
  Skydome, Toronto

TUESDAY 9

All-Star Break

WEDNESDAY 10

Winning Pitcher:

Losing Pitcher:

Home Runs:

Highlights:

Score by innings:

THURSDAY 11

J · U · L · Y

FRIDAY 12

_____ _____

Winning Pitcher:

Losing Pitcher:

Home Runs:

Highlights:

Score by innings:

SATURDAY 13

_____ _____

Winning Pitcher:

Losing Pitcher:

Home Runs:

Highlights:

Score by innings:

SUNDAY 14

_____ _____

Winning Pitcher:

Losing Pitcher:

Home Runs:

Highlights:

Score by innings:

CBS: Baltimore vs. Oakland
ESPN: Texas vs. Toronto

SCHEDULE

MONDAY
All-Star Break

TUESDAY
All-Star Game in Toronto

WEDNESDAY
All-Star Break

THURSDAY	Chi vs. Mil	*SF vs. Phil*
Cleve vs. Sea	KC vs. Det	*Hou vs. Chi*
Bal vs. Oak	Tex vs. Tor	*StL vs. Atl*
NY vs. Cal	*LA vs. Mon*	*Pitt vs. Cin*
Bos vs. Min	*SD vs. NY*	
FRIDAY	Chi vs. Mil	*SF vs. Phil*
Cleve vs. Sea	KC vs. Det	*Hou vs. Chi*
Bal vs. Oak	Tex vs. Tor	*StL vs. Atl*
NY vs. Cal	*LA vs. Mon*	*Pitt vs. Cin*
Bos vs. Min	*SD vs. NY*	
SATURDAY	Chi vs. Mil	*SF vs. Phil*
Cleve vs. Sea	KC vs. Det	*Hou vs. Chi*
Bal vs. Oak	Tex vs. Tor	*StL vs. Atl*
NY vs. Cal	*LA vs. Mon*	*Pitt vs. Cin*
Bos vs. Min	*SD vs. NY*	
SUNDAY	Chi vs. Mil	*SF vs. Phil*
Cleve vs. Sea	KC vs. Det	*Hou vs. Chi*
Bal vs. Oak	Tex vs. Tor	*StL vs. Atl*
NY vs. Cal	*LA vs. Mon*	*Pitt vs. Cin*
Bos vs. Min	*SD vs. NY*	

All-Star Game 1990

Scorecard

National	1	2	3	4	5	6	7	8	9	10	11	12	AB	R	H	RBI
TOTALS													R			
													H			
TOTALS													E			
													LOB			

SCORING KEY

/ Single	:: Double ::: Triple	◇ Home Run ◇ Run Scored

K = Strikeout	DP = Double Play	Ӿ = Called 3rd Strike
W = Walk	SB = Stolen Base	IW = Intentional Walk
FC = Fielder's Choice	PB = Passed Ball	SAC = Sacrifice
CS = Caught Stealing	FO = Foul Out	SF = Sacrifice Fly
WP = Wild Pitch	HP = Hit by Pitch	# of Fielder = Flyout

| # of Fielder plus "-" = Unassisted Groundout |
| # of Fielder "-" # of 2nd Fielder = Assisted Groundout |

BALANCE YOUR BOX SCORE

AB ____	RUNS ____
BB ____	OUTS ____
HP ____	
SAC ____	LOB ____
INT ____	
TOTALS ____	TOTALS ____

1990 Box Score

AMERICAN	ab	r	h	rbi
Henderson, lf	3	0	0	0
Gallego, ss	2	0	0	0
Boggs, 3b	2	0	1	0
Gruber, 3b	4	0	1	0
Ripken Jr, ss	2	0	0	0
Bell, lf	2	0	0	0
Griffey, cf	2	1	1	0
Puckett, cf	1	0	0	0
McGwire, 1b	2	0	0	0
Fielder, 1b	1	0	0	0
SAlomar, c	3	0	1	1
Trammell, ph	0	0	0	0
Finley, p	1	0	0	0
Eckersley, p	0	0	0	0
Sax, 2b	1	0	0	1
Saberhagen, p	0	0	0	0
Parrish, c	1	0	0	0
Welch, p	1	0	1	0
Jacoby, ph	0	0	0	0
Stieb, p	1	0	0	0
JuFranco, 2b	3	1	1	2

NATIONAL	ab	r	h	rbi
Dykstra, cf	4	0	0	0
Sandberg, 2b	3	0	1	0
RAlomar, 2b	1	0	0	0
Clark, 1b	3	0	0	0
Myers, p	0	0	0	0
JoFranco, p	0	0	0	0
Williams, ph	1	0	0	0
Mitchell, lf	2	0	1	0
Viola, p	0	0	0	0
Dawson, rf	2	0	1	0
Wallach, 3b	2	0	0	0
Strawberry, rf	1	0	0	0
Sabo, 3b	2	0	1	0
DSmith, p	0	0	0	0
Brantley, p	0	0	0	0
Dibble, p	1	0	0	0
Bonilla, 1b	2	0	1	0
Scioscia, c	1	0	0	0
Olson, c	1	0	0	0
OSmith, ss	1	0	0	0
Bonds, lf	1	0	0	0
JMartinez, p	0	0	0	0
Armstrong, p	0	0	0	0
RMartinez, p	0	0	0	0
Gwynn, ph	1	0	1	0
Dunston, ss	2	0	0	0

AMERICAN	IP	H	R	ER	BB	SO
Welch	2	1	0	0	0	2
Stieb	2	2	0	0	1	0
Saberhagen W, 1-0	1	1	0	0	1	1
Thigpen	1	1	0	0	1	1
Finley	1	0	0	0	0	2
Eckersley S, 1	1	0	0	0	0	2

NATIONAL	IP	H	R	ER	BB	SO
AMartinez	1	1	0	0	0	0
RMartinez	1	0	0	0	1	2
JMartinez	1	1	0	0	0	1
Viola	1	0	0	0	0	0
DSmith	1	1	0	0	0	0
Brantley L, 0-1	⅓	2	2	2	0	0
Dibble	⅔	0	0	0	0	2
Myers	1	0	0	0	0	2
JoFranco	1	0	0	0	0	2

E—Strawberry. DP—National League 2, LOB—American League 10, National League 4. SB—Sax, Gruber 2, Canseco. Larkin.

American League	000 000 200—2
National League	000 000 000—0

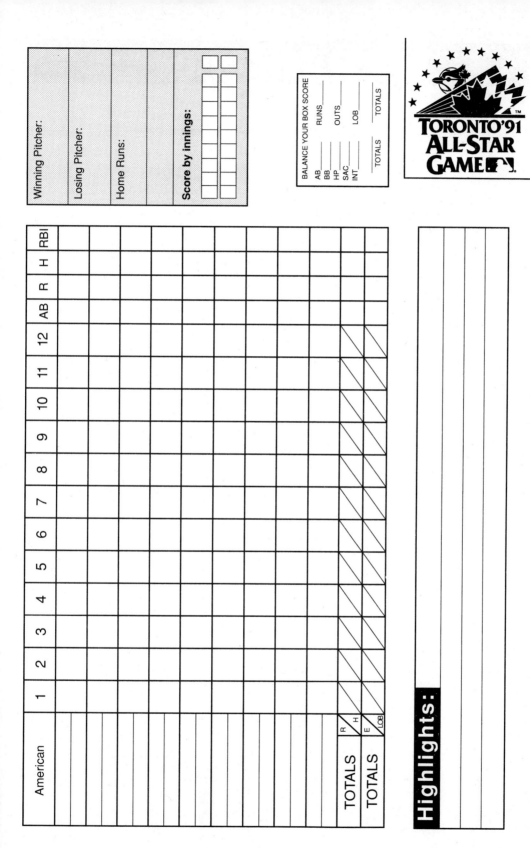

TORONTO '91
ALL-STAR
GAME

BALANCE YOUR BOX SCORE

AB		RUNS	
BB		OUTS	
HP		LOB	
SAC			
INT			
	TOTALS		TOTALS

Winning Pitcher:

Losing Pitcher:

Home Runs:

Score by innings:

American	1	2	3	4	5	6	7	8	9	10	11	12	AB	R	H	RBI
TOTALS													R			
													H			
TOTALS													E			
													LOB			

Highlights:

All-Star Game

YEAR	DATE	WINNER	SCORE	SITE
1933	July 6	American	4-2	Comiskey Park, Chicago
1934	July 10	American	9-7	Polo Grounds, New York
1935	July 8	American	4-1	Municipal Stadium, Cleveland
1936	July 7	National	4-3	Braves Field, Boston
1937	July 7	American	8-3	Griffith Stadium, Washington
1938	July 6	National	4-1	Crosley Field, Cincinnati
1939	July 11	American	3-1	Yankee Stadium, New York
1940	July 9	National	4-0	Sportsman's Park, St. Louis
1941	July 8	American	7-5	Briggs Stadium, Detroit
1942	July 6	American	3-1	Polo Grounds, New York
1943	July 13	American	5-3	Shibe Park, Philadelphia
1944	July 11	National	7-1	Forbes Field, Pittsburgh
1945	*No game due to wartime travel restrictions*			
1946	July 9	American	12-0	Fenway Park, Boston
1947	July 8	American	2-1	Wrigley Field, Chicago
1948	July 13	American	5-2	Sportsman's Park, St. Louis
1949	July 12	American	11-7	Ebbets Field, Brooklyn
1950	July 11	National	4-3	Comiskey Park, Chicago
1951	July 10	National	8-3	Briggs Stadium, Detroit
1952	July 8	National	3-2	Shibe Park, Philadelphia
1953	July 14	National	5-1	Crosley Field, Cincinnati
1954	July 13	American	11-9	Municipal Stadium, Cleveland
1955	July 12	National	6-5	County Stadium, Milwaukee
1956	July 10	National	7-3	Griffith Stadium, Washington
1957	July 9	American	6-5	Busch Stadium, St. Louis
1958	July 8	American	4-3	Memorial Stadium, Baltimore
1959 (1)	July 7	National	5-4	Forbes Field, Pittsburgh
1959 (2)	August 3	American	5-3	Memorial Coliseum, Los Angeles
1960 (1)	July 11	National	5-3	Municipal Stadium, Kansas City
1960 (2)	July 13	National	6-0	Yankee Stadium, New York
1961 (1)	July 11	National	5-4	Candlestick Park, San Francisco
1961 (2)	July 31	Tie*	1-1	Fenway Park, Boston
1962 (1)	July 10	National	3-1	D.C. Stadium, Washington
1962 (2)	July 30	American	9-4	Wrigley Field, Chicago
1963	July 9	National	5-3	Municipal Stadium, Cleveland
1964	July 7	National	7-4	Shea Stadium, New York
1965	July 13	National	6-5	Metropolitan Stadium, Minnesota
1966	July 12	National	2-1	Busch Memorial Stadium, St. Louis
1967	July 11	National	2-1	Anaheim Stadium, California
1968	July 9	National	1-0	Astrodome, Houston
1969	July 23	National	9-3	R.F. Kennedy Stadium, Washington
1970	July 14	National	5-4	Riverfront Stadium, Cincinnati
1971	July 13	American	6-4	Tiger Stadium, Detroit
1972	July 25	National	4-3	Atlanta Stadium, Atlanta
1973	July 24	National	7-1	Royals Stadium, Kansas City
1974	July 23	National	7-2	Three Rivers Stadium, Pittsburgh
1975	July 15	National	6-3	County Stadium, Milwaukee
1976	July 13	National	7-1	Veterans Stadium, Philadelphia
1977	July 19	National	7-5	Yankee Stadium, New York
1978	July 11	National	7-3	San Diego Stadium, San Diego
1979	July 17	National	7-6	Kingdome, Seattle
1980	July 8	National	4-2	Dodger Stadium, Los Angeles
1981	August 9	National	5-4	Municipal Stadium, Cleveland
1982	July 13	National	4-1	Olympic Stadium, Montreal
1983	July 6	American	13-3	Comiskey Park, Chicago
1984	July 10	National	3-1	Candlestick Park, San Francisco
1985	July 16	National	6-1	Metrodome, Minneapolis
1986	July 15	American	3-2	Astrodome, Houston
1987	July 14	National	2-0	Oakland Coliseum, Oakland
1988	July 12	American	2-1	Riverfront Stadium, Cincinnati
1989	July 11	American	5-3	Anaheim Stadium, Anaheim
1990	July 10	American	2-0	Wrigley Field, Chicago

Game called because of rain after nine innings

All-Star Game

TOP VOTE-GETTERS BY YEAR

YEAR	TOTAL BALLOTS	TOP VOTE-GETTER
1970	2,034,724	Hank Aaron, Atl (1,394,847)
1971	2,396,895	Hank Aaron, Atl (1,119,306)
1972	3,171,556	Johnny Bench, Cin (1,229,677)
1973	4,011,237	Johnny Bench, Cin (1,738,557)
1974	6,545,712	Reggie Jackson, Oak (3,497,358)
1975	7,357,811	Rod Carew, Min (3,165,614)
1976	8,370,145	Joe Morgan, Cin (3,079,082)
1977	12,562,476	Rod Carew, Min (4,292,740)
1978	12,245,544	Rod Carew, Min (4,010,136)
1979	12,392,340	Rod Carew, Cal (3,997,081)
1980	11,958,209	Davey Lopes, LA (3,862,403)
1981	3,243,674	George Brett, KC (1,144,272)
1982	9,347,447	Gary Carter, Mon (2,785,407)
1983	5,922,129	Robin Yount, Mil (1,956,964)
1984	6,333,903	Steve Garvey, SD (1,701,083)
1985	5,149,729	Dale Murphy, Atl (1,425,952)
1986	5,414,304	Darryl Strawberry, NY (1,619,511)
1987	5,572,493	Ozzie Smith, StL (2,254,409)
1988	6,146,477	Ozzie Smith, StL (2,106,757)
1989	6,051,313	Will Clark, SF (1,833,329)
1990	6,923,422	Jose Canseco, Oak (2,313,091)

MOST SELECTED PLAYERS

PLAYER	SEL.	POS.	TEAM	YEARS
Carew	15	2B	Min	1970-75
		1B	Min	1976-78
		1B	Cal	1979-84
Jackson	11	OF	Oak	1972-75
		OF	Yanks	1977-78, 80-81
		OF	Cal	1982-84
Brett	11	3B	KC	1976-86
Bench	10	C	Cin	1970-78, 80
Garvey	9	1B	LA	1974-80
		1B	SD	1984-85
Schmidt	9	3B	Phil	1979-84, 86-87, 89
Carter	8	C	Mon	1981-84
		C	Mets	1985-88
Smith	8	SS	StL	1983-1990
Winfield	8	OF	SD	1979
		OF	Yanks	1981, 83-88
Fisk	7	C	Bos	1973-74, 77-78, 80
		C	Chi (AL)	1981-82
Morgan	7	2B	Cin	1972-78
Rose	7	OF	Cin	1973-75
		3B	Cin	1976, 78
		1B	Phil	1981-82

ALL-STAR MVPs

YEAR	PLAYER TEAM	POSITION	PERFORMANCE
1962 (1)	Maury Wills, LA (NL)	SS	1-for1, 2R, 1 SB
1962 (2)	Leon Wagner, LA (AL)*	LF	3-For-4, 2RBI
1963	Willie Mays, SF*	CF	1-for-3, 2RBI, 2SB
1964	Johnny Callison, Phil	RF	1-for-3, HR, 3RBI
1965	Juan Marichal, SF*	P	3IP,OR,1H
1966	Brooks Robinson, Bal*	3B	3-for-4, triple
1967	Tony Perez, Cin	3B	1-for-2, HR, 1RBI
1968	Willie Mays, SF*	CF	1-for-4, 1R
1969	Willie McCovey, SF	1B	2-for-4, 2HR, 3RBI
1970	Carl Yastrzemski, Bos*	CF-1B	4-for-6, 1RBI
1971	Frank Robinson, Bal*	RF	1-for-2, HR, 2RBI
1972	Joe Morgan, Cin*	2B	1-for-4, 1RBI
1973	Bobby Bonds, SF	RF	2-for-2, double, HR, 2RBI
1974	Steve Garvey, LA*	1B	2-for-4, double, 1RBI
1975	Bill Madlock, Chi (NL)	3B	1-for-2, 2RBI
	Jon Matlack, NY (NL)	P	2IP, 0R, 2H, 4K (WP)
1976	George Foster, Cin*	CF-RF	1-for-3, HR, 3RBI
1977	Don Sutton, LA*	P	3IP, 0R, 1H, 4K (WP)
1978	Steve Garvey, LA*	1B	2-for-3, triple, 2RBI
1979	Dave Parker, Pitt*	RF	1-for-3, 1RBI
1980	Ken Griffey, Cin	LF	2-for-3, HR, 1RBI
1981	Gary Carter, Mon*	C	2-for-3, 2HR, 2RBI
1982	Dave Concepcion, Cin*	SS	1-for-3, HR, 2RBI (GWRBI)
1983	Fred Lynn, Cal*	CF	1-for-3, HR, 4RBI
1984	Gary Carter, Mon*	C	1-for-2, HR, 1 RBI (GWRBI)
1985	LaMarr Hoyt, SD*	P	3IP, 1R, 2H (WP)
1986	Roger Clemens, Bos*	P	3IP, 0R, 0H (WP)
1987	Tim Raines, Mon	LF	3-for-3, triple, 2RBI (GWRBI)
1988	Terry Steinbach, Oak*	C	1-for-1, HR, 2RBI
1989	Bo Jackson, KC	LF	2-for-4, HR, 2RBI
1990	Julio Franco, Tex	2B	1-for-3, 2B, 2RBI

*Started Game   W—Winning Pitcher   GWRBI—Game-Winning RBI

1990 STANDINGS

East	Won	Lost	Pct.	GB
Boston	47	39	.547	–
Toronto	48	41	.539	$\frac{1}{2}$
Cleveland	43	43	.500	4
Detroit	42	47	.472	$6\frac{1}{2}$
Baltimore	40	47	.460	$7\frac{1}{2}$
Milwaukee	38	47	.447	$8\frac{1}{2}$
New York	30	54	.357	16

East	Won	Lost	Pct.	GB
Pittsburgh	52	33	.612	–
New York	49	34	.590	2
Montreal	50	38	.568	$3\frac{1}{2}$
Philadelphia	41	43	.488	$10\frac{1}{2}$
Chicago	37	52	.416	17
St. Louis	36	51	.414	17

West	Won	Lost	Pct.	GB
Oakland	55	32	.632	–
Chicago	52	31	.627	1
Seattle	45	44	.506	11
California	44	45	.494	12
Texas	43	45	.489	$12\frac{1}{2}$
Minnesota	42	46	.477	$13\frac{1}{2}$
Kansas City	39	47	.453	$15\frac{1}{2}$

West	Won	Lost	Pct.	GB
Cincinnati	53	31	.631	–
San Francisco	47	40	.540	$7\frac{1}{2}$
Los Angeles	42	44	.488	12
San Diego	38	46	.452	15
Atlanta	34	50	.405	19
Houston	35	52	.402	$19\frac{1}{2}$

INDIVIDUAL LEADERS

AMERICAN LEAGUE

BATTING

Based on 3.1 plate appearances per game

	G	AB	R	H	Pct.
Griffey,K Sea	89	340	57	113	.332
Henderson,R Oak	81	293	69	97	.331
Guillen,O Chi	82	274	35	87	.318
Sheffield,G Mil	71	285	41	90	.316
Harper,B Min	75	260	32	81	.312
Parker,D Mil	82	321	39	100	.312
Palmeiro,R Tex	82	316	41	98	.310
Puckett,K Min	85	321	58	99	.308
Jacoby,B Cleve	82	292	45	90	.308
Burks,E Bos	80	304	49	92	.303

HOME RUNS

Fielder,C Det	29
Canseco,J Oak	24
McGwire,M Oak	22
Gruber,K Tor	20
McGriff,F Tor	20
Milligan,R Bal	18
Bell,G Tor	17
Henderson,R Oak	17
Parrish,L Cal	17

WINS

Welch,B Oak	14
Finley,C Cal	12
Clemens,R Bos	12
Brown,K Tex	11
Stieb,D Tor	11
Stewart,D Oak	11
Boddicker,M Bos	11

RBI

Fielder,C Det	76
Gruber,K Tor	66
Canseco,J Oak	60
Bell,G Tor	60
Parker,D Mil	58
McGwire,M Oak	57
Leonard,J Sea	56
Puckett,K Min	54
Milligan,R Bal	53
Sierra,R Tex	52

E.R.A.

Clemens,R Bos	2.46
Finley,C Cal	2.50
Hibbard,G Chi	2.58
Welch,B Oak	2.75
Stewart,D Oak	2.87
Black,B Cleve	2.93
Saberhagen,B KC	3.10
Stieb,D Tor	3.12
King,E Chi	3.20
Brown,K Tex	3.27

SLUGGING

Fielder,C Det	.604
Canseco,J Oak	.602
Henderson,R Oak	.587
Gruber,K Tor	.539
Milligan,R Bal	.530
Puckett,K Min	.526
Parrish,L Cal	.520
McGriff,F Tor	.516
Griffey,K Sea	.515
Burks,E Bos	.510

SAVES

Thigpen,B Chi	30
Eckersley,D Oak	28
Jones,D Cleve	25
Schooler,M Sea	23
Aguilera,R Min	21
Olson,G Bal	19
Henneman,M Det	18
Righetti,D NY	17
Henke,T Tor	16
Reardon,J Bos	15

NATIONAL LEAGUE

BATTING

	G	AB	R	H	Pct.
Dykstra,L Phil	78	304	60	110	.362
Bonds,B Pitt	77	276	58	94	.341
Dawson,A Chi	82	296	46	97	.328
Sandberg,R Chi	87	350	69	114	.326
McGee,W SF	87	347	55	112	.323
Mitchell,K SF	77	289	58	92	.318
Larkin,B Cin	84	332	46	104	.313
Gant,R Atl	75	276	53	86	.312
Lind,J Pitt	81	286	29	89	.311
Hatcher,B Cin	76	300	36	93	.310

HOME RUNS

Mitchell,K SF	24
Sandberg,R Chi	24
Strawberry,D NY	23
Davis,G Hou	19
Bonilla,B Pitt	19
Dawson,A Chi	19
Williams,M SF	17
Gant,R Atl	17
Bonds,B Pitt	17
Sabo,C Cin	16

WINS

Viola,F NY	13
Armstrong,J Cin	11
Martinez,R LA	10
Drabek,D Pitt	10
Heaton,N Pitt	10
Burkett,J SF	9
Browning,T Cin	9
Gooden,D NY	9

RBI

Williams,M SF	72
Bonds,B Pitt	67
Clark,W SF	64
Carter,J SD	62
Bonilla,B Pitt	62
Wallach,T Mon	61
Dawson,A Chi	59
Sandberg,R Chi	59
Strawberry,D NY	58
Mitchell,K SF	55

E.R.A.

Gardner,M Mon	2.32
Viola,F NY	2.39
Armstrong,J Cin	2.59
Martinez,De Mon	2.71
Whitson,E SD	2.81
Browning,T Cin	2.82
Tudor,J StL	2.91
Smith,Z Mon	2.93
Boyd,D Mon	3.04
Martinez,R LA	3.14

SLUGGING

Bonds,B Pitt	.627
Mitchell,K SF	.623
Dawson,A Chi	.598
Sandberg,R Chi	.591
Strawberry,D NY	.575
Gant,R Atl	.572
Wallach,T Mon	.536
Bonilla,B Pitt	.532
Sabo,C Cin	.518
Daniels,K LA	.515

SAVES

Myers,R Cin	20
Franco,J NY	18
Smith,D Hou	17
Brantley,J SF	15
McDowell,R Phil	13
Schmidt,D Mon	13
Landrum,B Pitt	12
Lefferts,C SD	12
Burke,T Mon	11
Smith,L StL	11

1991 STANDINGS

AMERICAN LEAGUE

East	Won	Lost	Pct.	GB

West	Won	Lost	Pct.	GB

NATIONAL LEAGUE

East	Won	Lost	Pct.	GB

West	Won	Lost	Pct.	GB

INDIVIDUAL LEADERS

AMERICAN LEAGUE

BATTING

HOME RUNS

WINS

RBI

E.R.A.

SLUGGING

SAVES

NATIONAL LEAGUE

BATTING

HOME RUNS

WINS

RBI

E.R.A.

SLUGGING

SAVES

J · U · L · Y

MONDAY 15

Winning Pitcher:

Losing Pitcher:

Home Runs:

Highlights:

Score by innings:

TUESDAY 16

Winning Pitcher:

Losing Pitcher:

Home Runs:

Highlights:

Score by innings:

WEDNESDAY 17

Winning Pitcher:

Losing Pitcher:

Home Runs:

Highlights:

Score by innings:

THURSDAY 18

Winning Pitcher:

Losing Pitcher:

Home Runs:

Highlights:

Score by innings:

J · U · L · Y

FRIDAY 19

Winning Pitcher:

Losing Pitcher:

Home Runs:

Highlights:

Score by innings:

SATURDAY 20

Winning Pitcher:

Losing Pitcher:

Home Runs:

Highlights:

Score by innings:

CBS: Los Angeles vs. Mets
Detroit vs. Kansas City

SUNDAY 21

Winning Pitcher:

Losing Pitcher:

Home Runs:

Highlights:

Score by innings:

ESPN: Cincinnati vs. Pittsburgh
Toronto vs. Texas

SCHEDULE

MONDAY	Bos vs. Chi	*LA vs. Phil*
NY vs. Sea	Min vs. Mil	*Hou vs. Pitt*
Cleve vs. Oak	Tex vs. Det	*Chi vs. Atl*
Bal vs. Cal	*SD vs. Mon*	*StL vs. Cin*
Tor vs. KC	*SF vs. NY*	
TUESDAY	Bos vs. Chi	*LA vs. Phil*
NY vs. Sea	Min vs. Mil	*Hou vs. Pitt*
Cleve vs. Oak	Tex vs. Det	*Chi vs. Atl*
Bal vs. Cal	*SD vs. Mon*	*StL vs. Cin*
Tor vs. KC	*SF vs. NY*	
WEDNESDAY	Tex vs. Det	*Chi vs. Atl*
Cleve vs. Oak	*SD vs. Mon*	*StL vs. Cin*
Bal vs. KC	*SF vs. NY*	
Bos vs. Chi	*LA vs. Phil*	
Sea vs. Mil	*Hou vs. Pitt*	
THURSDAY	Sea vs. Mil	
NY vs. Oak	Min vs. Bos	
Cleve vs. Cal	*LA vs. NY*	
Tor vs. Tex		
Bal vs. KC		
FRIDAY	Mil vs. Chi	*Cin vs. Pitt*
NY vs. Oak	Sea vs. Bal	*Atl vs. StL*
Cleve vs. Cal	Min vs. Bos	*Chi vs. Hou*
Tor vs. Tex	*SF vs. Mon*	*Phil vs. SD*
Det vs. KC	*LA vs. NY*	
SATURDAY	Mil vs. Chi	*Cin vs. Pitt*
NY vs. Oak	Sea vs. Bal	*Atl vs. StL*
Cleve vs. Cal	Min vs. Bos	*Chi vs. Hou*
Tor vs. Tex	*SF vs. Mon*	*Phil vs. SD*
Det vs. KC	*LA vs. NY*	
SUNDAY	Mil vs. Chi	*Cin vs. Pitt*
NY vs. Oak	Sea vs. Bal	*Atl vs. StL*
Cleve vs. Cal	Min vs. Bos	*Chi vs. Hou*
Tor vs. Tex	*SF vs. Mon*	*Phil vs. SD*
Det vs. KC	*LA vs. NY*	

1990 STANDINGS

East	Won	Lost	Pct.	GB	East	Won	Lost	Pct.	GB
Toronto	51	44	.537	–	Pittsburgh	55	36	.604	–
Boston	50	44	.532	½	New York	53	37	.589	1½
Baltimore	46	48	.489	4½	Montreal	51	44	.537	6
Cleveland	45	48	.484	5	Philadelphia	45	46	.495	10
Detroit	45	51	.469	6½	Chicago	43	52	.453	14
Milwaukee	42	50	.457	7½	St. Louis	41	53	.436	15½
New York	34	57	.374	15					

West	Won	Lost	Pct.	GB	West	Won	Lost	Pct.	GB
Oakland	59	35	.628	–	Cincinnati	58	33	.637	–
Chicago	54	36	.600	3	San Francisco	49	44	.527	10
Seattle	49	47	.510	11	Los Angeles	45	47	.489	13½
California	47	48	.495	12½	Houston	40	54	.426	19½
Texas	46	48	.489	13	San Diego	38	53	.418	20
Minnesota	45	50	.474	14½	Atlanta	36	55	.396	22
Kansas City	43	50	.462	15½					

INDIVIDUAL LEADERS

AMERICAN LEAGUE   NATIONAL LEAGUE

BATTING

Based on 3.1 plate appearances per game

	G	AB	R	H	Pct.
Henderson,R Oak	82	297	71	99	.333
Sheffield,G Mil	78	310	46	100	.323
Griffey,K Sea	95	366	60	117	.320
Harper,B Min	80	279	34	89	.319
Palmeiro,R Tex	88	339	45	107	.316
Martinez,E Sea	89	312	47	97	.311
Reed,J Bos	90	338	40	105	.311
Puckett,K Min	92	347	62	107	.308
Canseco,J Oak	74	274	57	84	.307
Parker,D Mil	89	346	44	106	.306

BATTING

	G	AB	R	H	Pct.
Dykstra,L Phil	85	331	69	117	.353
Bonds,B Pitt	83	292	63	99	.339
McGee,W StL	94	376	59	125	.332
Dawson,A Chi	87	311	48	103	.331
Sandberg,R Chi	93	370	73	120	.324
Larkin,B Cin	91	356	51	114	.320
Mitchell,K SF	83	310	60	97	.313
Gwynn,T SD	90	365	51	114	.312
Gant,R Atl	82	304	59	94	.309
Hatcher,B	82	322	39	99	.307

HOME RUNS

Fielder,C Det	31
Canseco,J Oak	28
McGwire,M Oak	24
McGriff,F Tor	22
Gruber,K Tor	21
Milligan,R Bal	20
Jackson,B KC	19
Bell,G Tor	18

WINS

Welch,B Oak	15
Finley,C Cal	13
Stieb,D Tor	12
Stewart,D Oak	12
Clemens,R Bos	12
Brown,K Tex	11
Sanderson,S Oak	11
Boddicker,M Bos	11

HOME RUNS

Sandberg,R Chi	25
Mitchell,K SF	24
Strawberry,D NY	24
Gant,R Atl	20
Bonilla,B Pitt	20
Williams,M SF	19
Davis,G Hou	19
Dawson,A Chi	19
Sabo,C Cin	17
Bonds,B Pitt	17

WINS

Viola,F NY	13
Armstrong,J Cin	11
Martinez,R LA	11
Drabek,D Pitt	11
Gooden,D NY	10
Heaton,N Pitt	10
Burkett,J SF	9
Browning,T Cin	9

RBI

Fielder,C Det	80
Gruber,K Tor	70
Canseco,J Oak	67
Parker,D Mil	64
McGwire,M Oak	61
Bell,G Tor	61
Leonard,J Sea	58
Milligan,R Bal	57
Palmeiro,R Tex	57
Jackson,B KC	57

E.R.A.

Clemens,R Bos	2.47
Finley,C Cal	2.47
Welch,B Oak	2.65
Stewart,D Oak	2.83
Hibbard,G Chi	2.84
Wells,D Tor	2.94
Appier,K KC	2.97
Stieb,D Tor	2.98
King,E Chi	3.00
Saberhagen,B KC	3.10

RBI

Williams,M SF	80
Bonds,B Pitt	70
Clark,W SF	65
Bonilla,B Pitt	65
Wallach,T Mon	63
Carter,J SD	63
Dawson,A Chi	62
Sandberg,R Chi	62
Strawberry,D NY	61
Guerrero,P StL	60

E.R.A.

Viola,F NY	2.27
Gardner,M Mon	2.52
Armstrong,J Cin	2.69
Martinez,De Mon	2.85
Browning,T Cin	2.87
Tudor,J StL	2.89
Whitson,E SD	2.93
Martinez,R LA	2.97
Boyd,D Mon	3.04
Drabek,D Pitt	3.10

SLUGGING

Canseco,J Oak	.639
Fielder,C Det	.602
Henderson,R Oak	.589
Milligan,R Bal	.536
Gruber,K Tor	.534
Parrish,L Cal	.521
McGriff,F Tor	.515
Puckett,K Min	.513
Jackson,B KC	.507
Parker,D Mil	.506

SAVES

Thigpen,B Chi	31
Eckersley,D Oak	30
Schooler,M Sea	26
Jones,D Cleve	26
Aguilera,R Min	23
Olson,G Bal	21
Righetti,D NY	20
Henke,T Tor	19
Henneman,M Det	18
Reardon,J Bos	18

SLUGGING

Bonds,B Pitt	.610
Mitchell,K SF	.597
Sandberg,R Chi	.592
Dawson,A Chi	.592
Gant,R Atl	.579
Strawberry,D NY	.548
Bonilla,B Pitt	.532
Wallach,T Mon	.524
Williams,M SF	.518
Daniels,K LA	.513

SAVES

Franco,J NY	21
Myers,R Cin	20
Smith,D Hou	18
Brantley,J SF	15
McDowell,R Phil	14
Smith,L StL	14
Schmidt,D Mon	13
Landrum,B Pitt	12
Burke,T Mon	12
Lefferts, SD	12

1991 STANDINGS

AMERICAN LEAGUE

East	Won	Lost	Pct.	GB

West	Won	Lost	Pct.	GB

NATIONAL LEAGUE

East	Won	Lost	Pct.	GB

West	Won	Lost	Pct.	GB

INDIVIDUAL LEADERS

AMERICAN LEAGUE

BATTING

HOME RUNS

WINS

RBI

E.R.A.

SLUGGING

SAVES

NATIONAL LEAGUE

BATTING

HOME RUNS

WINS

RBI

E.R.A.

SLUGGING

SAVES

J · U · L · Y

_____ ___

| Winning Pitcher: |
| Losing Pitcher: |
| Home Runs: |
| |
| Highlights: |
| |
| |
| **Score by innings:** |

Hall of Fame Game: Minnesota vs. San
Francisco, at Cooperstown

MONDAY 22

_____ ___

| Winning Pitcher: |
| Losing Pitcher: |
| Home Runs: |
| |
| Highlights: |
| |
| |
| **Score by innings:** |

TUESDAY 23

_____ ___

| Winning Pitcher: |
| Losing Pitcher: |
| Home Runs: |
| |
| Highlights: |
| |
| |
| **Score by innings:** |

WEDNESDAY 24

_____ ___

| Winning Pitcher: |
| Losing Pitcher: |
| Home Runs: |
| |
| Highlights: |
| |
| |
| **Score by innings:** |

THURSDAY 25

FRIDAY 26

_____ _____

Winning Pitcher:

Losing Pitcher:

Home Runs:

Highlights:

Score by innings:

SATURDAY 27

_____ _____

Winning Pitcher:

Losing Pitcher:

Home Runs:

Highlights:

Score by innings:

SUNDAY 28

_____ _____

Winning Pitcher:

Losing Pitcher:

Home Runs:

Highlights:

Score by innings:

ESPN: White Sox vs. Boston
Detroit vs. Texas

SCHEDULE

MONDAY		
Bos vs. Tex		
Mil vs. Chi		
Atl vs. Pitt		
Hou vs. StL		
TUESDAY	Oak vs. Cleve	*Hou vs. StL*
Bos vs. Tex	Cal vs. Bal	*Phil vs. LA*
Mil vs. KC	Sea vs. NY	*Mon vs. SD*
Tor vs. Chi	*Atl vs. Pitt*	*NY vs. SF*
Min vs. Det	*Cin vs. Chi*	
WEDNESDAY	Oak vs. Cleve	*Hou vs. StL*
Bos vs. Tex	Cal vs. Bal	*Phil vs. LA*
Mil vs. KC	Sea vs. NY	*Mon vs. SD*
Tor vs. Chi	*Atl vs. Pitt*	*NY vs. SF*
Min vs. Det	*Cin vs. Chi*	
THURSDAY	Cal vs. Bal	*NY vs. SF*
Mil vs. KC	Sea vs. NY	
Tor vs. Chi	*Cin vs. Chi*	
Min vs. Det	*Phil vs. LA*	
Oak vs. Cleve	*Mon vs. SD*	
FRIDAY	Oak vs. Bal	*Pitt vs. Hou*
Det vs. Tex	Cal vs. NY	*Mon vs. LA*
Mil vs. Min	Chi vs. Bos	*NY vs. SD*
Sea vs. Cleve	*Atl vs. Chi*	*Phil vs. SF*
KC vs. Tor	*Cin vs. StL*	
SATURDAY	Oak vs. Bal	*Pitt vs. Hou*
Det vs. Tex	Cal vs. NY	*Mon vs. LA*
Mil vs. Min	Chi vs. Bos	*NY vs. SD*
Sea vs. Cleve	*Atl vs. Chi*	*Phil vs. SF*
KC vs. Tor	*Cin vs. StL*	
SUNDAY	Oak vs. Bal	*Pitt vs. Hou*
Det vs. Tex	Cal vs. NY	*Mon vs. LA*
Mil vs. Min	Chi vs. Bos	*NY vs. SD*
Sea vs. Cleve	*Atl vs. Chi*	*Phil vs. SF*
KC vs. Tor	*Cin vs. StL*	

1990 STANDINGS

AMERICAN LEAGUE **Through July 29** **NATIONAL LEAGUE**

East	Won	Lost	Pct.	GB		East	Won	Lost	Pct.	GB
Toronto	54	47	.535	–		New York	58	40	.592	–
Boston	53	48	.525	1		Pittsburgh	57	41	.582	1
Baltimore	50	51	.495	4		Montreal	54	48	.529	6
Detroit	49	54	.476	6		Philadelphia	49	49	.500	9
Cleveland	47	54	.465	7		Chicago	47	55	.461	13
Milwaukee	45	53	.459	7½		St. Louis	45	57	.441	15
New York	38	61	.384	15						

West	Won	Lost	Pct.	GB		West	Won	Lost	Pct.	GB
Oakland	63	39	.618	–		Cincinnati	59	40	.596	–
Chicago	58	38	.604	2		San Francisco	54	46	.540	5½
Seattle	53	49	.520	10		Los Angeles	51	48	.515	8
Texas	50	50	.500	12		San Diego	44	55	.444	15
Minnesota	49	53	.480	14		Houston	42	60	.412	18½
California	49	53	.480	14		Atlanta	39	60	.394	20
Kansas City	46	54	.460	16						

INDIVIDUAL LEADERS

AMERICAN LEAGUE **NATIONAL LEAGUE**

BATTING

Based on 3.1 plate appearances per game

	G	AB	R	H	Pct.			G	AB	R	H	Pct.
Henderson,R Oak	90	329	79	111	.337		Dykstra,L Phil	92	359	75	126	.351
Sheffield,G Mil	84	336	49	111	.330		McGee,W StL	99	395	62	132	.334
Harper,B Min	87	305	40	99	.325		Bonds,B Pitt	90	314	67	104	.331
Palmeiro,R Tex	92	357	48	114	.319		Dawson,A Chi	93	330	49	109	.330
Griffey,K Sea	101	392	64	125	.319		Larkin,B Cin	98	382	54	122	.319
Quintana,C Bos	93	295	34	93	.315		Gwynn,T SD	98	396	55	125	.316
Reed,J Bos	97	365	47	114	.312		Mitchell,K SF	89	335	62	105	.313
Martinez,E Sea	95	330	50	103	.312		Sandberg,R Chi	100	402	76	125	.311
Canseco,J Oak	82	304	63	94	.309		Murray,E LA	93	321	54	99	.308
Guillen,O Chi	95	318	41	98	.308		Jefferies,G NY	92	365	63	111	.304

HOME RUNS / WINS (AL) — HOME RUNS / WINS (NL)

HOME RUNS		WINS		HOME RUNS		WINS	
Fielder,C Det	32	Welch,B Oak	16	Mitchell,K SF	25	Viola,F NY	14
Canseco,J Oak	32	Finley,C Cal	13	Strawberry,D NY	25	Martinez,R LA	13
McGwire,M Oak	27	Stieb,D Tor	13	Sandberg,R Chi	25	Drabek,D Pitt	13
McGriff,F Tor	23	Stewart,D Oak	13	Bonilla,B Pitt	21	Armstrong,J Cin	11
Gruber,K Tor	21	Clemens,R Bos	13	Williams,M SF	20	Gooden,D NY	11
Milligan,R Bal	20	Brown,K Tex	12	Gant,R Atl	20	Browning,T Cin	10
Henderson,R Oak	20	Hanson,E Sea	11	Davis,G Hou	19	Heaton,N Pitt	10
Jackson,B KC	19	Sanderson,S Oak	11	Dawson,A Chi	19		
Deer,R Mil	18	Candiotti,T Cleve	11	Bonds,B Pitt	18		
Bell,G Tor	18	Boddicker,M Bos	11				

RBI / E.R.A. (AL) — RBI / E.R.A. (NL)

RBI		E.R.A.		RBI		E.R.A.	
Fielder,C Det	84	Clemens,R Bos	2.33	Williams,M SF	83	Gardner,M Mon	2.34
Canseco,J Oak	77	Finley,C Cal	2.38	Bonds,B Pitt	73	Viola,F NY	2.36
Gruber,K Tor	72	McCaskill,K Cal	2.67	Carter,J SD	71	Tudor,J StL	2.66
McGwire,M Oak	66	Stieb,D Tor	2.81	Clark,W SF	68	Browning,T Cin	2.76
Parker,D Mil	66	Stewart,D Oak	2.87	Wallach,T Mon	68	Martinez,R LA	2.81
Leonard,J Sea	62	Hibbard,G Chi	2.91	Bonilla,B Pitt	67	Whitson,E SD	2.84
Bell,G Tor	62	Wells,D Tor	3.00	Strawberry,D NY	66	Martinez,De Mon	2.94
Sierra,R Tex	61	Welch,B Oak	3.06	Guerrero,P StL	65	Drabek,D Pitt	2.94
Palmeiro,R Tex	60	Harris,G Bos	3.07	Sandberg,R Chi	63	Boyd,D Mon	3.01
Puckett,K Min	60	Saberhagen,B KC	3.10			Fernandez,S NY	3.16

SLUGGING / SAVES (AL) — SLUGGING / SAVES (NL)

SLUGGING		SAVES		SLUGGING		SAVES	
Canseco,J Oak	.651	Thigpen,B Chi	32	Bonds,B Pitt	.596	Franco,J NY	23
Henderson,R Oak	.608	Eckersley,D Oak	31	Mitchell,K SF	.591	Myers,R Cin	20
Fielder,C Det	.591	Schooler,M Sea	28	Dawson,A Chi	.576	Smith,D Hou	18
Gruber,K Tor	.511	Jones,D Cleve	27	Sandberg,R Chi	.557	Brantley,J SF	16
McGriff,F Tor	.509	Olson,G Bal	23	Gant,R Atl	.545	Smith,L StL	16
Parrish,L Cal	.507	Aguilera,R Min	23	Strawberry,D NY	.540	McDowell,R Phil	15
Jackson,B KC	.507	Henke,T Tor	21	Wallach,T Mon	.523	Lefferts,C SD	14
Milligan,R Bal	.505	Righetti,D NY	21	Daniels,K LA	.523	Schmidt,D Mon	13
Burks,E Bos	.499	Henneman,M Det	18	Murray,E LA	.511		
Hrbek,K Min	.498	Reardon,J Bos	18	Bonilla,B Pitt	.503		

1991 STANDINGS

AMERICAN LEAGUE					NATIONAL LEAGUE				
East	**Won**	**Lost**	**Pct.**	**GB**	**East**	**Won**	**Lost**	**Pct.**	**GB**
West	**Won**	**Lost**	**Pct.**	**GB**	**West**	**Won**	**Lost**	**Pct.**	**GB**

INDIVIDUAL LEADERS

AMERICAN LEAGUE	NATIONAL LEAGUE
BATTING	**BATTING**

HOME RUNS	WINS	HOME RUNS	WINS

RBI	E.R.A.	RBI	E.R.A.

SLUGGING	SAVES	SLUGGING	SAVES

J · U · L · Y

MONDAY 29

_____ __
_____ __

Winning Pitcher:

Losing Pitcher:

Home Runs:

Highlights:

Score by innings:

TUESDAY 30

_____ __
_____ __

Winning Pitcher:

Losing Pitcher:

Home Runs:

Highlights:

Score by innings:

WEDNESDAY 31

_____ __
_____ __

Winning Pitcher:

Losing Pitcher:

Home Runs:

Highlights:

Score by innings:

THURSDAY 1

_____ __
_____ __

Winning Pitcher:

Losing Pitcher:

Home Runs:

Highlights:

Score by innings:

A · U · G · U · S · T

FRIDAY 2

_____
_____

Winning Pitcher:

Losing Pitcher:

Home Runs:

Highlights:

Score by innings:

SATURDAY 3

_____
_____

Winning Pitcher:

Losing Pitcher:

Home Runs:

Highlights:

Score by innings:

CBS: Toronto vs. Boston
Pittsburgh vs. St. Louis

SUNDAY 4

_____
_____

Winning Pitcher:

Losing Pitcher:

Home Runs:

Highlights:

Score by innings:

ESPN: *San Francisco vs. Cincinnati*

SCHEDULE

MONDAY	Oak vs. NY	*Mon vs. SF*
Bal vs. Sea	Tex vs. Bos	
Det vs. Min	*Pitt vs. Atl*	
Cal vs. Cleve	*StL vs. Hou*	
Chi vs. Tor	*NY vs. LA*	
TUESDAY	Chi vs. Tor	*Chi vs. Cin*
Bal vs. Sea	Oak vs. NY	*StL vs. Hou*
Det vs. Min	Tex vs. Bos	*NY vs. LA*
KC vs. Mil	*SD vs. Phil*	*Mon vs. SF*
Cal vs. Cleve	*Pitt vs. Atl*	
WEDNESDAY	Cleve vs. Tor	*Chi vs. Cin*
Bal vs. Sea	Min vs. NY	*StL vs. Hou*
Tex vs. Chi	Oak vs. Bos	*NY vs. LA*
KC vs. Mil	*SD vs. Phil*	
Cal vs. Det	*Pitt vs. Atl*	
THURSDAY	Min vs. NY	
Tex vs. Chi	Oak vs. Bos	
KC vs. Mil	*Phil vs. Mon*	
Cal vs. Det	*Pitt vs. StL*	
Cleve vs. Tor	*SF vs. Cin*	
FRIDAY	NY vs. Det	*Pitt vs. StL*
Min vs. Oak	KC vs. Cleve	*SD vs. Atl*
Sea vs. Cal	Tor vs. Bos	*SF vs. Cin*
Bal vs. Chi	*Phil vs. Mon*	*LA vs. Hou*
Tex vs. Mil	*Chi vs. NY*	
SATURDAY	NY vs. Det	*Pitt vs. StL*
Min vs. Oak	KC vs. Cleve	*SD vs. Atl*
Sea vs. Cal	Tor vs. Bos	*SF vs. Cin*
Bal vs. Chi	*Phil vs. Mon*	*LA vs. Hou*
Tex vs. Mil	*Chi vs. NY*	
SUNDAY	NY vs. Det	*Pitt vs. StL*
Min vs. Oak	KC vs. Cleve	*SD vs. Atl*
Sea vs. Cal	Tor vs. Bos	*SF vs. Cin*
Bal vs. Chi	*Phil vs. Mon*	*LA vs. Hou*
Tex vs. Mil	*Chi vs. NY*	

1990 STANDINGS

AMERICAN LEAGUE — Through August 5 — NATIONAL LEAGUE

East	Won	Lost	Pct.	GB	East	Won	Lost	Pct.	GB
Boston	58	49	.542	–	Pittsburgh	61	43	.587	–
Toronto	57	51	.528	1½	New York	61	43	.587	–
Baltimore	53	54	.495	5	Montreal	55	53	.509	8
Detroit	52	58	.473	7½	Philadelphia	51	53	.490	10
Cleveland	49	58	.458	9	Chicago	51	57	.472	12
Milwaukee	45	61	.425	12½	St. Louis	49	59	.454	14
New York	42	64	.396	15½					

West	Won	Lost	Pct.	GB	West	Won	Lost	Pct.	GB
Oakland	68	41	.624	–	Cincinnati	62	44	.585	–
Chicago	63	41	.606	2½	San Francisco	58	49	.542	4½
Texas	56	51	.523	11	Los Angeles	54	52	.509	8
Seattle	57	52	.523	11	San Diego	48	58	.453	14
California	52	57	.477	16	Houston	47	61	.435	16
Minnesota	51	58	.468	17	Atlanta	40	65	.381	21½
Kansas City	49	57	.462	17½					

INDIVIDUAL LEADERS

AMERICAN LEAGUE — NATIONAL LEAGUE

BATTING

Based on 3.1 plate appearances per game

	G	AB	R	H	Pct.		G	AB	R	H	Pct.
Henderson,R Oak	96	352	84	117	.332	Dykstra,L Phil	98	384	78	133	.346
Palmeiro,R Tex	99	390	51	128	.328	Dawson,A Chi	99	351	51	120	.342
Harper,B Min	94	331	44	107	.323	McGee,W StL	105	418	66	139	.333
Griffey,K Sea	108	419	69	134	.320	Bonds,B Pitt	96	338	73	108	.320
Reed,J Bos	103	388	52	123	.317	Larkin,B Cin	105	411	58	130	.316
Quintana,C Bos	99	319	38	101	.317	Murray,E LA	100	349	59	110	.315
Sheffield,G Mil	91	360	51	113	.314	Gwynn,T SD	105	426	59	134	.315
Martinez,E Sea	102	354	53	110	.311	Mitchell,K SF	93	348	65	108	.310
Boggs,W Bos	103	410	60	127	.310	Sandberg,R Chi	106	429	83	133	.310
Guillen,O Chi	103	345	45	106	.307	Jefferies,G NY	98	392	68	121	.309

HOME RUNS		WINS		HOME RUNS		WINS	
Fielder,C Det	34	Welch,B Oak	17	Mitchell,K SF	26	Viola,F NY	15
Canseco,J Oak	34	Stewart,D Oak	15	Strawberry,D NY	26	Martinez,R LA	14
McGwire,M Oak	28	Clemens,R Bos	15	Sandberg,R Chi	25	Drabek,D Pitt	14
McGriff,F Tor	24	Finley,C Cal	14	Bonilla,B Pitt	23	Armstrong,J Cin	11
Gruber,K Tor	22	Stieb,D Tor	14	Williams,M SF	21	Gooden,D NY	11
Henderson,R Oak	21	Brown,K Tex	12	Sabo,C Cin	21	Tudor,J StL	11
Milligan,R Bal	20			Dawson,A Chi	21	Harkey,M Chi	10
Bell,G Tor	20			Gant,R Atl	20	Burkett,J SF	10
Jackson,B KC	19					Browning,T Cin	10
						Heaton,N Pitt	10

RBI		E.R.A.		RBI		E.R.A.	
Fielder,C Det	89	Clemens,R Bos	2.14	Williams,M SF	86	Viola,F NY	2.28
Canseco,J Oak	82	Finley,C Cal	2.40	Carter,J SD	84	Tudor,J StL	2.49
Gruber,K Tor	78	Stewart,D Oak	2.58	Bonds,B Pitt	77	Whitson,E SD	2.76
McGwire,M Oak	69	Hibbard,G Chi	2.85	Bonilla,B Pitt	72	Martinez,R LA	2.76
Parker,D Mil	67	Stieb,D Tor	2.96	Strawberry,D NY	71	Drabek,D Pitt	2.76
Bell,G Tor	67	Saberhagen,B KC	3.10	Dawson,A Chi	70	Gardner,M Mon	2.89
Palmeiro,R Tex	66	Candiotti,T Cleve	3.10	Clark,W SF	69	Boyd,D Mon	3.05
Sierra,R Tex	65	Appier,K KC	3.11	Wallach,T Mon	68	Martinez,De Mon	3.08
Leonard,J Sea	64	Welch,B Oak	3.19	Guerrero,P StL	67	Browning,T Cin	3.12
Puckett,K Min	63	Brown,K Tex	3.20	Mitchell,K SF	64	Armstrong,J Cin	3.13

SLUGGING		SAVES		SLUGGING		SAVES	
Canseco,J Oak	.631	Thigpen,B Chi	35	Dawson,A Chi	.598	Franco,J NY	24
Henderson,R Oak	.597	Eckersley,D Oak	35	Mitchell,K SF	.589	Myers,R Cin	21
Fielder,C Det	.589	Schooler,M Sea	28	Bonds,B Pitt	.580	Smith,D Hou	18
McGriff,F Tor	.524	Jones,D Cleve	28	Sandberg,R Chi	.545	Smith,L StL	18
Gruber,K Tor	.509	Olson,G Bal	25	Gant,R Atl	.535	Brantley,T SF	16
Jackson,B KC	.507	Aguilera,R Min	23	Strawberry,D NY	.534	McDowell,R Phil	16
Burks,E Bos	.500	Henke,T Tor	23	Murray,E LA	.521	Lefferts,C SD	15
Hrbek,K Min	.499	Righetti,D NY	21	Bonilla,B Pitt	.521	Burke,T Mon	13
Griffey,K Sea	.496	Henneman,M Det	18	Wallach,T Mon	.511	Schmidt,D Mon	13
Milligan,R Bal	.493	Reardon,J Bos	18	Sabo,C Cin	.510		

1991 STANDINGS

AMERICAN LEAGUE

East	Won	Lost	Pct.	GB

West	Won	Lost	Pct.	GB

NATIONAL LEAGUE

East	Won	Lost	Pct.	GB

West	Won	Lost	Pct.	GB

INDIVIDUAL LEADERS

AMERICAN LEAGUE

BATTING

HOME RUNS

WINS

RBI

E.R.A.

SLUGGING

SAVES

NATIONAL LEAGUE

BATTING

HOME RUNS

WINS

RBI

E.R.A.

SLUGGING

SAVES

A · U · G · U · S · T

MONDAY 5

Winning Pitcher:

Losing Pitcher:

Home Runs:

Highlights:

Score by innings:

TUESDAY 6

Winning Pitcher:

Losing Pitcher:

Home Runs:

Highlights:

Score by innings:

WEDNESDAY 7

Winning Pitcher:

Losing Pitcher:

Home Runs:

Highlights:

Score by innings:

THURSDAY 8

Winning Pitcher:

Losing Pitcher:

Home Runs:

Highlights:

Score by innings:

FRIDAY 9

_____

Winning Pitcher:

Losing Pitcher:

Home Runs:

Highlights:

Score by innings:

SATURDAY 10

_____

Winning Pitcher:

Losing Pitcher:

Home Runs:

Highlights:

Score by innings:

SUNDAY 11

_____

Winning Pitcher:

Losing Pitcher:

Home Runs:

Highlights:

Score by innings:

ESPN: *Mets vs. Cubs*
Milwaukee vs. Texas

SCHEDULE

MONDAY	NY vs. Det	*SD vs. Hou*
Sea vs. Oak	Mil vs. Bal	
Min vs. Cal	*Chi vs. NY*	
Cleve vs. Tex	*SF vs. Atl*	
Bos vs. KC	*LA vs. Cin*	
TUESDAY	NY vs. Chi	*Mon vs. StL*
Sea vs. Oak	Det vs. Tor	*SF vs. Atl*
Min vs. Cal	Mil vs. Bal	*LA vs. Cin*
Cleve vs. Tex	*Pitt vs. NY*	*SD vs. Hou*
Bos vs. KC	*Chi vs. Phil*	
WEDNESDAY	NY vs. Chi	*Mon vs. StL*
Sea vs. Oak	Det vs. Tor	*SF vs. Atl*
Min vs. Cal	Mil vs. Bal	*LA vs. Cin*
Cleve vs. Tex	*Pitt vs. NY*	*SD vs. Hou*
Bos vs. KC	*Chi vs. Phil*	
THURSDAY	*Chi vs. Phil*	
NY vs. Chi	*Mon vs. StL*	
Det vs. Tor	*SF vs. Atl*	
Mil vs. Bal	*LA vs. Cin*	
Pitt vs. NY	*SD vs. Hou*	
FRIDAY	Bos vs. Tor	*NY vs. Chi*
Min vs. Sea	Chi vs. Bal	*Hou vs. Atl*
Oak vs. Cal	Det vs. NY	*Cin vs. SD*
Mil vs. Tex	*Mon vs. Phil*	*LA vs. SF*
Cleve vs. KC	*StL vs. Pitt*	
SATURDAY	Bos vs. Tor	*NY vs. Chi*
Min vs. Sea	Chi vs. Bal	*Hou vs. Atl*
Oak vs. Cal	Det vs. NY	*Cin vs. SD*
Mil vs. Tex	*Mon vs. Phil*	*LA vs. SF*
Cleve vs. KC	*StL vs. Pitt*	
SUNDAY	Bos vs. Tor	*NY vs. Chi*
Min vs. Sea	Chi vs. Bal	*Hou vs. Atl*
Oak vs. Cal	Det vs. NY	*Cin vs. SD*
Mil vs. Tex	*Mon vs. Phil*	*LA vs. SF*
Cleve vs. KC	*StL vs. Pitt*	

1990 STANDINGS

AMERICAN LEAGUE **Through August 12** **NATIONAL LEAGUE**

East	Won	Lost	Pct.	GB	East	Won	Lost	Pct.	GB
Boston	62	51	.549	–	New York	64	47	.577	–
Toronto	60	55	.522	3	Pittsburgh	64	48	.571	½
Baltimore	55	58	.487	7	Montreal	60	54	.526	5½
Cleveland	54	60	.474	8½	Chicago	55	59	.482	10½
Detroit	53	63	.457	10	St. Louis	54	61	.470	12
Milwaukee	48	65	.425	14	Philadelphia	52	60	.464	12½
New York	46	67	.407	16					

West	Won	Lost	Pct.	GB	West	Won	Lost	Pct.	GB
Oakland	73	42	.635	–	Cincinnati	65	47	.580	–
Chicago	66	45	.595	5	San Francisco	60	53	.531	5½
Texas	59	55	.518	13½	Los Angeles	58	54	.518	7
Seattle	58	57	.504	15	San Diego	54	59	.478	11½
Kansas City	55	59	.482	17½	Houston	49	65	.430	17
California	55	60	.478	18	Atlanta	42	70	.375	23
Minnesota	54	61	.470	19					

INDIVIDUAL LEADERS

AMERICAN LEAGUE **NATIONAL LEAGUE**

BATTING

Based on 3.1 plate appearances per game

	G	AB	R	H	Pct.		G	AB	R	H	Pct.
Henderson,R Oak	97	355	84	117	.330	Dykstra,L Phil	104	411	82	144	.350
Palmeiro,R Tex	106	418	53	135	.323	McGee,W StL	111	446	68	150	.336
Griffey,K Sea	114	445	71	143	.321	Dawson,A Chi	103	366	51	122	.333
Harper,B Min	98	347	47	111	.320	Bonds,B Pitt	104	363	79	117	.322
Quintana,C Bos	105	341	41	107	.314	Gwynn,T SD	111	451	66	144	.319
Brett,G KC	102	395	61	123	.311	Murray,E LA	106	373	64	119	.319
Reed,J Bos	108	412	53	128	.311	Larkin,B Cin	111	432	59	134	.310
Boggs,W Bos	109	439	66	136	.310	Sandberg,R Chi	112	456	86	141	.309
Trammell,A Det	109	421	52	130	.309	Jefferies,G NY	105	418	71	129	.309
Burks,E Bos	103	394	63	121	.307	Mitchell,K SF	99	375	66	114	.304

HOME RUNS / WINS

HOME RUNS		**WINS**		**HOME RUNS**		**WINS**	
Fielder,C Det	35	Welch,B Oak	19	Sandberg,R Chi	27	Martinez,R LA	15
Canseco,J Oak	34	Stewart,D Oak	16	Mitchell,K SF	26	Viola,F NY	15
McGwire,M Oak	29	Clemens,R Bos	16	Strawberry,D NY	26	Drabek,D Pitt	14
McGriff,F Tor	26	Finley,C Cal	15	Bonds,B Pitt	23	Browning,T Cin	12
Gruber,K Tor	23	Stieb,D Tor	15	Bonilla,B Pitt	23	Harkey,M Chi	11
Henderson,R Oak	21	Brown,K Tex	12	Sabo,C Cin	22	Armstrong,J Cin	11
Milligan,R Bal	20	Candiotti,T Cleve	12	Williams,M SF	21	Burkett,J SF	11
Deer,R Mil	20			Gant,R Atl	21	Gooden,D NY	11
Bell,G Tor	20			Dawson,A Chi	21	Tudor,J StL	11
						Heaton,N Pitt	10

RBI / E.R.A.

RBI		**E.R.A.**		**RBI**		**E.R.A.**	
Fielder,C Det	91	Clemens,R Bos	2.16	Carter,J SD	93	Tudor,J StL	2.45
Canseco,J Oak	82	Finley,C Cal	2.36	Bonds,B Pitt	88	Whitson,E SD	2.62
Gruber,K Tor	80	Stewart,D Oak	2.46	Williams,M SF	86	Viola,F NY	2.73
McGwire,M Oak	74	Welch,B Oak	3.08	Strawberry,D NY	75	Martinez,R LA	2.79
Sierra,R Tex	71	Saberhagen,B KC	3.10	Bonilla,B Pitt	74	Gardner,M Mon	2.85
Bell,G Tor	70	Stieb,D Tor	3.12	Clark,W SF	71	Boyd,D Mon	2.99
Palmeiro,R Tex	69	Hibbard,G Chi	3.12	Dawson,A Chi	71	Drabek,D Pitt	2.99
Parker,D Mil	68	Candiotti,T Cleve	3.27	Wallach,T Mon	70	Browning,T Cin	3.02
McGriff,F Tor	68	Brown,K Tex	3.32	Guerrero,P StL	69	Martinez,De Mon	3.02
		Wells,D Tor	3.33	Sandberg,R Chi	69	Cook,D Phil	3.28

SLUGGING / SAVES

SLUGGING		**SAVES**		**SLUGGING**		**SAVES**	
Canseco,J Oak	.618	Thigpen,B Chi	37	Bonds,B Pitt	.598	Franco,J NY	25
Henderson,R Oak	.592	Eckersley,D Oak	37	Dawson,A Chi	.579	Myers,R Cin	23
Fielder,C Det	.581	Jones,D Cleve	31	Mitchell,K SF	.565	Smith,L StL	21
McGriff,F Tor	.537	Schooler,M Sea	29	Sandberg,R Chi	.550	Smith,D Hou	19
Gruber,K Tor	.501	Olson,G Bal	26	Gant,R Atl	.534	Lefferts,C SD	18
Griffey,K Sea	.501	Aguilera,R Min	24	Strawberry,D NY	.524	Brantley,J SF	17
Burks,E Bos	.500	Henke,T Tor	24	Bonilla,B Pitt	.523	McDowell,R Phil	16
Milligan,R Bal	.494	Righetti,D NY	24	Murray,E LA	.517	Burke,T Mon	14
Hrbek,K Min	.493	Henneman,M Det	18	Daniels,K LA	.509	Williams,M Chi	13
Felix,J Tor	.487	Reardon,J Bos	18	Wallach,T Mon	.506	Schmidt,D Mon	13

1991 STANDINGS

AMERICAN LEAGUE

East	Won	Lost	Pct.	GB

West	Won	Lost	Pct.	GB

NATIONAL LEAGUE

East	Won	Lost	Pct.	GB

West	Won	Lost	Pct.	GB

INDIVIDUAL LEADERS

AMERICAN LEAGUE

BATTING

HOME RUNS

WINS

RBI

E.R.A.

SLUGGING

SAVES

NATIONAL LEAGUE

BATTING

HOME RUNS

WINS

RBI

E.R.A.

SLUGGING

SAVES

A · U · G · U · S · T

MONDAY 12

Winning Pitcher:

Losing Pitcher:

Home Runs:

Highlights:

Score by innings:

TUESDAY 13

Winning Pitcher:

Losing Pitcher:

Home Runs:

Highlights:

Score by innings:

WEDNESDAY 14

Winning Pitcher:

Losing Pitcher:

Home Runs:

Highlights:

Score by innings:

THURSDAY 15

Winning Pitcher:

Losing Pitcher:

Home Runs:

Highlights:

Score by innings:

A · U · G · U · S · T

FRIDAY 16

_____ ___
_____ ___

Winning Pitcher:

Losing Pitcher:

Home Runs:

Highlights:

Score by innings:

SATURDAY 17

_____ ___
_____ ___

Winning Pitcher:

Losing Pitcher:

Home Runs:

Highlights:

Score by innings:

SUNDAY 18

_____ ___
_____ ___

Winning Pitcher:

Losing Pitcher:

Home Runs:

Highlights:

Score by innings:

ESPN: Oakland vs. Minnesota

SCHEDULE

MONDAY	Chi vs. Bal	_Hou vs. SD_
Oak vs. Sea	_Mon vs. Phil_	_Atl vs. SF_
Mil vs. Tex	_StL vs. Pitt_	
Cal vs. Min	_NY vs. Chi_	
Bos vs. Tor	_Cin vs. LA_	
TUESDAY	Bos vs. Cleve	_NY vs. StL_
Oak vs. Sea	Tex vs. Bal	_Cin vs. LA_
Cal vs. Min	KC vs. NY	_Hou vs. SD_
Tor vs. Mil	_Phil vs. Pitt_	_Atl vs. SF_
Chi vs. Det	_Mon vs. Chi_	
WEDNESDAY	Bos vs. Cleve	_NY vs. StL_
Oak vs. Sea	Tex vs. Bal	_Cin vs. LA_
Cal vs. Min	KC vs. NY	_Hou vs. SD_
Tor vs. Mil	_Phil vs. Pitt_	_Atl vs. SF_
Chi vs. Det	_Mon vs. Chi_	
THURSDAY	Bos vs. Cleve	_NY vs. StL_
Oak vs. Sea	Tex vs. Bal	_Hou vs. LA_
Cal vs. Min	KC vs. NY	_Atl vs. SD_
Tor vs. Mil	_Phil vs. Pitt_	_Cin vs. SF_
Chi vs. Det	_Mon vs. Chi_	
FRIDAY	Tex vs. Cleve	_Phil vs. Chi_
Cal vs. Sea	Chi vs. NY	_Hou vs. LA_
Oak vs. Min	KC vs. Bos	_Atl vs. SD_
Bal vs. Mil	_StL vs. Mon_	_Cin vs. SF_
Tor vs. Det	_NY vs. Pitt_	
SATURDAY	Tex vs. Cleve	_Phil vs. Chi_
Cal vs. Sea	Chi vs. NY	_Hou vs. LA_
Oak vs. Min	KC vs. Bos	_Atl vs. SD_
Bal vs. Mil	_StL vs. Mon_	_Cin vs. SF_
Tor vs. Det	_NY vs. Pitt_	
SUNDAY	Tex vs. Cleve	_Phil vs. Chi_
Cal vs. Sea	Chi vs. NY	_Hou vs. LA_
Oak vs. Min	KC vs. Bos	_Atl vs. SD_
Bal vs. Mil	_StL vs. Mon_	_Cin vs. SF_
Tor vs. Det	_NY vs. Pitt_	

1990 STANDINGS

AMERICAN LEAGUE					Through August 19	NATIONAL LEAGUE				

East	Won	Lost	Pct.	GB	East	Won	Lost	Pct.	GB
Boston	64	55	.538	–	Pittsburgh	71	49	.592	–
Toronto	65	56	.537	–	New York	68	50	.576	2
Baltimore	57	62	.479	7	Montreal	63	57	.525	8
Cleveland	56	64	.467	8½	Chicago	58	62	.483	13
Detroit	56	66	.459	9½	Philadelphia	57	61	.483	13
Milwaukee	53	66	.445	11	St. Louis	56	65	.463	15½
New York	49	70	.412	15					

West	Won	Lost	Pct.	GB	West	Won	Lost	Pct.	GB
Oakland	77	44	.636	–	Cincinnati	68	51	.571	–
Chicago	69	49	.585	6½	Los Angeles	62	58	.517	6½
Texas	62	59	.512	15	San Francisco	61	59	.508	7½
Seattle	60	61	.496	17	San Diego	56	63	.471	12
California	60	61	.496	17	Houston	53	68	.438	16
Kansas City	58	62	.483	18½	Atlanta	45	75	.375	23½
Minnesota	55	66	.455	22					

INDIVIDUAL LEADERS

AMERICAN LEAGUE

NATIONAL LEAGUE

BATTING

Based on 3.1 plate appearances per game

	G	AB	R	H	Pct.
Henderson,R Oak	101	366	86	120	.328
Palmeiro,R Tex	113	446	56	143	.321
Griffey,K Sea	120	468	72	148	.316
Brett,G KC	108	418	63	131	.313
Sheffield,G Mil	104	413	57	129	.312
Trammell,A Det	115	446	58	139	.312
Reed,J Bos	113	432	55	134	.310
Boggs,W Bos	114	459	66	142	.309
Harper,B Min	103	363	49	112	.309
Martinez,E Sea	114	396	56	121	.306

BATTING

	G	AB	R	H	Pct.
Dykstra,L Phil	110	436	87	150	.344
McGee,W StL	117	472	69	160	.339
Magadan,D NY	103	313	54	105	.335
Dawson,A Chi	109	390	51	126	.323
Gwynn,T SD	117	480	67	153	.319
Bonds,B Pitt	112	387	83	122	.315
Grace,M Chi	117	437	50	136	.311
Sandberg,R Chi	118	476	90	147	.309
Murray,E LA	114	405	66	125	.309
Wallach,T Mon	119	460	51	140	.304

HOME RUNS

Fielder,C Det	39
Canseco,J Oak	34
McGwire,M Oak	32
McGriff,F Tor	28
Deer,R Mil	23
Gruber,K Tor	23
Henderson,R Oak	22
Milligan,R Bal	20
Bell,G Tor	20

WINS

Welch,B Oak	20
Clemens,R Bos	18
Stewart,D Oak	17
Finley,C Cal	16
Stieb,D Tor	16
Brown,K Tex	12
Witt,B Tex	12
Sanderson,S Oak	12
Candiotti,T Cleve	12

HOME RUNS

Bonilla,B Pitt	28
Sandberg,R Chi	28
Mitchell,K SF	27
Strawberry,D NY	27
Williams,M SF	24
Bonds,B Pitt	24
Sabo,C Cin	22
Gant,R Atl	21
Dawson,A Chi	21

WINS

Drabek,D Pitt	16
Martinez,R LA	15
Viola,F NY	15
Gooden,D NY	13
Harkey,M Chi	12
Armstrong,J Cin	12
Browning,T Cin	12
Burkett,J SF	11
Maddux,G Chi	11
Tudor,J StL	11

RBI

Fielder,C Det	99
McGwire,M Oak	83
Canseco,J Oak	83
Gruber,K Tor	83
Sierra,R Tex	75
Bell,G Tor	75
Palmeiro,R Tex	72
McGriff,F Tor	72
Parker,D Mil	71

E.R.A.

Clemens,R Bos	2.04
Finley,C Cal	2.24
Stewart,D Oak	2.43
Stieb,D Tor	2.99
McCaskill,K Cal	3.02
Welch,B Oak	3.09
Saberhagen,B KC	3.10
Hibbard,G Chi	3.13
Appier,K KC	3.14
Wells,D Tor	3.21

RBI

Carter,J SD	96
Williams,M SF	93
Bonds,B Pitt	90
Bonilla,B Pitt	83
Strawberry,D NY	78
Clark,W SF	76
Sandberg,R Chi	73
Murray,E LA	73
Wallach,T Mon	72
Dawson,A Chi	72

E.R.A.

Tudor,J StL	2.45
Whitson,E SD	2.53
Viola,F NY	2.79
Drabek,D Pitt	2.82
Martinez,De Mon	2.85
Boyd,D Mon	2.92
Browning,T Cin	3.05
Martinez,R LA	3.05
Gardner,M Mon	3.17
Smith,Z Pitt	3.27

SLUGGING

Fielder,C Det	.614
Canseco,J Oak	.607
Henderson,R Oak	.590
McGriff,F Tor	.554
Gruber,K Tor	.502
Milligan,R Bal	.494
Hrbek,K Min	.491
Griffey,K Sea	.489
Deer,R Mil	.489
McGwire,M Oak	.485

SAVES

Thigpen,B Chi	40
Eckersley,D Oak	38
Jones,D Cleve	33
Schooler,M Sea	29
Olson,G Bal	28
Henke,T Tor	26
Righetti,D NY	26
Aguilera,R Min	25
Plesac,D Mil	20

SLUGGING

Bonds,B Pitt	.584
Mitchell,K SF	.555
Dawson,A Chi	.554
Bonilla,B Pitt	.552
Sandberg,R Chi	.548
Gant,R Atl	.515
Strawberry,D NY	.514
Daniels,K LA	.509
Wallach,T Mon	.502
Murray,E LA	.501

SAVES

Franco,J NY	28
Myers,R Cin	24
Smith,L StL	21
Smith,D Hou	20
Lefferts,C SD	19
Brantley,J SF	17
McDowell,R Phil	17
Burke,T Mon	14
Williams, M Chi	13
Schmidt,D Mon	13

1991 STANDINGS

AMERICAN LEAGUE

East	Won	Lost	Pct.	GB

West	Won	Lost	Pct.	GB

NATIONAL LEAGUE

East	Won	Lost	Pct.	GB

West	Won	Lost	Pct.	GB

INDIVIDUAL LEADERS

AMERICAN LEAGUE

BATTING

HOME RUNS

WINS

RBI

E.R.A.

SLUGGING

SAVES

NATIONAL LEAGUE

BATTING

HOME RUNS

WINS

RBI

E.R.A.

SLUGGING

SAVES

A · U · G · U · S · T

MONDAY 19

Winning Pitcher:

Losing Pitcher:

Home Runs:

Highlights:

Score by innings:

TUESDAY 20

Winning Pitcher:

Losing Pitcher:

Home Runs:

Highlights:

Score by innings:

WEDNESDAY 21

Winning Pitcher:

Losing Pitcher:

Home Runs:

Highlights:

Score by innings:

THURSDAY 22

Winning Pitcher:

Losing Pitcher:

Home Runs:

Highlights:

Score by innings:

A · U · G · U · S · T

FRIDAY 23

_____
_____

Winning Pitcher:

Losing Pitcher:

Home Runs:

Highlights:

Score by innings:

SATURDAY 24

_____
_____

Winning Pitcher:

Losing Pitcher:

Home Runs:

Highlights:

Score by innings:

CBS: *Cincinnati vs. Mets*
Minnesota vs. Baltimore

SUNDAY 25

_____
_____

Winning Pitcher:

Losing Pitcher:

Home Runs:

Highlights:

Score by innings:

ESPN: *Cincinnati vs. Mets*
White Sox vs. Cleveland

SCHEDULE

MONDAY	Det vs. Chi	
Cal vs. Sea	Cleve vs. Bos	
Bal vs. Tex	*Chi vs. Mon*	
NY vs. KC	*SD vs. LA*	
Oak vs. Min		
TUESDAY	Det vs. Chi	*Pitt vs. Phil*
Cal vs. Oak	Mil vs. Tor	*Atl vs. Cin*
Bal vs. Tex	Cleve vs. Bos	*SF vs. Hou*
NY vs. KC	*Chi vs. Mon*	*SD vs. LA*
Sea vs. Min	*StL vs. NY*	
WEDNESDAY	Det vs. Chi	*Pitt vs. Phil*
Cal vs. Oak	Mil vs. Tor	*Atl vs. Cin*
Bal vs. Tex	Cleve vs. Bos	*SF vs. Hou*
NY vs. KC	*Chi vs. Mon*	*SD vs. LA*
Sea vs. Min	*StL vs. NY*	
THURSDAY	*StL vs. NY*	
Cal vs. Oak	*Pitt vs. Phil*	
Tex vs. KC	*Atl vs. Cin*	
Sea vs. Min	*SF vs. Hou*	
Mil vs. Tor		
FRIDAY	Chi vs. Cleve	*SD vs. Chi*
Mil vs. Oak	NY vs. Tor	*LA vs. StL*
Bos vs. Cal	Min vs. Bal	*Phil vs. Atl*
Tex vs. KC	*Cin vs. NY*	*Mon vs. Hou*
Sea vs. Det	*SF vs. Pitt*	
SATURDAY	Chi vs. Cleve	*SD vs. Chi*
Mil vs. Oak	NY vs. Tor	*LA vs. StL*
Bos vs. Cal	Min vs. Bal	*Phil vs. Atl*
Tex vs. KC	*Cin vs. NY*	*Mon vs. Hou*
Sea vs. Det	*SF vs. Pitt*	
SUNDAY	Chi vs. Cleve	*SD vs. Chi*
Mil vs. Oak	NY vs. Tor	*LA vs. StL*
Bos vs. Cal	Min vs. Bal	*Phil vs. Atl*
Tex vs. KC	*Cin vs. NY*	*Mon vs. Hou*
Sea vs. Det	*SF vs. Pitt*	

1990 STANDINGS

AMERICAN LEAGUE				Through August 26		NATIONAL LEAGUE			

East	Won	Lost	Pct.	GB	East	Won	Lost	Pct.	GB
Boston	69	57	.548	–	Pittsburgh	74	53	.583	–
Toronto	66	62	.516	4	New York	70	55	.560	3
Baltimore	59	66	.472	9½	Montreal	66	60	.524	7½
Detroit	60	68	.469	10	Chicago	60	66	.476	13½
Cleveland	59	67	.468	10	Philadelphia	59	66	.472	14
Milwaukee	58	68	.460	11	St. Louis	58	69	.457	16
New York	53	73	.421	16					

West	Won	Lost	Pct.	GB	West	Won	Lost	Pct.	GB
Oakland	79	48	.622	–	Cincinnati	73	53	.579	–
Chicago	73	52	.584	5	Los Angeles	67	60	.528	6½
Texas	66	61	.520	13	San Francisco	66	61	.520	7½
Kansas City	64	63	.504	15	San Diego	59	66	.472	13½
California	63	65	.492	16½	Houston	57	71	.445	17
Seattle	62	66	.484	17½	Atlanta	49	78	.386	24½
Minnesota	56	71	.441	23					

INDIVIDUAL LEADERS

AMERICAN LEAGUE

BATTING

Based on 3.1 plate appearances per game

	G	AB	R	H	Pct.
Henderson,R Oak	106	383	91	123	.321
Palmeiro,R Tex	119	466	57	148	.318
Trammell,A Det	121	470	63	149	.317
Brett,G KC	115	443	68	139	.314
Harper,B Min	108	383	52	120	.313
James,C Cleve	112	415	50	128	.308
Boggs,W Bos	121	487	70	149	.306
Reed,J Bos	120	461	56	141	.306
Griffey,K Sea	127	494	74	151	.306
Sheffield,G Mil	111	437	60	133	.304

HOME RUNS

Fielder,C Det	41
Canseco,J Oak	35
McGwire,M Oak	33
McGriff,F Tor	28
Deer,R Mil	26
Gruber,K Tor	23
Henderson,R Oak	22

WINS

Welch,B Oak	21
Clemens,R Bos	19
Stewart,D Oak	17
Finley,C Cal	16
Stieb,D Tor	16
Witt,B Tex	13
Sanderson,S Oak	13
Candiotti,T Cleve	13

RBI

Fielder,C Det	108
Canseco,J Oak	88
McGwire,M Oak	86
Gruber,K Tor	85
Parker,D Mil	82
Sierra,R Tex	78
Bell,G Tor	77
Trammell,A Det	76
Palmeiro,R Tex	73

E.R.A.

Clemens,R Bos	1.95
Finley,C Cal	2.47
Stewart,D Oak	2.73
Stieb,D Tor	2.97
Appier,K KC	3.00
Hibbard,G Chi	3.01
Wells,D Tor	3.09
Harris,G Bos	3.16
McCaskill,K Cal	3.16
Welch,B Oak	3.24

SLUGGING

Fielder,C Det	.620
Canseco,J Oak	.595
Henderson,R Oak	.574
McGriff,F Tor	.544
Deer,R Mil	.500
Milligan,R Bal	.494
Parker,D Mil	.483
Brett,G KC	.483
Burks,E Bos	.481
Griffey,K Sea	.480

SAVES

Thigpen,B Chi	43
Eckersley,D Oak	39
Jones,D Cleve	34
Schooler,M Sea	30
Olson,G Bal	29
Righetti,D NY	27
Aguilera,R Min	26
Henke,T Tor	26
Plesac,D Mil	21
Montgomery,J KC	19

NATIONAL LEAGUE

BATTING

	G	AB	R	H	Pct.
Dykstra,L Phil	117	463	90	159	.343
McGee,W StL	123	493	74	166	.337
Magadan,D NY	110	338	56	113	.334
Gwynn,T SD	123	501	68	158	.315
Dawson,A Chi	113	407	53	127	.312
Murray,E LA	121	431	72	134	.311
Grace,M Chi	123	459	55	142	.309
Bonds,B Pitt	118	408	87	125	.306
Coleman,V StL	114	455	71	138	.303
Mitchell,K SF	113	423	75	128	.303

HOME RUNS

Bonilla,B Pitt	30
Sandberg,R Chi	29
Mitchell,K SF	28
Strawberry,D NY	28
Williams,M SF	26
Bonds,B Pitt	25
Gant,R Atl	24
Sabo,C Cin	22
Dawson,A Chi	21

WINS

Drabek,D Pitt	16
Viola,F NY	16
Martinez,R LA	15
Gooden,D NY	14
Harkey,M Chi	12
Armstrong,J Cin	12
Browning,T Cin	12

RBI

Williams,M SF	97
Carter,J SD	96
Bonds,B Pitt	92
Bonilla,B Pitt	90
Strawberry,D NY	80
Clark,W SF	77
Mitchell,K SF	76
Murray,E LA	76
Wallach,T Mon	75
Sandberg,R Chi	74

E.R.A.

Whitson,E SD	2.41
Tudor,J StL	2.45
Viola,F NY	2.71
Martinez,De Mon	2.82
Drabek,D Pitt	2.86
Martinez,R LA	3.03
Browning,T Cin	3.05
Gardner,M Mon	3.08
Boyd,D Mon	3.10
Smith,Z Pitt	3.24

SLUGGING

Bonds,B Pitt	.571
Bonilla,B Pitt	.557
Mitchell,K SF	.551
Gant,R Atl	.539
Sandberg,R Chi	.537
Dawson,A Chi	.536
Strawberry,D NY	.509
Murray,E LA	.499
Daniels,K LA	.493
Williams,M SF	.492

SAVES

Franco,J NY	30
Myers,R Cin	25
Smith,L StL	22
Lefferts,C SD	21
Smith,D Hou	20
Brantley,J SF	18
McDowell,R Phil	17
Burke,T Mon	14

1991 STANDINGS

AMERICAN LEAGUE

East	Won	Lost	Pct.	GB

West	Won	Lost	Pct.	GB

NATIONAL LEAGUE

East	Won	Lost	Pct.	GB

West	Won	Lost	Pct.	GB

INDIVIDUAL LEADERS

AMERICAN LEAGUE

BATTING

HOME RUNS

WINS

RBI

E.R.A.

SLUGGING

SAVES

NATIONAL LEAGUE

BATTING

HOME RUNS

WINS

RBI

E.R.A.

SLUGGING

SAVES

Winning Pitcher:

Losing Pitcher:

Home Runs:

Highlights:

Score by innings:

MONDAY 26

Winning Pitcher:

Losing Pitcher:

Home Runs:

Highlights:

Score by innings:

TUESDAY 27

Winning Pitcher:

Losing Pitcher:

Home Runs:

Highlights:

Score by innings:

WEDNESDAY 28

Winning Pitcher:

Losing Pitcher:

Home Runs:

Highlights:

Score by innings:

THURSDAY 29

S · E · P · T · E · M · B · E · R

FRIDAY 30

_____ _____

_____

Winning Pitcher:

Losing Pitcher:

Home Runs:

Highlights:

Score by innings:

SATURDAY 31

_____ _____

_____

Winning Pitcher:

Losing Pitcher:

Home Runs:

Highlights:

Score by innings:

SUNDAY 1

_____ _____

_____

Winning Pitcher:

Losing Pitcher:

Home Runs:

Highlights:

Score by innings:

ESPN: *Pittsburgh vs. San Diego*
Boston vs. Seattle

SCHEDULE

MONDAY	Min vs. Cleve	*SF vs. StL*
Mil vs. Sea	Tor vs. Bal	*Mon vs. Atl*
Bos vs. Oak	Tex vs. NY	*Phil vs. Cin*
Det vs. Cal	*SD vs. Pitt*	*NY vs. Hou*
Chi vs. KC	*LA vs. Chi*	
TUESDAY	Min vs. Cleve	*SF vs. StL*
Mil vs. Sea	Tor vs. Bal	*Mon vs. Atl*
Bos vs. Oak	Tex vs. NY	*Phil vs. Cin*
Det vs. Cal	*SD vs. Pitt*	*NY vs. Hou*
Chi vs. KC	*LA vs. Chi*	
WEDNESDAY	Min vs. Cleve	*NY vs. Atl*
Mil vs. Sea	Tor vs. Bal	*Mon vs. Cin*
Bos vs. Oak	Tex vs. NY	*Pitt vs. LA*
Det vs. Cal	*Hou vs. Phil*	*Chi vs. SF*
Chi vs. KC	*SD vs. StL*	
THURSDAY	*NY vs. Atl*	
Cleve vs. Chi	*Mon vs. Cin*	
Tor vs. NY	*Pitt vs. LA*	
Hou vs. Phil	*Chi vs. SF*	
SD vs. StL		
FRIDAY	Cleve vs. Chi	*NY vs. Cin*
Bos vs. Sea	Cal vs. Mil	*Chi vs. LA*
Det vs. Oak	Tor vs. NY	*Pitt vs. SD*
KC vs. Tex	*Hou vs. Mon*	*StL vs. SF*
Bal vs. Min	*Atl vs. Phil*	
SATURDAY	Cleve vs. Chi	*NY vs. Cin*
Bos vs. Sea	Cal vs. Mil	*Chi vs. LA*
Det vs. Oak	Tor vs. NY	*Pitt vs. SD*
KC vs. Tex	*Hou vs. Mon*	*StL vs. SF*
Bal vs. Min	*Atl vs. Phil*	
SUNDAY	Cleve vs. Chi	*NY vs. Cin*
Bos vs. Sea	Cal vs. Mil	*Chi vs. LA*
Det vs. Oak	Tor vs. NY	*Pitt vs. SD*
KC vs. Tex	*Hou vs. Mon*	*StL vs. SF*
Bal vs. Min	*Atl vs. Phil*	

1990 STANDINGS

AMERICAN LEAGUE Through September 2 NATIONAL LEAGUE

East	Won	Lost	Pct.	GB	East	Won	Lost	Pct.	GB
Boston	76	57	.571	–	New York	76	55	.580	–
Toronto	70	64	.522	6½	Pittsburgh	76	56	.576	½
Detroit	64	70	.478	12½	Montreal	69	63	.523	7½
Milwaukee	63	69	.477	12½	Philadelphia	62	70	.470	14½
Baltimore	60	72	.455	15½	Chicago	62	70	.470	14½
Cleveland	59	74	.444	17	St. Louis	60	73	.451	17
New York	56	77	.421	20					

West	Won	Lost	Pct.	GB	West	Won	Lost	Pct.	GB
Oakland	83	50	.624	–	Cincinnati	77	55	.583	–
Chicago	76	56	.576	6½	Los Angeles	71	62	.534	6½
Texas	67	66	.504	16	San Francisco	67	66	.504	10½
California	67	67	.500	16½	San Diego	61	71	.462	16
Kansas City	66	67	.496	17	Houston	60	73	.451	17½
Seattle	65	69	.485	18½	Atlanta	53	80	.398	24½
Minnesota	60	74	.448	23½					

INDIVIDUAL LEADERS

AMERICAN LEAGUE NATIONAL LEAGUE

BATTING

Based on 3.1 plate appearances per game

	G	AB	R	H	Pct.		G	AB	R	H	Pct.
Henderson,R Oak	112	406	96	132	.325	Dykstra,L Phil	124	490	91	167	.341
Brett,G KC	119	457	72	146	.319	McGee,W StL	125	501	76	168	.335
Palmeiro,R Tex	125	485	59	154	.318	Magadan,D NY	116	355	60	117	.330
Trammell,A Det	127	493	65	154	.312	Murray,E LA	127	454	76	142	.313
Burks,E Bos	123	471	77	147	.312	Gwynn,T SD	129	525	70	164	.312
Boggs,W Bos	128	517	78	161	.311	Grace,M Chi	129	484	55	151	.312
McGriff,F Tor	125	446	80	138	.309	Wallach,T Mon	131	506	55	156	.308
Parker,D Mil	129	501	63	155	.309	Bonds,B Pitt	123	426	89	131	.308
Harper,B Min	113	402	53	124	.308	Dawson,A Chi	119	430	54	132	.307
Reed,J Bos	126	490	60	150	.306	Mitchell,K SF	119	447	80	137	.306

HOME RUNS		WINS		HOME RUNS		WINS	
Fielder,C Det	42	Welch,B Oak	22	Mitchell,K SF	31	Drabek,D Pitt	17
Canseco,J Oak	35	Clemens,R Bos	20	Sandberg,R Chi	31	Viola,F NY	17
McGwire,M Oak	33	Finley,C Cal	17	Strawberry,D NY	30	Martinez,R LA	16
McGriff,F Tor	31	Stieb,D Tor	17	Bonilla,B Pitt	30	Gooden,D NY	14
Deer,R Mil	26	Stewart,D Oak	17	Williams,M SF	27		
Gruber,K Tor	24	Witt,B Tex	14	Gant,R Atl	25		
Henderson,R Oak	23	Boddicker,M Bos	14	Bonds,B Pitt	25		
Jackson,B KC	22	Johnson,R Sea	13	Sabo,C Cin	23		
Hrbek,K Min	21	Sanderson,S Oak	13				
Parrish,L Cal	21	Candiotti,T Cleve	13				

RBI		E.R.A.		RBI		E.R.A.	
Fielder,C Det	111	Clemens,R Bos	1.95	Williams,M SF	100	Whitson,E SD	2.31
Canseco,J Oak	89	Finley,C Cal	2.43	Carter,J SD	99	Tudor,J StL	2.54
Gruber,K Tor	88	Stewart,D Oak	2.81	Bonds,B Pitt	97	Viola,F NY	2.72
McGwire,M Oak	87	Appier,K KC	2.81	Bonilla,B Pitt	93	Drabek,D Pitt	2.77
Parker,D Mil	85	Stieb,D Tor	2.91	Strawberry,D NY	89	Martinez,De Mon	2.92
Sierra,R Tex	79	McCaskill,K Cal	2.96	Wallach,T Mon	83	Martinez,R LA	3.02
Burks,E Bos	79	Hibbard,G Chi	3.11	Mitchell,K SF	82	Boyd,D Mon	3.02
McGriff,F Tor	78	Welch,B Oak	3.16	Sandberg,R Chi	80	Smith,Z Pitt	3.08
Bell,G Tor	77	Harris,G Bos	3.17	Johnson,H NY	80	Rijo,J Cin	3.20
Trammell,A Det	77	Wells,D Tor	3.24			Browning,T Cin	3.21

SLUGGING		SAVES		SLUGGING		SAVES	
Fielder,C Det	.612	Thigpen,B Chi	46	Mitchell,K SF	.566	Franco,J NY	31
Henderson,R Oak	.579	Eckersley,D Oak	41	Bonds,B Pitt	.566	Myers,R Cin	27
Canseco,J Oak	.574	Jones,D Cleve	34	Bonilla,B Pitt	.545	Lefferts,C SD	22
McGriff,F Tor	.565	Schooler,M Sea	30	Sandberg,R Chi	.537	Smith,L StL	22
Burks,E Bos	.524	Olson,G Bal	29	Gant,R Atl	.537	Smith,D Hou	20
Parker,D Mil	.495	Righetti,D NY	29	Dawson,A Chi	.526	Brantley,J SF	18
Brett,G KC	.495	Aguilera,R Min	27	Strawberry,D NY	.516	McDowell,R Phil	18
Milligan,R Bal	.494	Henke,T Tor	26	Daniels,K LA	.505	Burke,T Mon	15
Hrbek,K Min	.492	Plesac,D Mil	22	Wallach,T Mon	.500		
Griffey Jr,K Sea	.481	Harvey,B Cal	20	Murray,E LA	.496		

1991 STANDINGS

AMERICAN LEAGUE

East	Won	Lost	Pct.	GB

West	Won	Lost	Pct.	GB

NATIONAL LEAGUE

East	Won	Lost	Pct.	GB

West	Won	Lost	Pct.	GB

INDIVIDUAL LEADERS

AMERICAN LEAGUE

BATTING

HOME RUNS

WINS

RBI

E.R.A.

SLUGGING

SAVES

NATIONAL LEAGUE

BATTING

HOME RUNS

WINS

RBI

E.R.A.

SLUGGING

SAVES

S · E · P · T · E · M · B · E · R

MONDAY 2

Winning Pitcher:

Losing Pitcher:

Home Runs:

Highlights:

Score by innings:

TUESDAY 3

Winning Pitcher:

Losing Pitcher:

Home Runs:

Highlights:

Score by innings:

WEDNESDAY 4

Winning Pitcher:

Losing Pitcher:

Home Runs:

Highlights:

Score by innings:

THURSDAY 5

Winning Pitcher:

Losing Pitcher:

Home Runs:

Highlights:

Score by innings:

S · E · P · T · E · M · B · E · R

FRIDAY 6

_____

_____

Winning Pitcher:

Losing Pitcher:

Home Runs:

Highlights:

Score by innings:

SATURDAY 7

_____

_____

Winning Pitcher:

Losing Pitcher:

Home Runs:

Highlights:

Score by innings:

SUNDAY 8

_____

_____

Winning Pitcher:

Losing Pitcher:

Home Runs:

Highlights:

Score by innings:

ESPN: Milwaukee vs. California

SCHEDULE

MONDAY	Cal vs. Mil	StL vs. LA
Det vs. Sea	Bal vs. Tor	Chi vs. SD
NY vs. Tex	Atl vs. Mon	Pitt vs. SF
Cleve vs. Min	Hou vs. NY	
KC vs. Chi	Cin vs. Phil	
TUESDAY	Bal vs. Tor	StL vs. LA
Det vs. Sea	Cal vs. Bos	Chi vs. SD
NY vs. Tex	Atl vs. Mon	Pitt vs. SF
KC vs. Chi	Hou vs. NY	
Oak vs. Mil	Cin vs. Phil	
WEDNESDAY	Bal vs. Tor	StL vs. LA
NY vs. Tex	Cal vs. Bos	Chi vs. SD
Cleve vs. Min	Atl vs. Mon	Pitt vs. SF
KC vs. Chi	Hou vs. NY	
Oak vs. Mil	Cin vs. Phil	
THURSDAY	StL vs. SD	
KC vs. Chi		
Oak vs. Det		
Tor vs. Cleve		
Sea vs. Bos		
FRIDAY	Tor vs. Cleve	LA vs. Pitt
Mil vs. Cal	KC vs. Bal	SF vs. Chi
Chi vs. Tex	Sea vs. Bos	Phil vs. Hou
NY vs. Min	Cin vs. Mon	StL vs. SD
Oak vs. Det	Atl vs. NY	
SATURDAY	Tor vs. Cleve	LA vs. Pitt
Mil vs. Cal	KC vs. Bal	SF vs. Chi
Chi vs. Tex	Sea vs. Bos	Phil vs. Hou
NY vs. Min	Cin vs. Mon	StL vs. SD
Oak vs. Det	Atl vs. NY	
SUNDAY	Tor vs. Cleve	LA vs. Pitt
Mil vs. Cal	KC vs. Bal	SF vs. Chi
Chi vs. Tex	Sea vs. Bos	Phil vs. Hou
NY vs. Min	Cin vs. Mon	StL vs. SD
Oak vs. Det	Atl vs. NY	

1990 STANDINGS

AMERICAN LEAGUE — Through September 9 — NATIONAL LEAGUE

East	Won	Lost	Pct.	GB	East	Won	Lost	Pct.	GB
Boston	78	61	.561	–	Pittsburgh	82	58	.586	–
Toronto	74	66	.529	4½	New York	78	61	.561	3½
Detroit	67	74	.475	12	Montreal	73	66	.525	8½
Milwaukee	66	73	.475	12	Philadelphia	65	74	.468	16½
Baltimore	63	75	.457	14½	Chicago	65	74	.468	16½
Cleveland	62	78	.443	16½	St. Louis	64	76	.457	18
New York	57	82	.410	21					

West	Won	Lost	Pct.	GB	West	Won	Lost	Pct.	GB
Oakland	89	50	.640	–	Cincinnati	79	60	.568	–
Chicago	79	59	.572	9½	Los Angeles	74	66	.529	5½
Texas	73	67	.521	16½	San Francisco	72	68	.514	7½
Seattle	69	71	.493	20½	San Diego	64	75	.460	15
California	69	71	.493	20½	Houston	63	77	.450	16½
Kansas City	66	74	.471	23½	Atlanta	58	82	.414	21½
Minnesota	65	76	.461	25					

INDIVIDUAL LEADERS

AMERICAN LEAGUE

BATTING

Based on 3.1 plate appearances per game

	G	AB	R	H	Pct.
Henderson,R Oak	118	429	104	139	.324
Brett,G KC	126	483	75	156	.323
Palmeiro,R Tex	132	513	64	165	.322
Trammell,A Det	133	510	67	160	.314
McGriff,F Tor	131	470	83	147	.313
Burks,E Bos	129	495	78	153	.309
Puckett,K Min	128	479	79	148	.309
Harper,B Min	119	429	58	132	.308
Boggs,W Bos	134	539	81	165	.306
Parker,D Mil	136	528	64	161	.305

HOME RUNS

Fielder,C Det	45
McGwire,M Oak	36
Canseco,J Oak	36
McGriff,F Tor	33
Deer,R Mil	27
Gruber,K Tor	26
Henderson,R Oak	26
Jackson,B KC	23
Barfield,J NY	22

WINS

Welch,B Oak	23
Clemens,R Bos	20
Stewart,D Oak	19
Stieb,D Tor	18
Finley,C Cal	17
Witt,B Tex	15
Sanderson,S Oak	15
Candiotti,T Cleve	14
Boddicker,M Bos	14

RBI

Fielder,C Det	116
McGwire,M Oak	99
Gruber,K Tor	92
Canseco,J Oak	90
Sierra,R Tex	86
Parker,D Mil	85
Maldonado,C Cleve	84
McGriff,F Tor	82
Trammell,A Det	82
Palmeiro,R Tex	81

E.R.A.

Clemens,R Bos	1.98
Finley,C Cal	2.51
Stewart,D Oak	2.77
Stieb,D Tor	2.78
McCaskill,K Cal	2.81
Appier,K KC	2.82
Hibbard,G Chi	2.95
Welch,B Oak	3.03
Wells,D Tor	3.27
Witt,B Tex	3.29

SLUGGING

Fielder,C Det	.612
Henderson,R Oak	.585
Canseco,J Oak	.572
McGriff,F Tor	.570
Burks,E Bos	.513
Brett,G KC	.499
Milligan,R Bal	.494
McGwire,M Oak	.489
Hrbek,K Min	.486
Gruber,K Tor	.485

SAVES

Thigpen,B Chi	48
Eckersley,D Oak	42
Jones,D Cleve	34
Olson,G Bal	30
Schooler,M Sea	30
Righetti,D NY	30
Aguilera,R Min	28
Henke,T Tor	28
Plesac,D Mil	22

NATIONAL LEAGUE

BATTING

	G	AB	R	H	Pct.
Dykstra,L Phil	131	517	97	176	.340
McGee,W StL	125	501	76	168	.335
Magadan,D NY	122	375	64	124	.331
Murray,E LA	134	480	80	151	.315
Grace,M Chi	135	508	58	157	.309
Dawson,A Chi	125	454	57	140	.308
Gwynn,T SD	136	555	74	171	.308
Bonds,B Pitt	131	451	92	138	.306
Smith,L Atl	116	390	57	119	.305
Wallach,T Mon	138	532	58	162	.305

HOME RUNS

Mitchell,K SF	33
Sandberg,R Chi	33
Strawberry,D NY	31
Bonilla,B Pitt	31
Williams,M SF	29
Gant,R Atl	28
Bonds,B Pitt	26
Daniels,K LA	24

WINS

Drabek,D Pitt	19
Martinez,R LA	17
Viola,F NY	17
Gooden,D NY	16
Smoltz,J Atl	13
Browning,T Cin	13

RBI

Williams,M SF	107
Carter,J SD	105
Bonds,B Pitt	102
Bonilla,B Pitt	102
Strawberry,D NY	92
Mitchell,K SF	87
Wallach,T Mon	86
Sandberg,R Chi	83
Johnson,H NY	83
Murray,E LA	83

E.R.A.

Whitson,E SD	2.37
Tudor,J StL	2.43
Viola,F NY	2.62
Drabek,D Pitt	2.63
Martinez,De Mon	2.92
Smith,Z Pitt	2.93
Boyd,D Mon	2.96
Rijo,J Cin	3.12
Martinez,R LA	3.22
Harkey,M Chi	3.26

SLUGGING

Mitchell,K SF	.560
Bonds,B Pitt	.557
Bonilla,B Pitt	.545
Gant,R Atl	.543
Sandberg,R Chi	.541
Dawson,A Chi	.524
Daniels,K LA	.515
Strawberry,D NY	.514
Murray,E LA	.502
Williams,M SF	.497

SAVES

Franco,J NY	31
Myers,R Cin	28
Smith,L StL	25
Lefferts,C SD	23
Smith,D Hou	23
Brantley,J SF	19
McDowell,R Phil	19
Burke,T Mon	17
Williams,M Chi	14
Howell,J LA	14

1991 STANDINGS

AMERICAN LEAGUE

East	Won	Lost	Pct.	GB

West	Won	Lost	Pct.	GB

NATIONAL LEAGUE

East	Won	Lost	Pct.	GB

West	Won	Lost	Pct.	GB

INDIVIDUAL LEADERS

AMERICAN LEAGUE

BATTING

HOME RUNS

WINS

RBI

E.R.A.

SLUGGING

SAVES

NATIONAL LEAGUE

BATTING

HOME RUNS

WINS

RBI

E.R.A.

SLUGGING

SAVES

S • E • P • T • E • M • B • E • R

MONDAY 9

Winning Pitcher:

Losing Pitcher:

Home Runs:

Highlights:

Score by innings:

TUESDAY 10

Winning Pitcher:

Losing Pitcher:

Home Runs:

Highlights:

Score by innings:

WEDNESDAY 11

Winning Pitcher:

Losing Pitcher:

Home Runs:

Highlights:

Score by innings:

THURSDAY 12

Winning Pitcher:

Losing Pitcher:

Home Runs:

Highlights:

Score by innings:

FRIDAY 13

_____ ___

_____ ___

Winning Pitcher:

Losing Pitcher:

Home Runs:

Highlights:

Score by innings:

SATURDAY 14

_____ ___

_____ ___

Winning Pitcher:

Losing Pitcher:

Home Runs:

Highlights:

Score by innings:

CBS: White Sox vs. California
Oakland vs. Toronto

SUNDAY 15

_____ ___

_____ ___

Winning Pitcher:

Losing Pitcher:

Home Runs:

Highlights:

Score by innings:

ESPN: Boston vs. Yankees

SCHEDULE

MONDAY	Mon vs. NY	SD vs. Hou
Chi vs. Oak	Pitt vs. Chi	
Tex vs. Cal	Phil vs. StL	
Min vs. KC	SF vs. Atl	
NY vs. Bal	LA vs. Cin	
TUESDAY	Bos vs. Det	Phil vs. StL
Chi vs. Oak	Sea vs. Tor	SF vs. Atl
Tex vs. Cal	NY vs. Bal	LA vs. Cin
Min vs. KC	Mon vs. Atl	SD vs. Hou
Cleve vs. Mil	Pitt vs. Chi	
WEDNESDAY	Bos vs. Det	Pitt vs. StL
Chi vs. Oak	Sea vs. Tor	SD vs. Atl
Tex vs. Cal	NY vs. Bal	SF vs. Cin
Min vs. KC	Mon vs. Phil	LA vs. Hou
Cleve vs. Mil	NY vs. Chi	
THURSDAY	Bos vs. NY	SF vs. Cin
Chi vs. Cal	Mon vs. Phil	LA vs. Hou
Min vs. Tex	NY vs. Chi	
Det vs. Mil	Pitt vs. StL	
Cleve vs. Bal	SD vs. Atl	
FRIDAY	Oak vs. Tor	NY vs. StL
Chi vs. Cal	Cleve vs. Bal	LA vs. Atl
Min vs. Tex	Bos vs. NY	Hou vs. Cin
Sea vs. KC	Pitt vs. Phil	SD vs. SF
Det vs. Mil	Mon vs. Chi	
SATURDAY	Oak vs. Tor	NY vs. StL
Chi vs. Cal	Cleve vs. Bal	LA vs. Atl
Min vs. Tex	Bos vs. NY	Hou vs. Cin
Sea vs. KC	Pitt vs. Phil	SD vs. SF
Det vs. Mil	Mon vs. Chi	
SUNDAY	Oak vs. Tor	NY vs. StL
Chi vs. Cal	Cleve vs. Bal	LA vs. Atl
Min vs. Tex	Bos vs. NY	Hou vs. Cin
Sea vs. KC	Pitt vs. Phil	SD vs. SF
Det vs. Mil	Mon vs. Chi	

1990 STANDINGS

AMERICAN LEAGUE   **Through September 16**   NATIONAL LEAGUE

East	Won	Lost	Pct.	GB
Boston	80	67	.544	–
Toronto	79	68	.537	1
Detroit	71	77	.480	9½
Milwaukee	69	77	.473	10½
Cleveland	67	80	.456	13
Baltimore	65	80	.448	14
New York	60	86	.411	19½

East	Won	Lost	Pct.	GB
Pittsburgh	84	63	.571	–
New York	83	63	.568	½
Montreal	78	68	.534	5½
Chicago	70	76	.479	13½
Philadelphia	67	79	.459	16½
St. Louis	66	81	.449	18

West	Won	Lost	Pct.	GB
Oakland	94	52	.644	–
Chicago	84	62	.575	10
Texas	77	69	.527	17
California	74	73	.503	20½
Seattle	72	75	.490	22½
Kansas City	68	78	.466	26
Minnesota	66	82	.446	29

West	Won	Lost	Pct.	GB
Cincinnati	82	63	.566	–
Los Angeles	77	69	.527	5½
San Francisco	75	71	.514	7½
San Diego	68	77	.469	14
Houston	67	79	.459	15½
Atlanta	59	87	.404	23½

INDIVIDUAL LEADERS

AMERICAN LEAGUE   NATIONAL LEAGUE

BATTING

Based on 3.1 plate appearances per game

	G	AB	R	H	Pct.
Henderson,R Oak	123	444	109	145	.327
Brett,G KC	132	510	78	166	.325
Palmeiro,R Tex	138	537	66	171	.318
Trammell,A Det	137	525	68	165	.314
Boggs,W Bos	142	569	84	177	.311
Parker,D Mil	143	554	67	169	.305
McGriff,F Tor	138	495	85	151	.305
Harper,B Min	125	447	59	136	.304
James,C Cleve	129	480	55	146	.304
Burks,E Bos	137	528	80	159	.301

BATTING

	G	AB	R	H	Pct.
McGee,W StL	125	501	76	168	.335
Dykstra,L Phil	138	545	98	182	.334
Magadan,D NY	129	400	68	129	.323
Murray,E LA	139	497	85	158	.318
Doran,B Cin	120	378	57	118	.312
Dawson,A Chi	132	478	61	149	.312
Grace,M Chi	142	533	65	166	.311
Gwynn,T SD	141	573	79	177	.309
Bonds,B Pitt	138	478	96	147	.308
Smith,L Atl	122	413	62	127	.308

HOME RUNS

Fielder,C Det	47
McGwire,M Oak	37
Canseco,J Oak	37
McGriff,F Tor	34
Gruber,K Tor	28
Deer,R Mil	27
Henderson,R Oak	26
Jackson,B KC	25
Barfield,J NY	23
Hrbek,K Min	22

WINS

Welch,B Oak	24
Stewart,D Oak	20
Clemens,R Bos	20
Finley,C Cal	18
Stieb,D Tor	18
Sanderson,S Oak	16
Hanson,E Sea	15
Witt,B Tex	15
Boddicker,M Bos	15
Candiotti,T Cleve	14

HOME RUNS

Sandberg,R Chi	36
Mitchell,K SF	34
Strawberry, NY	34
Bonilla,B Pitt	31
Williams,M SF	30
Gant,R Atl	29
Bonds,B Pitt	29
Daniels,K LA	26
Justice,D Atl	25

WINS

Drabek,D Pitt	19
Viola,F NY	19
Martinez,R LA	18
Gooden,D NY	17
Smoltz,J Atl	13
Maddux,G Chi	13
Browning,T Cin	13
Valenzuela,F LA	13

RBI

Fielder,C Det	120
Gruber,K Tor	106
McGwire,M Oak	103
Canseco,J Oak	95
Parker,D Mil	90
Sierra,R Tex	88
Trammell,A Det	88
Maldonado,C Cleve	86
Palmeiro,R Tex	84
Burks,E Bos	84

E.R.A.

Clemens,R Bos	1.98
Finley,C Cal	2.45
Stewart,D Oak	2.70
McCaskill,K Cal	2.87
Appier,K KC	2.91
Stieb,D Tor	2.93
Hibbard,G Chi	3.01
Welch,B Oak	3.04
Wells,D Tor	3.16
Ryan,N Tex	3.36

RBI

Williams,M SF	111
Bonds,B Pitt	107
Carter,J SD	107
Bonilla,B Pitt	106
Strawberry,D NY	101
Mitchell,K SF	91
Boyd,D Mon	91
Wallach,T Mon	91
Sandberg,R Chi	89
Dawson,A Chi	88
Murray,E LA	85

E.R.A.

Whitson,E SD	2.42
Viola,F NY	2.55
Drabek,D Pitt	2.75
Smith,Z Pitt	2.85
Martinez,De Mon	2.92
Boyd,D Mon	2.94
Rijo,J Cin	3.00
Martinez,R LA	3.08
Harkey,M Chi	3.26
Hurst,B SD	3.30

SLUGGING

Fielder,C Det	.607
Henderson,R Oak	.586
Canseco,J Oak	.558
McGriff,F Tor	.556
Brett,G KC	.508
Gruber,K Tor	.501
Burks,E Bos	.500
McGwire,M Oak	.493
Parker,D Mil	.484
Hrbek,K Min	.482

SAVES

Thigpen,B Chi	51
Eckersley,D Oak	43
Jones,D Cleve	35
Righetti,D NY	32
Olson,G Bal	31
Schooler,M Sea	30
Aguilera,R Min	28
Henke,T Tor	28
Harvey,B Cal	23
Plesac,D Mil	23

SLUGGING

Bonds,B Pitt	.569
Mitchell,K SF	.561
Sandberg,R Chi	.554
Bonilla,B Pitt	.534
Gant,R Atl	.533
Dawson,A Chi	.529
Daniels,K LA	.525
Strawberry,D NY	.524
Murray,E LA	.513
Williams,M SF	.491

SAVES

Franco,J NY	33
Myers,R Cin	29
Smith,L StL	26
Lefferts,C SD	23
Smith,D Hou	23
Brantley,J SF	19
Burke,T Mon	19
McDowell,R Phil	19
Howell,J LA	15
Williams,M Chi	14

1991 STANDINGS

AMERICAN LEAGUE

East	Won	Lost	Pct.	GB

West	Won	Lost	Pct.	GB

NATIONAL LEAGUE

East	Won	Lost	Pct.	GB

West	Won	Lost	Pct.	GB

INDIVIDUAL LEADERS

AMERICAN LEAGUE

BATTING

HOME RUNS

WINS

RBI

E.R.A.

SLUGGING

SAVES

NATIONAL LEAGUE

BATTING

HOME RUNS

WINS

RBI

E.R.A.

SLUGGING

SAVES

S · E · P · T · E · M · B · E · R

Winning Pitcher:

Losing Pitcher:

Home Runs:

Highlights:

Score by innings:

MONDAY 16

Winning Pitcher:

Losing Pitcher:

Home Runs:

Highlights:

Score by innings:

TUESDAY 17

Winning Pitcher:

Losing Pitcher:

Home Runs:

Highlights:

Score by innings:

WEDNESDAY 18

Winning Pitcher:

Losing Pitcher:

Home Runs:

Highlights:

Score by innings:

THURSDAY 19

S·E·P·T·E·M·B·E·R

Winning Pitcher:

Losing Pitcher:

Home Runs:

Highlights:

Score by innings:

FRIDAY 20

Winning Pitcher:

Losing Pitcher:

Home Runs:

Highlights:

Score by innings:

CBS: Yankees vs. Boston
San Francisco vs. San Diego

SATURDAY 21

Winning Pitcher:

Losing Pitcher:

Home Runs:

Highlights:

Score by innings:

ESPN: Toronto vs. Oakland

SUNDAY 22

SCHEDULE

MONDAY	*NY vs. Mon*	*Atl vs. SF*
Tor vs. Sea	*StL vs. Phil*	
KC vs. Min	*Chi vs. Pitt*	
Mil vs. NY	*Cin vs. LA*	
Bal vs. Bos	*Hou vs. SD*	
TUESDAY	Det vs. Cleve	*Chi vs. Pitt*
Tor vs. Sea	Mil vs. NY	*Cin vs. LA*
Cal vs. Tex	Bal vs. Bos	*Hou vs. SD*
KC vs. Min	*NY vs. Mon*	*Atl vs. SF*
Oak vs. Chi	*StL vs. Phil*	
WEDNESDAY	Det vs. Cleve	*StL vs. Pitt*
Tor vs. Sea	Mil vs. NY	*Hou vs. LA*
Cal vs. Tex	Bal vs. Bos	*Atl vs. SD*
KC vs. Min	*Phil vs. Mon*	*Cin vs. SF*
Oak vs. Chi	*Chi vs. NY*	
THURSDAY	*StL vs. Pitt*	
KC vs. Sea	*Hou vs. LA*	
Cal vs. Tex	*Atl vs. SD*	
Phil vs. Mon	*Cin vs. SF*	
Chi vs. NY		
FRIDAY	Mil vs. Det	*Phil vs. Pitt*
KC vs. Sea	Bal vs. Cleve	*Cin vs. Hou*
Tor vs. Oak	NY vs. Bos	*Atl vs. LA*
Tex vs. Min	*Chi vs. Mon*	*SF vs. SD*
Cal vs. Chi	*StL vs. NY*	
SATURDAY	Mil vs. Det	*Phil vs. Pitt*
KC vs. Sea	Bal vs. Cleve	*Cin vs. Hou*
Tor vs. Oak	NY vs. Bos	*Atl vs. LA*
Tex vs. Min	*Chi vs. Mon*	*SF vs. SD*
Cal vs. Chi	*StL vs. NY*	
SUNDAY	Mil vs. Det	*Phil vs. Pitt*
KC vs. Sea	Bal vs. Cleve	*Cin vs. Hou*
Tor vs. Oak	NY vs. Bos	*Atl vs. LA*
Tex vs. Min	*Chi vs. Mon*	*SF vs. SD*
Cal vs. Chi	*StL vs. NY*	

1990 STANDINGS

AMERICAN LEAGUE   Through September 23   **NATIONAL LEAGUE**

East	Won	Lost	Pct.	GB	East	Won	Lost	Pct.	GB
Toronto	83	70	.542	–	Pittsburgh	88	65	.575	–
Boston	82	71	.536	1	New York	85	67	.559	2½
Detroit	74	79	.484	9	Montreal	81	71	.533	6½
Cleveland	73	81	.474	10½	Philadelphia	72	80	.474	15½
Baltimore	70	81	.464	12	Chicago	72	80	.474	15½
Milwaukee	69	83	.454	13½	St. Louis	68	85	.444	20
New York	62	91	.405	21					

West	Won	Lost	Pct.	GB	West	Won	Lost	Pct.	GB
Oakland	97	55	.638	–	Cincinnati	87	66	.569	–
Chicago	89	64	.582	8½	Los Angeles	82	71	.536	5
Texas	80	72	.526	17	San Francisco	78	75	.510	9
California	75	77	.493	22	San Diego	71	82	.464	16
Seattle	74	80	.481	24	Houston	70	83	.458	17
Kansas City	71	81	.467	26	Atlanta	62	91	.405	25
Minnesota	70	84	.455	28					

INDIVIDUAL LEADERS

AMERICAN LEAGUE   **NATIONAL LEAGUE**

BATTING

Based on 3.1 plate appearances per game

	G	AB	R	H	Pct.		G	AB	R	H	Pct.
Brett,G KC	136	527	80	175	.332	McGee,W StL	125	501	76	168	.335
Palmeiro,R Tex	144	559	69	180	.322	Dykstra,L Phil	143	569	102	186	.327
Henderson,R Oak	129	461	112	148	.321	Murray,E LA	146	522	92	170	.326
Trammell,A Det	142	548	70	169	.308	Magadan,D NY	134	417	70	135	.324
Boggs,W Bos	148	593	85	181	.305	Dawson,A Chi	138	496	66	156	.315
James,C Cleve	134	501	60	152	.303	Grace,M Chi	147	553	69	173	.313
Parker,D Mil	149	577	70	175	.303	Gwynn,T SD	141	573	79	177	.309
Martinez,E Sea	141	479	70	145	.303	Bonds,B Pitt	144	496	103	153	.308
Puckett,K Min	140	526	82	159	.302	Roberts,L SD	142	541	101	166	.307
Burks,E Bos	143	551	84	166	.301	Sandberg,R Chi	147	585	110	179	.306

HOME RUNS		WINS		HOME RUNS		WINS	
Fielder,C Det	48	Welch,B Oak	25	Strawberry,D NY	37	Drabek,D Pitt	20
McGwire,M Oak	39	Stewart,D Oak	21	Sandberg,R Chi	37	Martinez,R LA	19
Canseco,J Oak	37	Clemens,R Bos	20	Mitchell,K SF	35	Viola,F NY	19
McGriff,F Tor	34	Finley,C Cal	18	Bonds,B Pitt	33	Gooden,D NY	18
Gruber,K Tor	30	Stieb,D Tor	18	Bonilla,B Pitt	32	Burkett,J SF	14
Deer,R Mil	27	Witt,B Tex	17	Williams,M SF	31	Maddux,G Chi	14
Henderson,R Oak	27	Sanderson,S Oak	17	Gant,R Atl	29	Browning,T Cin	14
Jackson,B KC	26	Hanson,E Sea	16	Justice,D Atl	27		
Barfield,J NY	24	Boddicker,M Bos	16	Daniels,K LA	26		
Incaviglia,P Tex	23	Candiotti,T Cleve	14				

RBI		E.R.A.		RBI		E.R.A.	
Fielder,C Det	126	Clemens,R Bos	1.98	Williams,M SF	114	Darwin,D Hou	2.31
Gruber,K Tor	112	Finley,C Cal	2.49	Carter,J SD	114	Whitson,E SD	2.63
McGwire,M Oak	105	Stewart,D Oak	2.67	Bonilla,B Pitt	114	Viola,F NY	2.66
Canseco,J Oak	95	Appier,K KC	2.76	Bonds,B Pitt	113	Smith,Z Pitt	2.73
Parker,D Mil	92	Stieb,D Tor	2.96	Strawberry,D NY	107	Boyd,D Mon	2.75
Sierra,R Tex	91	McCaskill,K Cal	3.01	Wallach,T Mon	95	Rijo,J Cin	2.75
Maldonado,C Cleve	90	Welch,B Oak	3.02	Sandberg,R Chi	95	Drabek,D Pitt	2.87
Trammell,A Det	89	Wells,D Tor	3.07	Dawson,A Chi	94	Martinez,De Mon	2.92
Burks,E Bos	87	Hibbard,G Chi	3.21	Mitchell,K SF	93	Martinez,R LA	3.04
Palmeiro,R Tex	85	Witt,B Tex	3.29	Murray,E LA	91	Hurst,B SD	3.23

SLUGGING		SAVES		SLUGGING		SAVES	
Fielder,C Det	.601	Thigpen,B Chi	53	Bonds,B Pitt	.585	Franco,J NY	33
Henderson,R Oak	.577	Eckersley,D Oak	44	Sandberg,R Chi	.556	Myers,R Cin	30
Canseco,J Oak	.553	Jones,D Cleve	40	Mitchell,K SF	.550	Smith,L StL	27
McGriff,F Tor	.541	Righetti,D NY	34	Dawson,A Chi	.542	Lefferts,C SD	23
Gruber,K Tor	.524	Olson,G Bal	33	Bonilla,B Pitt	.531	Smith,D Hou	23
Brett,G KC	.518	Schooler,M Sea	30	Daniels,K LA	.526	Burke,T Mon	20
Burks,E Bos	.503	Henke,T Tor	30	Strawberry,D NY	.526	McDowell,R Phil	20
McGwire,M Oak	.500	Aguilera,R Min	29	Gant,R Atl	.523	Brantley,J SF	19
Griffey Jr,K Sea	.481	Harvey,B Cal	23	Murray,E LA	.519	Howell,J LA	16
Parker,D Mil	.475	Plesac,D Mil	23	Williams,M SF	.490	Williams,M Chi	14

1991 STANDINGS

AMERICAN LEAGUE

East	Won	Lost	Pct.	GB

West	Won	Lost	Pct.	GB

NATIONAL LEAGUE

East	Won	Lost	Pct.	GB

West	Won	Lost	Pct.	GB

INDIVIDUAL LEADERS

AMERICAN LEAGUE

BATTING

HOME RUNS

WINS

RBI

E.R.A.

SLUGGING

SAVES

NATIONAL LEAGUE

BATTING

HOME RUNS

WINS

RBI

E.R.A.

SLUGGING

SAVES

S · E · P · T · E · M · B · E · R

MONDAY 23

_____ __ __

Winning Pitcher:

Losing Pitcher:

Home Runs:

Highlights:

Score by innings:

TUESDAY 24

_____ __ __

Winning Pitcher:

Losing Pitcher:

Home Runs:

Highlights:

Score by innings:

WEDNESDAY 25

_____ __ __

Winning Pitcher:

Losing Pitcher:

Home Runs:

Highlights:

Score by innings:

THURSDAY 26

_____ __ __

Winning Pitcher:

Losing Pitcher:

Home Runs:

Highlights:

Score by innings:

S • E • P • T • E • M • B • E • R

FRIDAY 27

Winning Pitcher:

Losing Pitcher:

Home Runs:

Highlights:

Score by innings:

SATURDAY 28

Winning Pitcher:

Losing Pitcher:

Home Runs:

Highlights:

Score by innings:

CBS: To be announced

SUNDAY 29

Winning Pitcher:

Losing Pitcher:

Home Runs:

Highlights:

Score by innings:

ESPN: *San Francisco vs. Los Angeles*

SCHEDULE

MONDAY	Cleve vs. Det	
Tex vs. Sea	Bos vs. Bal	
KC vs. Oak	*Phil vs. Chi*	
Tor vs. Cal	*Mon vs. StL*	
NY vs. Mil	*SF vs. Hou*	
TUESDAY	NY vs. Mil	*Mon vs. StL*
Tex vs. Sea	Cleve vs. Det	*Cin vs. Atl*
KC vs. Oak	Bos vs. Bal	*SF vs. Hou*
Tor vs. Cal	*Pitt vs. NY*	*LA vs. SD*
Chi vs. Min	*Phil vs. Chi*	
WEDNESDAY	NY vs. Mil	*Mon vs. StL*
Tex vs. Sea	Cleve vs. Det	*Cin vs. Atl*
KC vs. Oak	Bos vs. Bal	*SF vs. Hou*
Tor vs. Cal	*Pitt vs. NY*	*LA vs. SD*
Chi vs. Min	*Phil vs. Chi*	
THURSDAY	*Pitt vs. NY*	
Tex vs. Oak	*Cin vs. Atl*	
Cal vs. KC		
NY vs. Mil		
Cleve vs. Det		
FRIDAY	Bal vs. Det	*Chi vs. StL*
Tex vs. Oak	NY vs. Cleve	*SD vs. Cin*
Cal vs. KC	Min vs. Tor	*Atl vs. Hou*
Sea vs. Chi	*Pitt vs. Mon*	*SF vs. LA*
Bos vs. Mil	*Phil vs. NY*	
SATURDAY	Bal vs. Det	*Chi vs. StL*
Tex vs. Oak	NY vs. Cleve	*SD vs. Cin*
Cal vs. KC	Min vs. Tor	*Atl vs. Hou*
Sea vs. Chi	*Pitt vs. Mon*	*SF vs. LA*
Bos vs. Mil	*Phil vs. NY*	
SUNDAY	Bal vs. Det	*Chi vs. StL*
Tex vs. Oak	NY vs. Cleve	*SD vs. Cin*
Cal vs. KC	Min vs. Tor	*Atl vs. Hou*
Sea vs. Chi	*Pitt vs. Mon*	*SF vs. LA*
Bos vs. Mil	*Phil vs. NY*	

1990 STANDINGS

AMERICAN LEAGUE   Through September 30   **NATIONAL LEAGUE**

East	Won	Lost	Pct.	GB		East	Won	Lost	Pct.	GB
Boston	86	73	.541	–		Pittsburgh	94	65	.591	–
Toronto	85	74	.535	1		New York	89	70	.560	5
Detroit	77	82	.484	9		Montreal	82	77	.516	12
Cleveland	75	85	.469	11½		Philadelphia	76	83	.478	18
Baltimore	74	84	.468	11½		Chicago	75	84	.472	19
Milwaukee	72	87	.453	14		St. Louis	70	89	.440	24
New York	66	93	.415	20						

West	Won	Lost	Pct.	GB		West	Won	Lost	Pct.	GB
Oakland	102	57	.642	–		Cincinnati	89	70	.560	–
Chicago	93	66	.585	9		San Francisco	84	75	.528	5
Texas	82	77	.516	20		Los Angeles	84	75	.528	5
California	78	81	.491	24		San Diego	74	85	.465	15
Seattle	76	83	.478	26		Houston	74	85	.465	15
Kansas City	75	84	.472	27		Atlanta	63	96	.396	26
Minnesota	72	87	.453	30						

INDIVIDUAL LEADERS

AMERICAN LEAGUE   **NATIONAL LEAGUE**

BATTING

Based on 3.1 plate appearances per game

	G	AB	R	H	Pct.			G	AB	R	H	Pct.
Brett,G KC	141	543	82	178	.328		McGee,W StL	125	501	76	168	.335
Henderson,R Oak	133	478	116	156	.326		Magadan,D NY	141	440	74	145	.330
Palmeiro,R Tex	151	585	72	187	.320		Murray,E LA	152	546	95	177	.324
Trammell,A Det	145	555	70	169	.305		Dykstra,L Phil	147	583	104	188	.322
Boggs,W Bos	152	608	88	185	.304		Roberts,L Phil	146	552	104	172	.312
Martinez,E Sea	144	487	71	147	.302		Dawson,A Chi	145	524	71	163	.311
McGriff,F Tor	150	545	89	164	.301		Grace,M Chi	154	579	72	180	.311
Griffey Jr,K Sea	155	597	91	179	.300		Gwynn,T SD	141	573	79	177	.309
Greenwell,M Bos	156	599	69	178	.297		Butler,B SF	157	612	105	189	.309
James,C Cleve	138	519	61	154	.297		Sandberg,R Chi	154	613	115	187	.305

HOME RUNS		WINS		HOME RUNS		WINS	
Fielder,C Det	49	Welch,B Oak	26	Sandberg,R Chi	39	Drabek,D Pitt	22
McGwire,M Oak	39	Stewart,D Oak	22	Strawberry,D NY	37	Martinez,R LA	19
Canseco,J Oak	37	Clemens,R Bos	21	Mitchell,K SF	35	Gooden,D NY	19
McGriff,F Tor	34	Finley,C Cal	18	Williams,M SF	33	Viola,F NY	19
Gruber,K Tor	31	Stieb,D Tor	18	Bonds,B Pitt	33	Browning,T Cin	15
Jackson,B KC	28	Hanson,E Sea	17	Bonilla,B Pitt	32	Burkett,J SF	14
Henderson,R Oak	28	Witt,B Tex	17	Gant,R Atl	31	Maddux,G Chi	14
Deer,R Mil	27	Sanderson,S Oak	17	Justice,D Atl	28	Rijo,J Cin	14
Barfield,J NY	25	Boddicker,M Bos	16	Daniels,K LA	27	Whitson,E SD	14
				Dawson,A Chi	27		

RBI		E.R.A.		RBI		E.R.A.	
Fielder,C Det	127	Clemens,R Bos	1.93	Williams,M SF	121	Darwin,D Hou	2.21
Gruber,K Tor	117	Finley,C Cal	2.40	Bonilla,B Pitt	118	Whitson,E SD	2.60
McGwire,M Oak	108	Stewart,D Oak	2.58	Carter,J SD	115	Smith,Z Pitt	2.61
Canseco,J Oak	99	Appier,K KC	2.76	Bonds,B Pitt	114	Viola,F NY	2.63
Sierra,R Tex	95	Stieb,D Tor	2.95	Strawberry,D NY	108	Rijo,J Cin	2.70
Maldonado,C Cleve	94	Welch,B Oak	3.00	Dawson,A Chi	98	Drabek,D Pitt	2.76
Parker,D Mil	92	Wells,D Tor	3.05	Sandberg,R Chi	98	Boyd,D Mon	2.93
Palmeiro,R Tex	89	Hibbard,G Chi	3.13	Wallach,T Mon	97	Martinez,De Mon	2.95
Burks,E Bos	89	McCaskill,K Cal	3.25	Daniels,K LA	94	Martinez,R LA	3.00
Trammell,A Det	89	Hanson,E Sea	3.37			Hurst,B SD	3.14

SLUGGING		SAVES		SLUGGING		SAVES	
Fielder,C Det	.590	Thigpen,B Chi	57	Bonds,B Pitt	.566	Franco,J NY	33
Henderson,R Oak	.584	Eckersley,D Oak	47	Sandberg,R Chi	.555	Myers,R Cin	30
Canseco,J Oak	.544	Jones,D Cleve	42	Mitchell,K SF	.544	Smith,L StL	27
McGriff,F Tor	.530	Olson,G Bal	36	Dawson,A Chi	.538	Lefferts,C SD	23
Gruber,K Tor	.516	Righetti,D NY	35	Gant,R Atl	.532	Smith,D Hou	23
Brett,G KC	.514	Aguilera,R Min	31	Daniels,K LA	.531	McDowell,R Phil	21
McGwire,M Oak	.494	Henke,T Tor	31	Bonilla,B Pitt	521	Burke,T Mon	20
Burks,E Bos	.488	Schooler,M Sea	30	Strawberry,D NY	.518	Brantley,J SF	19
Griffey Jr,K Sea	.481	Montgomery,J KC	24	Murray,E LA	.516	Bedrosian,S SF	17
Hrbek,K Min	.474	Harvey,B Cal	24	Williams,M SF	.493	Howell,J LA	16

1991 STANDINGS

AMERICAN LEAGUE					NATIONAL LEAGUE				
East	Won	Lost	Pct.	GB	East	Won	Lost	Pct.	GB
West	Won	Lost	Pct.	GB	West	Won	Lost	Pct.	GB

INDIVIDUAL LEADERS

AMERICAN LEAGUE	NATIONAL LEAGUE
BATTING	**BATTING**
HOME RUNS / **WINS**	**HOME RUNS** / **WINS**
RBI / **E.R.A.**	**RBI** / **E.R.A.**
SLUGGING / **SAVES**	**SLUGGING** / **SAVES**

O · C · T · O · B · E · R

Winning Pitcher:

Losing Pitcher:

Home Runs:

Highlights:

Score by innings:

MONDAY 30

Winning Pitcher:

Losing Pitcher:

Home Runs:

Highlights:

Score by innings:

TUESDAY 1

Winning Pitcher:

Losing Pitcher:

Home Runs:

Highlights:

Score by innings:

WEDNESDAY 2

Winning Pitcher:

Losing Pitcher:

Home Runs:

Highlights:

Score by innings:

THURSDAY 3

O · C · T · O · B · E · R

_____

_____

Winning Pitcher:

Losing Pitcher:

Home Runs:

Highlights:

Score by innings:

FRIDAY 4

_____

_____

Winning Pitcher:

Losing Pitcher:

Home Runs:

Highlights:

Score by innings:

CBS: To be announced

SATURDAY 5

_____

_____

Winning Pitcher:

Losing Pitcher:

Home Runs:

Highlights:

Score by innings:

Season closes

SUNDAY 6

SCHEDULE

MONDAY	Bal vs. Det	*NY vs. Pitt*
Sea vs. Tex	NY vs. Cleve	*Atl vs. Cin*
Oak vs. KC	Cal vs. Tor	*SD vs. LA*
Min vs. Chi	*StL vs. Mon*	*Hou vs. SF*
Bos vs. Mil	*Chi vs. Phil*	
TUESDAY	Cal vs. Tor	*NY vs. Pitt*
Sea vs. Tex	Bal vs. NY	*Atl vs. Cin*
Oak vs. KC	Det vs. Bos	*SD vs. LA*
Min vs. Chi	*StL vs. Mon*	*Hou vs. SF*
Mil vs. Cleve	*Chi vs. Phil*	
WEDNESDAY	Cal vs. Tor	*NY vs. Pitt*
Sea vs. Tex	Bal vs. NY	*Atl vs. Cin*
Oak vs. KC	Det vs. Bos	*SD vs. LA*
Min vs. Chi	*StL vs. Mon*	*Hou vs. SF*
Mil vs. Cleve	*Chi vs. Phil*	
THURSDAY		
Min vs. Chi		
Mil vs. Cleve		
Bal vs. NY		
Det vs. Bos		
FRIDAY	Det vs. Bal	*StL vs. Chi*
Chi vs. Sea	Cleve vs. NY	*Hou vs. Atl*
KC vs. Cal	Mil vs. Bos	*Cin vs. SD*
Oak vs. Tex	*NY vs. Phil*	*LA vs. SF*
Tor vs. Min	*Mon vs. Pitt*	
SATURDAY	Det vs. Bal	*StL vs. Chi*
Chi vs. Sea	Cleve vs. NY	*Hou vs. Atl*
KC vs. Cal	Mil vs. Bos	*Cin vs. SD*
Oak vs. Tex	*NY vs. Phil*	*LA vs. SF*
Tor vs. Min	*Mon vs. Pitt*	
SUNDAY	Det vs. Bal	*StL vs. Chi*
Chi vs. Sea	Cleve vs. NY	*Hou vs. Atl*
KC vs. Cal	Mil vs. Bos	*Cin vs. SD*
Oak vs. Tex	*NY vs. Phil*	*LA vs. SF*
Tor vs. Min	*Mon vs. Pitt*	

1990 STANDINGS

AMERICAN LEAGUE			Through October 3		NATIONAL LEAGUE				

East	Won	Lost	Pct.	GB	East	Won	Lost	Pct.	GB
Boston	88	74	.543	–	Pittsburgh	95	67	.586	–
Toronto	86	76	.531	2	New York	91	71	.562	4
Detroit	79	83	.488	9	Montreal	85	77	.525	10
Cleveland	77	85	.475	11	Philadelphia	77	85	.475	18
Baltimore	76	85	.472	11½	Chicago	77	85	.475	18
Milwaukee	74	88	.457	14	St. Louis	70	92	.432	25
New York	67	95	.414	21					

West	Won	Lost	Pct.	GB	West	Won	Lost	Pct.	GB
Oakland	103	59	.636	–	Cincinnati	91	71	.562	–
Chicago	94	68	.580	9	Los Angeles	86	76	.531	5
Texas	83	79	.512	20	San Francisco	85	77	.525	6
California	80	82	.494	23	San Diego	75	87	.463	16
Seattle	77	85	.475	26	Houston	75	87	.463	16
Kansas City	75	86	466	27½	Atlanta	65	97	.401	26
Minnesota	74	88	.457	29					

INDIVIDUAL LEADERS

AMERICAN LEAGUE

BATTING

Based on 3.1 plate appearances per game

	G	AB	R	H	Pct.
Brett,G KC	142	544	82	179	.329
Henderson,R Oak	136	489	119	159	.325
Palmeiro,R Tex	154	598	72	191	.319
Trammell,A Det	146	559	71	170	.304
Boggs,W Bos	155	619	89	187	.302
Martinez,E Sea	144	487	71	147	.302
Griffey Jr,K Sea	155	597	91	179	.300
McGriff,F Tor	153	557	91	167	.300
James,C Cleve	140	528	62	158	.299
Puckett,K Min	146	551	82	164	.298

HOME RUNS

			WINS	
Fielder,C Det	51		Welch,B Oak	27
McGwire,M Oak	39		Stewart,D Oak	22
Canseco,J Oak	37		Clemens,R Bos	21
McGriff,F Tor	35		Hanson,E Sea	18
Gruber,K Tor	31		Finley,C Cal	18
Jackson,B KC	28		Stieb,D Tor	18
Henderson,R Oak	28		Witt,B Tex	17
Deer,R Mil	27		Sanderson,S Oak	17
Barfield,J NY	25		Boddicker,M Bos	17

RBI

			E.R.A.	
Fielder,C Det	132		Clemens,R Bos	1.93
Gruber,K Tor	118		Finley,C Cal	2.40
McGwire,M Oak	108		Stewart,D Oak	2.56
Canseco,J Oak	101		Appier,K KC	2.76
Sierra,R Tex	96		Stieb,D Tor	2.93
Maldonado,C Cleve	95		Welch,B Oak	2.95
Parker,D Mil	92		Wells,D Tor	3.14
Palmeiro,R Tex	89		Hibbard,G Chi	3.16
Burks,E Bos	89		Hanson,E Sea	3.24
Trammell,A Det	89		McCaskill,K Cal	3.25

SLUGGING

			SAVES	
Fielder,C Det	.592		Thigpen,B Chi	57
Henderson,R Oak	.577		Eckersley,D Oak	48
Canseco,J Oak	.543		Jones,D Cleve	43
McGriff,F Tor	.530		Olson,G Bal	37
Brett,G KC	.515		Righetti,D NY	36
Gruber,K Tor	.512		Aguilera,R Min	32
McGwire,M Oak	.489		Henke,T Tor	32
Burks,E Bos	.486		Schooler,M Sea	30
Griffey Jr,K Sea	.481		Harvey,B Cal	25
Hrbek,K Min	.474			

NATIONAL LEAGUE

BATTING

	G	AB	R	H	Pct.
McGee,W StL	125	501	76	168	.335
Murray,E LA	155	558	96	184	.330
Magadan,D NY	144	451	74	148	.328
Dykstra,L Phil	149	590	106	192	.325
Dawson,A Chi	147	529	72	164	.310
Roberts,L SD	149	556	104	172	.309
Grace,M Chi	157	589	72	182	.309
Gwynn,T SD	141	573	79	177	.309
Butler,B SF	160	622	108	192	.309
Sandberg,R Chi	155	615	116	188	.306

HOME RUNS

			WINS	
Sandberg,R Chi	40		Drabek,D Pitt	22
Strawberry,D NY	37		Martinez,R LA	20
Mitchell,K SF	35		Viola,F NY	20
Williams,M SF	33		Gooden,D NY	19
Bonds,B Pitt	33		Maddux,G Chi	15
Gant,R Atl	32		Browning,T Cin	15
Bonilla,B Pitt	32			
Justice,D Atl	28			
Daniels,K LA	27			
Dawson,A Chi	27			

RBI

			E.R.A.	
Williams,M SF	122		Darwin,D Hou	2.21
Bonilla,B Pitt	120		Smith,Z Pitt	2.55
Carter,J SD	115		Whitson,E SD	2.60
Bonds,B Pitt	114		Viola,F NY	2.67
Strawberry,D NY	108		Rijo,J Cin	2.70
Dawson,A Chi	100		Drabek,D Pitt	2.76
Sandberg,R Chi	100		Martinez,R LA	2.92
Wallach,T Mon	98		Boyd,D Mon	2.93
Clark,W SF	95		Martinez,De Mon	2.95
Murray,E LA	95		Hurst,B SD	3.14

SLUGGING

			SAVES	
Bonds,B Pitt	.565		Franco,J NY	33
Sandberg,R Chi	.559		Myers,R Cin	31
Mitchell,K SF	.544		Smith,L StL	27
Gant,R Atl	.539		Lefferts,C SD	23
Justice,D Atl	.535		Smith,D Hou	23
Dawson,A Chi	.535		McDowell,R Phil	22
Daniels,K LA	.531		Burke,T Mon	20
Murray,E LA	.520		Brantley,J SF	19
Strawberry,D NY	.518		Bedrosian,S SF	17
Bonilla,B Pitt	.518			

1991 STANDINGS

AMERICAN LEAGUE

East	Won	Lost	Pct.	GB

West	Won	Lost	Pct.	GB

NATIONAL LEAGUE

East	Won	Lost	Pct.	GB

West	Won	Lost	Pct.	GB

INDIVIDUAL LEADERS

AMERICAN LEAGUE

BATTING

HOME RUNS

WINS

RBI

E.R.A.

SLUGGING

SAVES

NATIONAL LEAGUE

BATTING

HOME RUNS

WINS

RBI

E.R.A.

SLUGGING

SAVES

SCORECARDS

3-1   1-3

PITTSBURGH PIRATES vs. CHICAGO CUBS

DATE: 4/13/91

PLAYER'S NUMBERS
- 1—Pitcher
- 2—Catcher
- 3—First Base
- 4—Second Base
- 5—Third Base
- 6—Shortstop
- 7—Left Field
- 8—Center Field
- 9—Right Field
- DH—Designated Hitter

BALANCE YOUR BOX SCORE

AB ___	RUNS ___	
BB ___	OUTS ___	
HP ___	LOB ___	
SAC ___		
INT ___		
TOTALS ___	TOTALS ___	

VISITOR	1	2	3	4	5	6	7	8	9	10	11	12	AB	R	H	RBI
REDUS 3	9		1b		5-3	5-0		8	1							
BELL 6	7		9			9	3		2B							
VAN SLYKE 8	9		8	1		9			1b							
BONILLA 9		HP		1B					HR 3RBI							
BONDS 7		4-6-3		4-6			3		Sco							
McCLENDON LF 5																
KING 5	6-3					5-3										
LAVALLIERE 2	6-3						4-3		4-3							
LIND 4			8	1	3			E6								
DRABEK P			1B	9	9			6-3 DP								
PATTERSON P5																
TOTALS	R: 0 0 0 0 1 0 0 0 0 = 3															
	H: 0 0 1 1 0 0 0 0 0 = 3															
TOTALS	E: 0 0 1 0 1 0 0 0 0 = 0															
	LOB: 0 0 0 0 0 0 0 0 0 = 0															

VARSHO/RIES
HEATON
PRINCE
A8
LANDB

SCORING KEY

. (Single)	/ (Double)	HR (Home Run)
◇ (Run Scored)		

K = Strikeout	⅄ = Called 3rd Strike
W = Walk	IW = Intentional Walk
FC = Fielder's Choice	SAC = Sacrifice
CS = Caught Stealing	SF = Sacrifice Fly
WP = Wild Pitch	# of Fielder = Flyout

DP = Double Play	# of Fielder plus "·" = Unassisted Groundout
SB = Stolen Base	# of Fielder "-" # of 2nd Fielder = Assisted Groundout
PB = Passed Ball	
FO = Foul Out	
HP = Hit by Pitch	

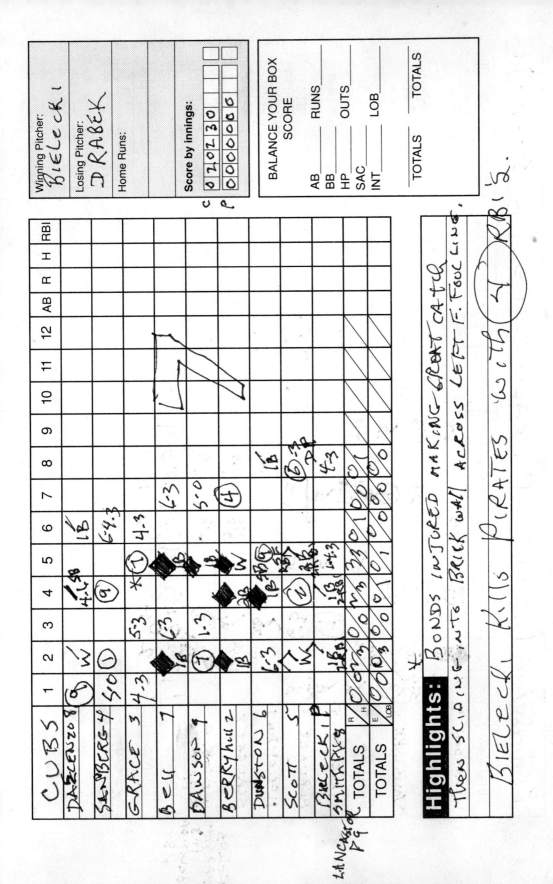

PITTSBURGH PIRATES vs. CHICAGO CUBS   DATE: 4-14-91

VISITOR	1	2	3	4	5	6	7	8	9	10	11	12	AB	R	H	RBI
Wilkerson 4	1	1B		(4)		6-3			5-0							
Bell 6	5-4	1 W		5-3			6-3		4-3							
VanSlyke 8	(3)	1B RBI		4-3			(9)		1B							
Bonilla 9	W	5-4			6-3		HR RBI		4-3							
King 5	1B RBI		(1)		1B	PC	1B									
Martinez 3	3		6-3		(4)		5-0	0-0-6								
McClendon 7		1	2B					6-3								
Slaught 2		1 3	W			5-3		6-3								
Walk P		K	(4)			6-3										
Kipper PL																
TOTALS	R: 1	1	2	0	0	0	1	0	0							
	H: 1	2	3	0	0	0	2	0	0							
TOTALS	E: 0	2	0	0	0	1	0	0	0							
	LOB:															

Redus
TARTABLE P#8
Belinda P8

Winning Pitcher: SLOCUMBE

Losing Pitcher: BELINDA

Home Runs: BEREHIM, SANDBERG, BONILLA WALK

Score by innings:

BALANCE YOUR BOX SCORE

AB	_____	RUNS	_____
BB	_____	OUTS	_____
HP	_____	LOB	_____
SAC	_____		
INT	_____		
TOTALS	_____	TOTALS	_____

CUBS	1	2	3	4	5	6	7	8	9	10	11	12	AB	R	H	RBI
DASCENZO 8			6-3		E-3		1-3									
SANDBERG 4	HR RBI	5-3	5-3		E-3	6-3	5-3	5-0								
GRACE 3	W		6-3		W		4-4 RBI									
BELL 7	1B			1	5		7 2B	6-4								
DAWSON 9	RBI			5-0 2-3		6-3	W									
BEREHILL 2	1			4-3	5-0	HR RBI	5	1B								
DUNSTON 6		5-3			W	K		1B								
SCOTT 5		4			W	W										
JACKSON P		5-3			1-4 SAC	5-0		W								
SLOCUMB P							Or	2								
TOTALS	R 2 3	0	0	0	0	1	0	2								
TOTALS	H 6 6	0	0	0	0	0	0	0								
	E 0 0	0	0	0	3	0	1	3								
	LOB															

Highlights:

— AT PITTSBURGH 3-3

PITTSBURGH PIRATES vs. NEW YORK METS   DATE: 4/15/91

VISITOR	1	2	3	4	5	6	7	8	9	10	11	12	AB	R	H	RBI
Redus 3	⑨		①	5-0			1B	5-0	⑧							
Bell 6	⑨		6-3	⑧			SAC		①							
Van Slyke 8	W		⑨		3		W		3							
Bonilla 9	W			⑧	2B		①									
Varsho 7	Ⓛ			1B	4-3		2B RBI	①								
King 5	5-0			1B	5-0	3	③	⑨								
Lavalliere 2	OUT			W		8										
Lind 4		1B		1/		1BEN		1B								
Martinez P-8				2RBI												
Smith P		①		1B												
Merced PH																
TOTALS	R 0	6 0	0 0	4 0	1 0	0	2 0	0 0								
TOTALS	E 0	2 0	0 0	6 3	0	1	2 0	0								

LANDRUM P9-7
TOMLIN PR9→
PATTERSON PT
KIPPER P-9

Winning Pitcher:
CONE N.Y.

Losing Pitcher:
RIPPER PHA.

Home Runs:
Johnson

Score by innings:

BALANCE YOUR BOX
SCORE

AB ____	RUNS ____
BB ____	OUTS ____
HP ____	LOB ____
SAC ____	
INT ____	
TOTALS ____	TOTALS ____

METS	1	2	3	4	5	6	7	8	9	10	11	12	AB	R	H	RBI
COLEMAN 8	1B 3B		5-0	1B		7 (BATE)			1B HE							
MILLER 9	(9)			5-3		(8)			1B HE							
MAGADAN 3	5-0		1B		1B		W		1B RBI							
CARREON 7	5-0		5-3		1B		6-4-3									
JOHNSON 5		HR RBI			5-0		5-6	5-3	1B RBI							
HERR 4		6-3	4-3	5-0	(3)			4-3 5-0	RBI							
CERONEZ Boston LF		1B		6-3	(9)	1B		(9)	1B P.C.							
ELSTER 6		5-0		7		1-6-3 DP			3B RBI							
PENA P 9		5-0		W					W 50							
CONE P																
JEFFRIES PH 9																
TOTALS	R 0	1	1	3	0	2	0	0								
	H 0	1	0	0	0	2	1	0								
TOTALS	E 1	0	0	0	0	0	0	0								
	LOB															

Highlights:

REDUS FOOLED BY A OUTSIDE CURVE S.O. WITH BASES LOADED IN THE 4TH TO END A POTENTIAL BIG INNING

J SMITH VERY EFFECTIVE (GREAT DP IN 6TH)

VARSHO'S DOUBLE IN THE 7TH RULED 6-RULE ONLY ONE SCORES)

RIPPER BLOWS GAME, WALKS FIRST TWO IN 9TH, THROWS WILDLY ON BUNT 2 GAMES IN A ROW, APPALLING DEFENSE COSTS GAMES —

NEW YORK METS vs. PITTSBURGH PIRATES DATE: 4/16/91

6-2   3-4

VISITOR	1	2	3	4	5	6	7	8	9	10	11	12	AB	R	H	RBI
COLEMAN 8	5-0				(7)		(4)									
JEFFRIES 5	1B	W	SB	W			1-3	5-0								
BROOKS 9	1-3	W	W		HR RBI	(9)										
JOHNSON L 6	5-0		(7)		OUT			2B								
McREYNOLDS 7		6-3		(9)		(9)		(8)	5-0							
MAGADAN 3		W		(9)		6-3		(7)	5-0							
HERR 4	6-3			1B		1B 2-c										
O'BRIEN 2		(7)				1-3										
INNIS P 9																
WHITEHURST P			5-0-5				HR RBI		(2)							
CARREON PH 7																
TOTALS R/H	0	1	0	0	0	1	0	1	0							
TOTALS E/LOB	0	1	0	2	0	0	0	0	2							

BOSTON→ PH 9
LASSER → PH 9

Winning Pitcher: TOMLIN

Losing Pitcher: WHITEHURST

Home Runs: BROOKS, VAN SLYKE, CARREON

Score by innings:

BALANCE YOUR BOX SCORE

AB	____	RUNS	____
BB	____	OUTS	____
HP	____	LOB	____
SAC	____		
INT	____		

TOTALS ____ TOTALS ____

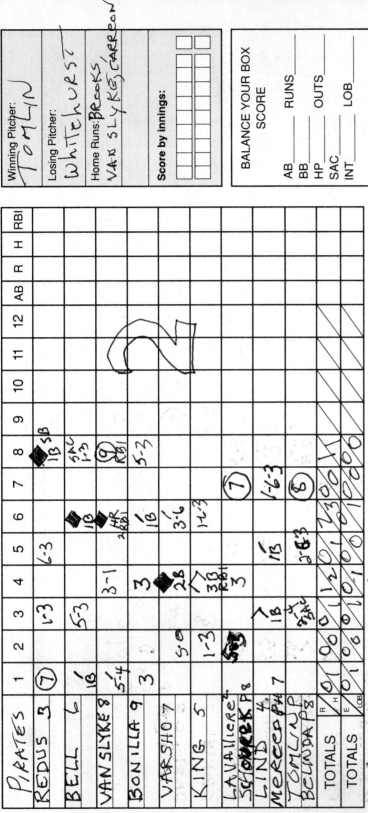

PIRATES	1	2	3	4	5	6	7	8	9	10	11	12	AB	R	H	RBI
REDUS 3	⑦	1-3	1-3		6-3			1B SB								
BELL 6	1B	5-3	5-3	3-1		1B		SAC 1-3								
VAN SLYKE 8	5-4					HR 2RBI		⑨ RBI								
BONILLA 9	3			3	1B			5-3								
VARSHO 7		5-0		2B		3-6										
KING 5		1-3		7 3B RBI 3		1-3										
LAVALLIERE 2 / SCHOOLER P8			7 1B				⑦									
LIND 4				1B			1-6-3									
MERCED PH4 7																
TOMLIN P / BELINDA P8			SAC	2-6-3			⑥									
TOTALS	R 01	00	00	12	0	23	00	11								
	H 01	00	01	00	0	02	00	00								
	E															
	LOB															

Highlights:

IN THE 4th, BROOKS MISPLAYED A LINER INTO R.CENTER INTO A TRIPLE & THEN HITS A SOLO HOMER TO REDEEM HIMSELF — TOMLIN PITCHED A SUPERB 7 IN. 1 GOPHER PITCHES HURT — QUESTION TAKING HIM OUT IN THE 8th — VAN SLYKE S.F, 3RD RBI, ON 0-2 CURVE FROM LEFT HANDER

BELINDA KILLS TWO BATTERS WITH WICKED FAST BALLS ON OUTSIDE CORNER IN 9th —

NEW YORK METS vs. PITTSBURGH PIRATES DATE: 4/17/91

6-3   4-4

VISITOR	1	2	3	4	5	6	7	8	9	10	11	12	AB	R	H	RBI
JOHNSON 6	5-3		5-3			5-0			⑦							
JEFFRIES 5	④			6-3			⑦									
MAGADAN 3	⑦			①			5-0									
BROOKS 9		6-3		6-3			④									
McREYNOLDS 8		7 2B			④			E3 6-3								
CARREON 7		5-3			5-3	6-3		④								
HERR 4					④			5-3								
GIBBEN 2	⑨		⑥			6-0			5-3							
DARLING P			6-0			6-3			⑥							
SIMONS P																
TOTALS	R 0 0	0 0	0 0	0 0	0 0	0 0	0 0	0 0	0 0							
TOTALS	H 0 0	0 0	0 0	0 0	0 0	0 0	0 0	0 0	0 0							
	E									LOB						

Teufel PH 9

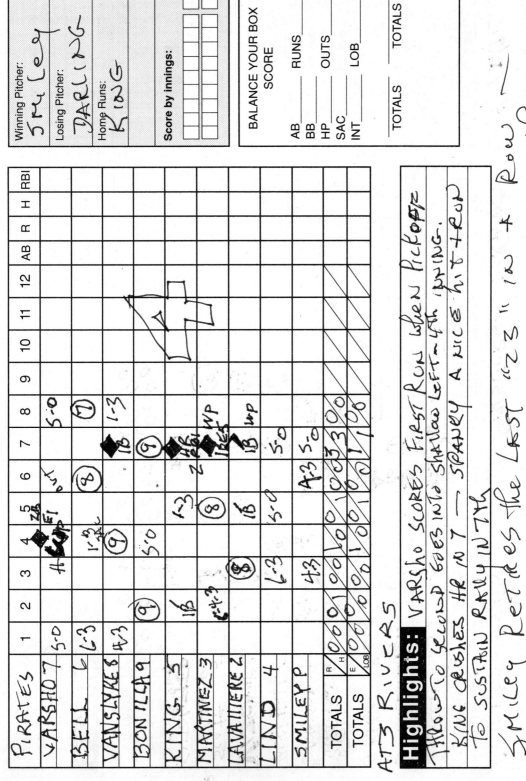

Winning Pitcher: Smiley

Losing Pitcher: Darling

Home Runs: King

Score by innings:

BALANCE YOUR BOX
SCORE

AB	_____	RUNS	_____
BB	_____	OUTS	_____
HP	_____	LOB	_____
SAC	_____		
INT	_____		
TOTALS	_____	TOTALS	_____

PIRATES	1	2	3	4	5	6	7	8	9	10	11	12	AB	R	H	RBI
VARSHO 7	5-0			2B	FL	out		5-0								
BELL 6	6-3			1-3				⑦								
VANSLYKE 8	4-3			⑨			1B	1-3								
BONILLA 9		⑨		5-0			⑨									
KING 5		1B			1-3											
MARTINEZ 3		6-4-3			⑧		2B WP									
LAVALLIERE 2			⑧		1B		1B WP									
LIND 4			4-3		5-0	6-3	5-0									
SMILEY P			4-3			4-3 5-0										
TOTALS R H	0 0 0	0 0 0	0 0 0	1 0 0	0 0 0	0 0 0	3 3 0	0 0 0								
TOTALS E LOB	0 0 0	0 0 0	0 0 0	0 0 1	0 0 0	0 0 1	1 0 6									

AT 3 RIVERS

Highlights: VARSHO SCORES FIRST RUN when PICKOFF throw to second goes into shallow left in 4th inning.
KING CRUSHES HR in 7 - SPANKEY A NICE HIT + RUN to sustain rally in 7th

SMILEY RETIRES the LAST "23" in 4 Row —
ONLY HIT A BADLY PLAYED line DRIVE that we kept for A DOUBLE in the 2nd INN.

5-4 3RD

CHICAGO CUBS vs. PITTSBURGH PIRATES DATE: 4/18/91

VISITOR	1	2	3	4	5	6	7	8	9	10	11	12	AB	R	H	RBI
DASCENZO LF 8	(3)		1-3			5-3 (4SB RBI)										
SANDBERG 4	5-3		(7)			1B	(7)									
GRACE 3	6-3			5-3		3B RBI		(8)								
BELL 7	(8)	(8)		6-0		1B RBI	5-0									
WALTON CF 8																
DAWSON 9		5-0		6 1B		6-4-3		5-3								
BERRYHILL 2		6-3	1B	(8)	4-3		◆		(6)							
VIZCAINO 6			1B		6-3		1B		4-3							
SCOTT 5					5-0		1-3 SAC		(3)							
SLOCUMB P 7			1-3RC				◆ W									
SUTCLIFFE P																
SMITH P 1																

	R	0	0	2	0	1	0	0	2	1	0	0	0			
TOTALS	H	0	0	0	0	0	1	0	0	3	0	0	0			
TOTALS	E	0	0	0	1	0	0	0	0	0	0	0	0			
	LOB															

Winning Pitcher: ___

Losing Pitcher: ___

Home Runs: ___

Score by innings:

PIRATES	1	2	3	4	5	6	7	8	9	10	11	12	AB	R	H	RBI
KING 5	⑨		3-u		L-3			3-1								
BELL 6	⑨		1-3		5-0			6-10 v-3								
VAN SLYKE 8	W		W			3			⑨							
BONILLA 9	⑧		2-1B 2RBI			⑨			③							
BONDS 7	4-3 5-0		5-0			⑧	6-3		5-0							
MARTINEZ (VARSHO P7)	LBB	1B.		5-3			④									
LAVALLIERE 2	4-6-3			1-3				4-3								
LIND 4			③	3-1			④									
DRABEK P8 / HULSMANN P8			1B		①											
TOTALS	R 0 0 1 0 0 0 0 0 0															
TOTALS	H 1 0 0 N 3 0 0 0 0 / E 0															

WILKERSON P8S / SANDRUM P9

Highlights: Run scores when drawn in
Infield can not turn a double play
on a grounder on the short stops
of second. Bonds running catch in

AT DOME (IN PERSON)

OAKLAND A'S   vs. MINNESOTA TWINS   DATE: 4/22/91

VISITOR	1	2	3	4	5	6	7	8	9	10	11	12	AB	R	H	RBI
16 WILSON LF	4-3		◆ 1B NN		4-3	Ẇ		1B SB								
4 HENDERSON CF	⑨		1B-1-3	⑦		5-0		③	PC							
33 CANSECO RF	1B SB			5-0				⑦ Ẇ								
3 BAINES DH	⑧	⑧		⑦		⑧		5-0	5-0							
36 STEINBACH C / JENNINGS PH9		⑧		2B		5-0	2B PC									
25 McGUIRE 1B		⑧	Ẇ	④	A-7		1-3		4-3							
HEMOND DR 7		⑥			1B SB				1B							
11 RILES 3B			6-4-3	1-3			⑧									
12 BLANKENSHIP 2B / QUIRK PH7																
9 GALLEGO SS / MANRIQUE PH9									③							

TOTALS R 0 1 0 6 1 0 0 0 0 0
       H 0 1 0 0 0 0 0 0 0 0
TOTALS E 0 1 0 0 0 0 0 0 0 0
       LOB

MOORE P BLINK P7 BK (SCC) P6

12,998

TWINS	1	2	3	4	5	6	7	8	9	10	11	12	AB	R	H	RBI
32 GLADDEN LF	6⁴		④		⑦	⑨		⑦								
25 BUSH RF 5-0	5-0	5-0	W		W		3									
34 MACK RF/LF																
34 PUCKETT CF	1B	5-0			(8) F-8	5-0	5-0	5-3								
14 HRBEK 1B	1 W			W	1B ROE	1B	5-0	2-U E5								
44 DAVIS	3			1B	5-0			W								
12 HARPER C		5-0		⑧		1B		1B								
Newman PR 8																
13 PAGLIARULO 3B		4-3		3-6 DP		1B		1B								
Leius PH 8																
11 Knoblock 2B		⑧			①	1-5		1B								
7 GAGNE SS			5-0			5-0										

	R	0	2	0	0	6	0	0	1	2	0	1	0	12
TOTALS	H	0	2	0	0	1	0	0	2	0	1	0	12
TOTALS	E	0	2	0	0	1	0	0	2	0	1	0	12
	LOB													

P. TAPAN L CASSIAN P 7 BEDROSIAN P 8

Highlights: GAGNE DR IVES IN G0 AHEAD RUN IN 8TH

8TH: 0-2 Pitch Hit to Right — I turn out

STEALING

Winning Pitcher:

Losing Pitcher:

Home Runs:

Score by innings:

BALANCE YOUR BOX SCORE

AB	_____	RUNS	_____
BB	_____	OUTS	_____
HP	_____	LOB	_____
SAC	_____		
INT	_____		
TOTALS	_____	TOTALS	_____

SEED AT DOME

MINNESOTA TWINS vs. SEATTLE MARINERS DATE: 4/26/91

	VISITOR	1	2	3	4	5	6	7	8	9	10	11	12	AB	R	H	RBI
2B	REYNOLDS	⑧	4-3	1-3		1-3		1B									
LF	GRIFFEY SR. (TOKES)	W		1-3				4-3									
CF	GRIFFEY JR.	6-4		4-3		①											
S	MARTINEZ	1B		4F			K										
DH	DAVIS	W		4-6													
1B	O'BRIEN	⑧	①		⑧		⑧										
RF	RILEY				4-3		4-F	4-3									
C	BRADLEY		4-3		4-3												
SS	VIZQUEL		1B			3		⑥									
	TOTALS	R 0	0	0	0	0	0	0									
		H 0	0	0	0	0	0	0									
	TOTALS	E 0	0	0	0	0	0	0									

JOHNSON P KREUGER PL

PLAYER'S NUMBERS

1—Pitcher
2—Catcher
3—First Base
4—Second Base
5—Third Base
6—Shortstop
7—Left Field
8—Center Field
9—Right Field
DH—Designated Hitter

BALANCE YOUR BOX SCORE

AB ___ RUNS ___
BB ___ OUTS ___
HP ___
SAC ___ LOB ___
INT ___

TOTALS ___   TOTALS ___

SCORING KEY

Single	Double	Triple
	Home Run	Run Scored

K = Strikeout
W = Walk
FC = Fielder's Choice
CS = Caught Stealing
WP = Wild Pitch

DP = Double Play
SB = Stolen Base
PB = Passed Ball
FO = Foul Out
HP = Hit by Pitch

ϰ = Called 3rd Strike
IW = Intentional Walk
SAC = Sacrifice
SF = Sacrifice Fly
# of Fielder = Flyout

# of Fielder plus "—" = Unassisted Groundout
# of Fielder "-" # of 2nd Fielder = Assisted Groundout

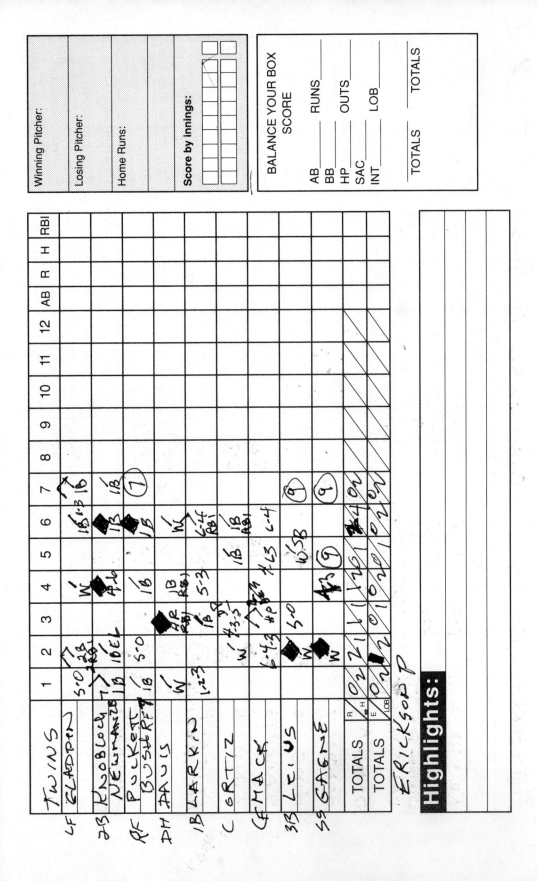

PITTSBURGH PIRATES vs. CINCINNATI REDLEGS DATE: 4-30-91

VISITOR	1	2	3	4	5	6	7	8	9	10	11	12	AB	R	H	RBI
REDUS 3	6-3		6-3			⑧			5-0							
MERCED PR																
BELL 6			6-3			①			5-0							
Wilkerson PH 9																
VAN SLYKE 8	④ HR RBI			①		⑦			5-0							
BONILLA 9	①	⑧		①			⑧									
BONDS 7		⑧		⊗	1B		4-3									
KING 5		⑨	5-3 →		1B E1 4-3		5-3									
SLAUGHT 2		◆ The RBI			1B E1			5-0								
LIND 4			→		4-3			6-3								
DRABEK P		⑤			4-3			5-0								
MARTINEZ PH8																
TOTALS	R 1 0 0 1 0 1 0 0 0 H E															
TOTALS	0 0 0 0 0 0 0 0 0															

LIND CP 8

PLAYER'S NUMBERS

1—Pitcher
2—Catcher
3—First Base
4—Second Base
5—Third Base
6—Shortstop
7—Left Field
8—Center Field
9—Right Field
DH—Designated Hitter

BALANCE YOUR BOX SCORE

AB ____	RUNS ____
BB ____	OUTS ____
HP ____	
SAC ____	LOB ____
INT ____	
TOTALS ____	TOTALS ____

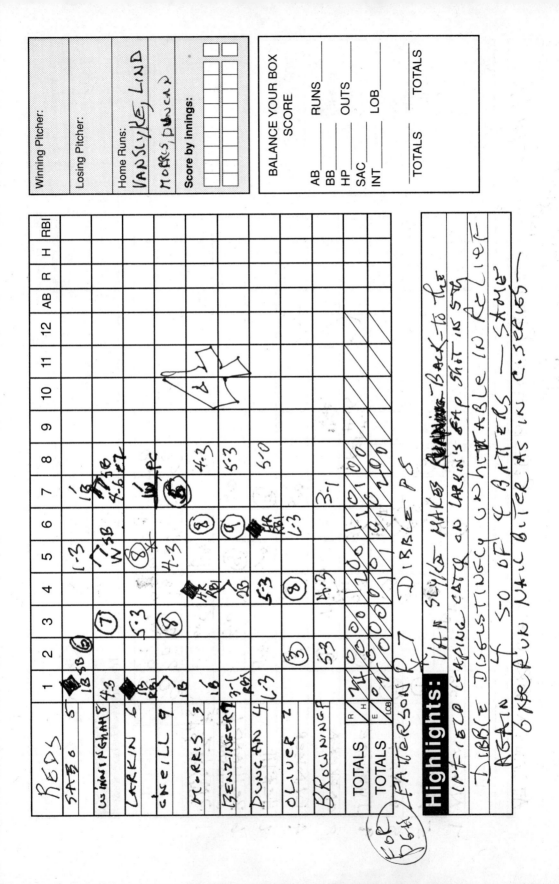

18-9   3 Rivers Pl. 2½

ATLANTA BRAVES   vs. PITTSBURGH PIRATES 1st   DATE: 5/10/91

	VISITOR	1	2	3	4	5	6	7	8	9	10	11	12	AB	R	H	RBI
1	NIXON	5-0		1B 1F			2 3		9								
5	PENDLETON	4		1B	2B		1B 4-6		5								
8	GANT	1			1-3		4-5-2										
6	JUSTICE		8		4-3 RBI		3-2			BREATH HIR							
3	CABRERA		9		7-2 1B 30		8			2nd to 3rd							
4	BLAUSER		W		1B			5-0									
2	HEATH		5-3			5-0		9									
6	BELLIARD			5-0		8		5-0									
1	STARTER P8					6-3											
1	SMOLZ P			6 OT				5-0									
	SMITH P48																

TOTALS	R	0	0	0	3	0	0	1	0	0							
	H	0	0	1	6	0	2	0	0	0							
TOTALS	E	0	6	0													
	LOB																

PLAYER'S NUMBERS
1—Pitcher
2—Catcher
3—First Base
4—Second Base
5—Third Base
6—Shortstop
7—Left Field
8—Center Field
9—Right Field
DH—Designated Hitter

BALANCE YOUR BOX SCORE

AB ___	RUNS ___
BB ___	
HP ___	OUTS ___
SAC ___	
INT ___	LOB ___
TOTALS ___	TOTALS ___

Winning Pitcher:

Losing Pitcher:

Home Runs: MERCED, BREAM

Score by innings:

BALANCE YOUR BOX
SCORE

AB ___	RUNS ___		
BB ___	OUTS ___		
HP ___	LOB ___		
SAC ___			
INT ___			
TOTALS ___	TOTALS ___		

PIRATES	1	2	3	4	5	6	7	8	9	10	11	12	AB	R	H	RBI
MERCED 3	5-0		1B		HR RBI		4-3									
BELL	6-0		8	WP	6-3		6-3									
VAN SLYKE 8	4-3		3		8		1B									
BONILLA 5		1B		4-3		1B WP	5	1B SB 1B								
BONDS 7		5-0		1B 3B WP		7 W										
VATCHER 9 / McCLENDON P4B		6	8	7 W		3										
LAVALLIERE 2		4-3		3-6		1		1B 6 K								
LIND 4			4-3	1		4-1		9								
SMILEY P			7 W		5-0	8										
BELINDA P 8																
TOTALS	R H	0 0	0 1 0	1 0	1 1	1 0										
TOTALS	E LOB	0 0	1 0 0	0 0	0 2	0 1										

Highlights:

BONDS BRILLIANT THROW ENDS POTENTIAL
BIG INNING FOR BRAVES IN 4th — GACHT D IN 6th SAVES
TODAY MERCED THROWS 6st RUNNER AT PLATE (MERCED H.R. too)
SMILEY PITCHES 7 STRONG INNINGS —

ATLANTA BRAVES vs. PITTSBURGH PIRATES   DATE: 5/12/91

VISITOR	1	2	3	4	5	6	7	8	9	10	11	12	AB	R	H	RBI
Nixon 9	1B		1-3 SAC		1-3 SAC		8	1B								
Gant 8	HR		5-0		5-0			1B								
Pendleton 5	6-3			5		1B		4-3								
Justice 9	5-0	7				K		4-3								
Bream 3	5-0			1B		1B		1B								
Blauser 4		5-3		#P	1 #P	1-3	4-3	HR RBI								
Olson 2		7		6-4-3	1B	2	4-3	6								
Bellard 6		5-3			out											
Avery P			7													
Smith P67			W													
TOTALS	R	2	0	0	0	1	2	0	0							
TOTALS	H 0	0	0	0	1	6	0	6								
	E															
	LOB															

BERENGUER P7

SCORING KEY

Single	Double	Triple	Home Run	Run Scored

PLAYER'S NUMBERS
1—Pitcher
2—Catcher
3—First Base
4—Second Base
5—Third Base
6—Shortstop
7—Left Field
8—Center Field
9—Right Field
DH—Designated Hitter

BALANCE YOUR BOX SCORE

AB ___	RUNS ___
BB ___	OUTS ___
HP ___	
SAC ___	LOB ___
INT ___	
TOTALS ___	TOTALS ___

K = Strikeout	DP = Double Play	⅄ = Called 3rd Strike
W = Walk	SB = Stolen Base	IW = Intentional Walk
FC = Fielder's Choice	PB = Passed Ball	SAC = Sacrifice
CS = Caught Stealing	FO = Foul Out	SF = Sacrifice Fly
WP = Wild Pitch	HP = Hit by Pitch	# of Fielder = Flyout

# of Fielder plus "-" = Unassisted Groundout
# of Fielder "-" # of 2nd Fielder = Assisted Groundout

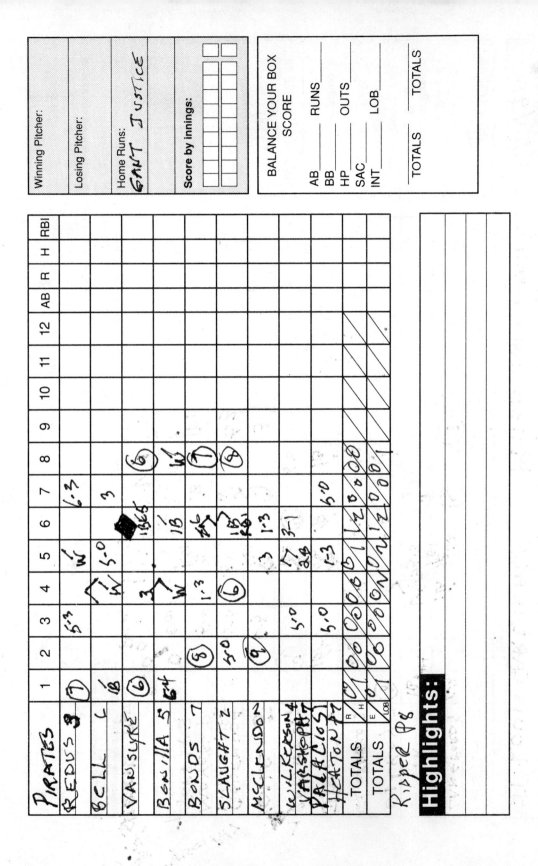

Winning Pitcher:

Losing Pitcher:

Home Runs: GANT JUSTICE

Score by innings:

BALANCE YOUR BOX
SCORE

AB ____ RUNS ____
BB ____ OUTS ____
HP ____
SAC ____ LOB ____
INT ____

TOTALS ____ TOTALS ____

PIRATES	1	2	3	4	5	6	7	8	9	10	11	12	AB	R	H	RBI
REDUS 3																
BELL 6																
VAN SLYKE																
Bonilla 5																
BONDS 7																
SLAUGHT 2																
McCLENDON																
WILKERSON 4																
VARSHO PH																
PALACIOS																

Rasper P8

Highlights:

ST. LOUIS CARDINALS vs. PITTSBURGH PIRATES DATE: 5/24/91

20-16 -2½ (3RD)   22-13 1ST +2

VISITOR	1	2	3	4	5	6	7	8	9	10	11	12	AB	R	H	RBI
LANGFORD 8	5-3			1B	1SB	5-0	⑧		⑦							
SMITH 6	1B3#4			1-4-3S-3	1B		⑨	W								
GILKEY 7	③			2B		5-0										
GuERRERO 3		5-0		⑦		6-3 5-4-3		1B								
JOSE 9		1B1-3b			2B	1B	⑧	1B								
PAGNOZZI 2		⑦	6-3		5-3		W	5-0								
ZEILE 5			5-0				1B		3							
OQUENDO 4			5-0		⑧ RBI		1B		K-3							
WILSON PH5																
MOYER P																
TERRY P 3																
TOTALS	0	0	0	0	3	3	0	0	0							
TOTALS	0	0	0	0	1	0	2	2	0							

PErry P4 9

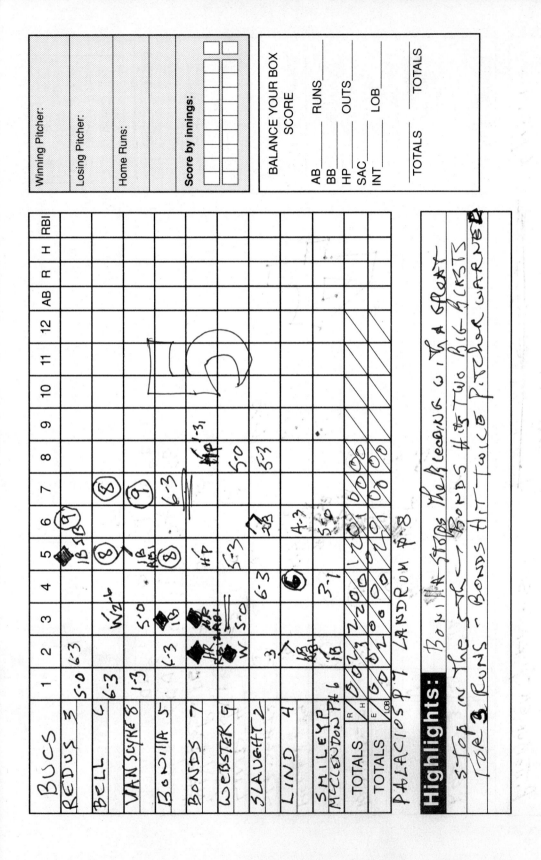

Winning Pitcher:		
Losing Pitcher:		
Home Runs:		
Score by innings:		

BALANCE YOUR BOX SCORE

AB _____ RUNS _____
BB _____ OUTS _____
HP _____ LOB _____
SAC _____
INT _____

TOTALS _____ TOTALS _____

BUCS	1	2	3	4	5	6	7	8	9	10	11	12	AB	R	H	RBI
REDUS 3	5-0	6-3				⑨										
BELL 6	6-3		W2-4		1B ⑧	⑨	⑧									
VAN SYKE 8	1-3		5-0		1B RBI		⑨									
BONILLA 5		6-3	5-0 1B		⑧	6-3	6-3	HR 1-3								
BONDS 7		HR RBI	HR RBI	#P	#P	⑦		#P 1-3								
WEBSTER 9		W	5-0		5-3	4-3		5-0								
SLAUGHT 2		-3		6-3				5-3								
LIND 4		T		⑥	5-0	4-3										
SMILEY P / McCLENDON Pt 6		RBI 1B	3-1													
TOTALS	R	0 0 2 3 2 2 0 0														
TOTALS	E	0 0 2 0 0 0 0 0														
	LOB															

PALACIOS P 9   LANDRUM Pt 8

Highlights: Bonilla stops the record w/ a great
stop in the 5th. Bonds #15 two big hits.
For 3 runs. Bonds hit twice. Pitcher warned.

36 -22 +6 1ST   25 -37

SAN FRANCISCO GIANTS

PITTSBURGH PIRATES   vs.   LOS ANGELES DODGERS   DATE: 6/16/91

VISITOR	1	2	3	4	5	6	7	8	9	10	11	12	AB	R	H	RBI
REDUS 3	8		A				0	4-3								
BELL 6	1-3															
WEBSTER 8	3			9				6								
BONILLA 5		3-1		8				T	W							
BONDS 7		6		6-3	5-3	SB			1-6							
McCLENDON 9		7			W	3	4		5-4-3							
SLAUGHT 2							OUT									
LIND 4			4-3													
LANDRUM P9			4-3													
WALK P					5-0											
PATTERSON PG																
TOTALS	R 0	0	0	0	0	3	0	0	0							
TOTALS	H 0	0	0	0	0	1	0	0	0							
	E 0	LOB														

SCORING KEY

K = Strikeout	DP = Double Play	ꓘ = Called 3rd Strike
W = Walk	SB = Stolen Base	IW = Intentional Walk
FC = Fielder's Choice	PB = Passed Ball	SAC = Sacrifice
CS = Caught Stealing	FO = Foul Out	SF = Sacrifice Fly
WP = Wild Pitch	HP = Hit by Pitch	# of Fielder = Flyout

# of Fielder plus "—" = Unassisted Groundout
# of Fielder "-" # of 2nd Fielder = Assisted Groundout

Single Double Triple Home Run Run Scored

PLAYER'S NUMBERS

1—Pitcher
2—Catcher
3—First Base
4—Second Base
5—Third Base
6—Shortstop
7—Left Field
8—Center Field
9—Right Field
DH—Designated Hitter

BALANCE YOUR BOX SCORE

AB _____ RUNS _____
BB _____ OUTS _____
HP _____
SAC _____ LOB _____
INT _____

TOTALS _____ TOTALS _____

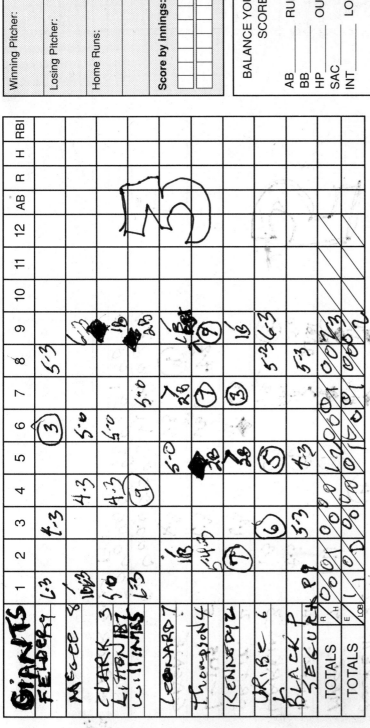

GIANTS	1	2	3	4	5	6	7	8	9	10	11	12	AB	R	H	RBI
FELDER 9	6-3		4-3			③		5-3								
MCGEE 8	10-23			4-3		2-5	5-0									
CLARK 3	5-0			4-3		5-0										
LEITON 187 WILLIAMS	6-3			⑨												
LEONARD 7					6-0		7-26									
THOMPSON 4					2B		⑦									
KENNEDY 2		⑦			1B				1B							
URIBE 6			⑥		⑤		③	5-2 6-3								
BLACK P SEGUR P9			5-3		4-2			5-3								
TOTALS	R 0 0	1 0 0	0 0 0	0 0 0	2 0 0	0 0 0	0 0 1	0 0 3								
TOTALS	E 1 0	0 0	0 0	0 0	0 0	0 1	0 1	0 0 2								
	LOB															

WON
42-27
2D out of 4R
1ST PLACE BY 3

MINNESOTA TWINS vs. NEW YORK YANKEES DATE: 6/24/91

VISITOR	1	2	3	4	5	6	7	8	9	10	11	12	AB	R	H	RBI
GLADDEN 7	⑨			⑨				4-3	④							
KNOBLOCK 4	5-3			4-3		5-3			1-3							
PUCKETT 8	L-3			④												
MACK 9		⑦			⑦				5-0							
MUNOZ 34		4-3			⑨				③							
LARKIN 3		1-3	1-3		L-3		6-3									
ORTIZ 2						W										
LEIUS 5			L-3					4-3								
GAGNE 6			4-3			L-3		⑨							
TOTALS	0 0	0 0	0 0	0 0	0 0	1	2 3	0 0	2 2							
TOTALS	0 0	0 0	0 0	0 0	0 0	0	1	0 0	0 0							

ERICKSON P
GOES FOR 12TH STR.

PLAYER'S NUMBERS
1—Pitcher
2—Catcher
3—First Base
4—Second Base
5—Third Base
6—Shortstop
7—Left Field
8—Center Field
9—Right Field
DH—Designated Hitter

BALANCE YOUR BOX SCORE

AB ___ RUNS ___
BB ___ OUTS ___
HP ___
SAC ___
INT ___ LOB ___

TOTALS ___ TOTALS ___

K = Strikeout	DP = Double Play
W = Walk	SB = Stolen Base
FC = Fielder's Choice	PB = Passed Ball
CS = Caught Stealing	FO = Foul Out
WP = Wild Pitch	HP = Hit by Pitch

⋊ = Called 3rd Strike
IW = Intentional Walk
SAC = Sacrifice
SF = Sacrifice Fly
# of Fielder = Flyout

# of Fielder plus "·" = Unassisted Groundout
# of Fielder "·" = # of 2nd Fielder = Assisted Groundout

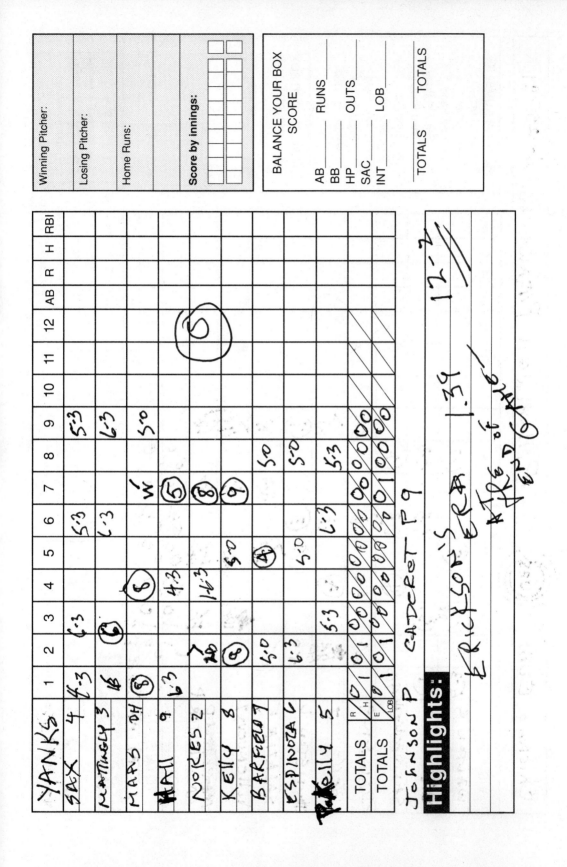

Chicago Cubs vs. Pittsburgh Pirates DATE: 6-25-91

VISITOR	1	2	3	4	5	6	7	8	9	10	11	12	AB	R	H	RBI
WALTON 6	6-3		1-3		⑧			6-3	5-3							
GRACE 3		①	⑥	⑥		4-3		4-3								
SANDBERG 4	4-3			④		6-3		②								
DAWSON 9	out	HR		5-0	HR	1B			W							
BELL 7		HR		Ⓐ	1-0	1B			W							
DUNSTON 6	5-0	out	1B63		L13		4-3		W							
SALAZAR 5					HR		5-0									
VILLANUEVA 2			FC		1-3 SAC		5-0		1B							
LANCASTER P	00	00	00	00	00	00	00	00	00							

		R	H
TOTALS			
TOTALS	E		LOB

ASSENMACHER P8

40-26 1ST PLACE +5

PIRATES	1	2	3	4	5	6	7	8	9	10	11	12	AB	R	H	RBI
MERCED 3	5-0	4-3			5-0		⑦									
BELL 6	⑧		4-3		Ⓖ	3-1		1Bz-4								
VAN SLYKE 8	1B		⑥			2B		②								
BONILLA 5	W		W						5-0							
BONDS 7	1B RBI		Ⓐ	5-0		⑥										
WEBSTER 9	5-0			5-3		out	4-3									
LAVALLIERE 2		⑦					⑤									
SLAUGHT PH 4 2B		2B														
LIND 4		3-1		5-3			1B									
VARSHO PH 7																
SMILEY P		4-0		4-3												
PALACIOS PH																
TOTALS R H	1 1	0 0	0 0	0 0	0 0	0 0	0 0	0 0								
TOTALS E LOB	0 0	1 0	1 0	0 0	0 0	0 0	1 0	0 0								

6-4 Ripper P9

Winning Pitcher:
Losing Pitcher:
Home Runs:
Score by innings:

BALANCE YOUR BOX
SCORE
AB ____ RUNS ____
BB ____ OUTS ____
HP ____
SAC ____ LOB ____
INT ____
____ TOTALS ____ TOTALS

Highlights:

IN Person

1ST By 2

Chicago White Sox vs. Minnesota Twins   DATE: 6/29/91

VISITOR	1	2	3	4	5	6	7	8	9	10	11	12	AB	R	H	RBI
RAINES LF 1B		4-6-3			9	8	2B	9								
VENTURA 5 1B			W			6-3	W									
Thomas DH 1B			5-3			6-3	9									
PASQUA RF 1B 5-0				1B		1B 2B	7 2B									
FISK 1B 5-4-3						4	9									
SOSA RF 4-3				1B			1B	1B								
MERULLO 1B	A-3			3U												
JOHNSON 8	4-3			1-3				4-3								
CORA 4		7			5-3		1									
GUILLEN 6			1B 1B		5	3	1B RBI 1B RBI									
TOTALS (R H LOB)	0 3	0	0 0	0 1	0 0	0 0	4 4	1 1	0 1							
TOTALS (E)	0 2															

HIBBARD

SCORING KEY

Single · Double · Triple   Home Run   Run Scored

K = Strikeout	DP = Double Play
W = Walk	SB = Stolen Base
FC = Fielder's Choice	PB = Passed Ball
CS = Caught Stealing	FO = Foul Out
WP = Wild Pitch	HP = Hit by Pitch

⅄ = Called 3rd Strike	# of Fielder plus "·" = Unassisted Groundout
IW = Intentional Walk	# of Fielder "·" = # of 2nd
SAC = Sacrifice	Fielder = Assisted
SF = Sacrifice Fly	Groundout
# of Fielder = Flyout	

PLAYER'S NUMBERS

1—Pitcher
2—Catcher
3—First Base
4—Second Base
5—Third Base
6—Shortstop
7—Left Field
8—Center Field
9—Right Field
DH—Designated Hitter

BALANCE YOUR BOX SCORE

AB ___	RUNS ___
BB ___	OUTS ___
HP ___	LOB ___
SAC ___	
INT ___	
TOTALS ___	TOTALS ___

TWINS

Player	1	2	3	4	5	6	7	8	9	10	11	12	AB	R	H	RBI
KNOBLOCH ④ 1B	■		5-3		⑦			⑨								
LEIUS ⑥ 5-4		4-3				6-3		⑧								
PUCKETT ⑧ HR	■		④	①		1B	⑦	①								
DAVIS DH HR	■					1BES										
MACK ⑦ 3				6-3		6-4-3										
[ ] ⑨ 5-0				6 1B			6-3									
MUNOZ ⑥ 3		4-3		⑤			HR 1RBI									
HARBER ③					W											
ORTIZ ②		⑨			⑤ 3		5-3									
ERICKSON P / GAGNE ⑥							⑧									

	R															
TOTALS	3	3	0	0	0	0	1	0	0							
TOTALS (E)	0	0	0	0	6	1	0	0	0							
LOB	0	0	0	0	0	1	9	1	0							

→ ERICKSON P GOES FOR 13 STR.

Winning Pitcher:
Losing Pitcher:
Home Runs:
Score by innings:

BALANCE YOUR BOX SCORE

AB ___		RUNS ___	
BB ___		OUTS ___	
HP ___			
SAC ___		LOB ___	
INT ___			
TOTALS ___		TOTALS ___	

Highlights:
Puckett's 425 FT HR. GETS BACK the Lead in the FIRST (ERICKSON → YIELDS ONE R. IN FIRST DESPITE BIG IAK) Davis Follows with 418 FT. ONE — HRBEK HR. 25.

VS.

VISITOR	1	2	3	4	5	6	7	8	9	10	11	12
TOTALS	R	H										
TOTALS	E	LOB										

BERS

se
Base
Shortstop
7—Left Field
8—Center Field
9—Right Field
DH—Designated Hitter

BALANCE YOUR BOX SCORE

AB _____ RUNS _____
BB _____ OUTS _____
HP _____ LOB _____
SAC _____
INT _____

TOTALS _____ TOTALS _____

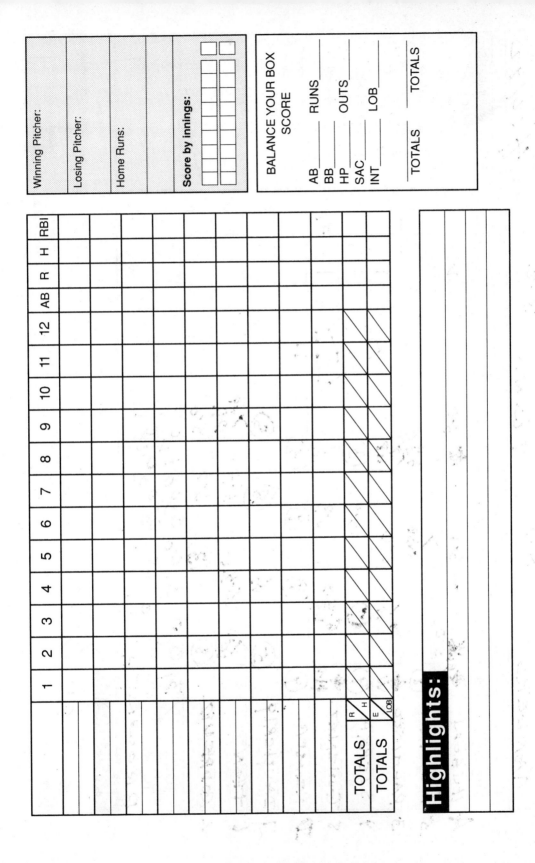

Winning Pitcher:

Losing Pitcher:

Home Runs:

Score by innings:

BALANCE YOUR BOX
SCORE

AB _____ RUNS _____
BB _____
HP _____ OUTS _____
SAC _____
INT _____ LOB _____

TOTALS _____ TOTALS _____

	1	2	3	4	5	6	7	8	9	10	11	12	AB	R	H	RBI
TOTALS													R		H	
TOTALS													E		LOB	

Highlights:

RANGERS 5-1 vs. TWINS 3-2   DATE: 4/12/92

VISITOR	1	2	3	4	5	6	7	8	9	10	11	12	AB	R	H	RBI
4 HUSON / MURPHY PH	⑨	W BB			3-1			1B	5-0					2		
5 NEWMAN	⑧	5-0			W SB 7			3-4 3rd HP								
3 PALMEIRO	W		9-1 W		5-0			⑦ HP								
9 SIERRA	⑨		⑦			5-0		③						1		
8 GONZALEZ	HR		6-4-3 DP	①		6-3	①	1B								
D REIMER	⑨			①	③	①	⑧	⑤	⑧					1	3-1	
7 DAUGHERTY		⑤		W			5-3		7 WP							
6 THON		7 1B		5-4-3			6-3		1B4							
2 RODRIGUEZ		⑧			③				5-0							

	R	3	1	0	0	0	0	0	0	1	0	1	
TOTALS	H	3	1	0	0	1	0	0	1	1	0	1	
TOTALS	E	0	1	0	0	0	0	0	2	0			

BROWN P.

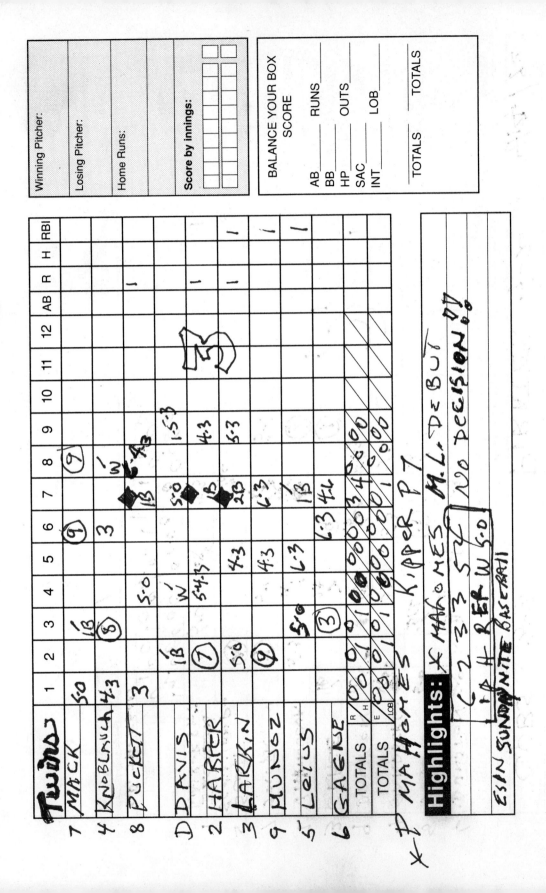

Twins

		1	2	3	4	5	6	7	8	9	10	11	12	AB	R	H	RBI
7	MACK	50		1B			9		9						1		
4	KNOBLAUCH	4-3		8			3	1B	3B 6 4-3	4-3							
8	PUCKET	3			5-0												
D	DAVIS		1B		W	4-3		5-0 1B	1-5-3					1	1		
2	HARPER		7		5-4-3	4-3		1B	4-3								
3	LARKIN		5-0			4-3		2B	6-3					1	1		1
9	MUNOZ		9	5-0		L-3		1									
5	LEIUS			3		L-3	L-3 4L	1B							1		1
6	GAGNE																
	TOTALS	R 0 0	0 1	0 1	0 0	0 0	0 0	3 4	0 0	0 0							
	TOTALS	E 0 0	0 1	0 1	0 0	0 0	0 0	1 0	0 0	0 0							

x-P MAHOMES   KiPPER P7

Highlights: x MAHOMES M.L. DEBUT
6 2 3 3 5 4 No DECISION
1 H R ER W 5-0

E5 IN SUNDAY NITE BASEBALL

Winning Pitcher:

Losing Pitcher:

Home Runs:

Score by innings:

BALANCE YOUR BOX
SCORE

AB _____   RUNS _____
BB _____   OUTS _____
HP _____   LOB _____
SAC _____
INT _____

TOTALS _____   TOTALS _____

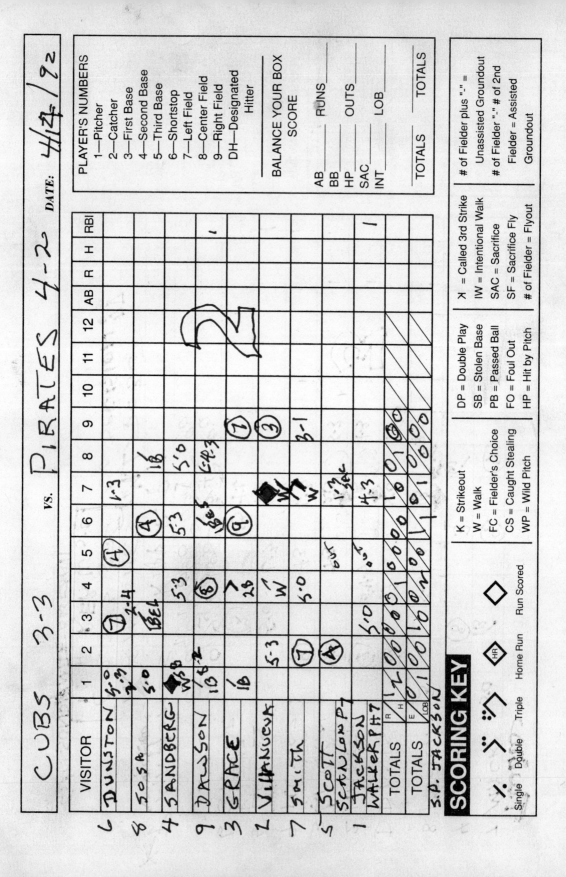

CUBS 3-3 vs. PIRATES 4-2 DATE: 4/4/92

PLAYER'S NUMBERS
1—Pitcher
2—Catcher
3—First Base
4—Second Base
5—Third Base
6—Shortstop
7—Left Field
8—Center Field
9—Right Field
DH—Designated Hitter

BALANCE YOUR BOX SCORE

AB ___		RUNS ___	
BB ___		OUTS ___	
HP ___		LOB ___	
SAC ___			
INT ___			
TOTALS ___		TOTALS ___	

VISITOR	1	2	3	4	5	6	7	8	9	10	11	12	AB	R	H	RBI
6 DUNSTON	6-0 3-3	⑦ 2-4			Ⓐ		1-3									
8 SOSA	5-0		BELL			④		1B								
4 SANDBERG	WP			5-3		5-3		5-0								
9 DAWSON	7K-2 1B	①	⑧			BG5	G4-3									1
3 GRACE	1B	Ⓐ		2B		Ⓢ										
2 VILLANUEVA		5-3		W			W		①							
7 SMITH		①		5-0			W		③							
5 SCOTT		Ⓐ			OUT		1-3 SAC		3-1							
SCANLON P7																
1 JACKSON			5-0	2-0			4-3									1
WALKER P#7																
TOTALS R H	1 2	0 0	0 0	0 1	0 0	0 0	0 0	0 1	0 1							
TOTALS E LOB	0 1	0 0	0 0	0 0	0 2	0 1	0 0	0 0	0 0							

S.P. JACKSON

SCORING KEY

✗	⟩⟩	⟩	◇	HR◇
Single	Double	Triple	Home Run	Run Scored

K = Strikeout	DP = Double Play	✗ = Called 3rd Strike	# of Fielder plus "+" = Unassisted Groundout
W = Walk	SB = Stolen Base	IW = Intentional Walk	# of Fielder "-" # of 2nd
FC = Fielder's Choice	PB = Passed Ball	SAC = Sacrifice	Fielder = Assisted Groundout
CS = Caught Stealing	FO = Foul Out	SF = Sacrifice Fly	
WP = Wild Pitch	HP = Hit by Pitch	# of Fielder = Flyout	

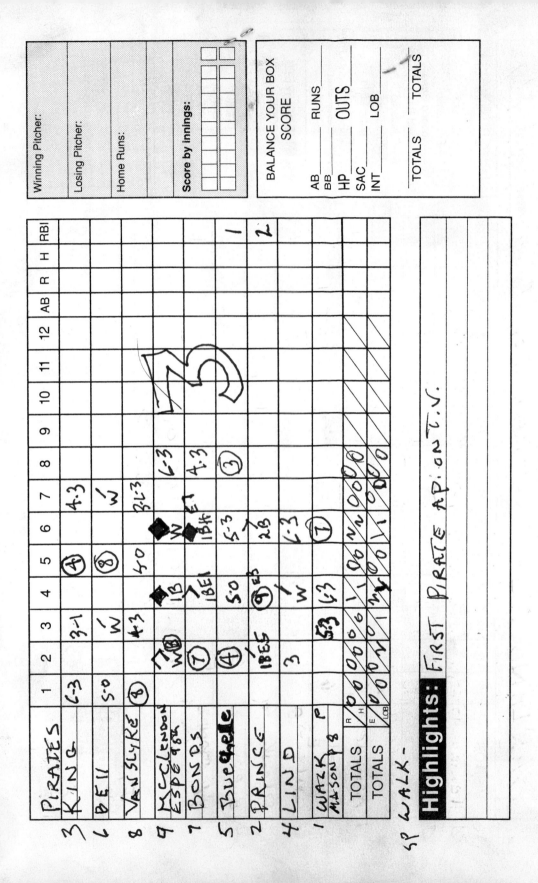

Winning Pitcher:

Losing Pitcher:

Home Runs:

Score by innings:

BALANCE YOUR BOX SCORE

AB ___ RUNS
BB ___
HP ___ OUTS
SAC ___
INT ___ LOB
___ TOTALS ___ TOTALS

PIRATES	1	2	3	4	5	6	7	8	9	10	11	12	AB	R	H	RBI
3 KING	6-3		3-1		④		4-3									
6 BELL	5-0		W		⑧	W										
8 VANSLYKE	⑧		4-3	4-0		3L-3		6-3								
9 MCCLENDON / ESPE48R		W⑧		1B	BB	W	BB-1	4-3								
7 BONDS		⑦		1BEN	5-0	5-3		③							1	
5 BUECHELE		④		⑨ 2B3		2B										
2 PRINCE		1BE5		1 W		6-3									2	
4 LIND		3	5-3			⑦										
1 WALK P / MASON 8				6-3												
TOTALS	R 0	0	0	0	1	2	0	0	0							
	H 0	0	0	0	0	2	0	0	0							
TOTALS	E 0	0	0	0	0	1	0	0	0							
	LOB															

Highlights: FIRST PIRATE AP. on T.V.

SP WALK -

LIVE AND "P.P.-YSON"

26,706

OAKLAND A'S vs. MINNESOTA Twins DATE: 4/24/92

VISITOR	1	2	3	4	5	6	7	8	9	10	11	12	AB	R	H	RBI
24 Henderson 7	7	8		5-0			7		2B							1
4 Lansford 5	1B	7 2B		4-3					1-4 SAC					1	1	1
33 Canseco 9	5-0	3	HR		5-0				5-0					2	1	1
26 McGuire 3	1B		W		8		8	W	W					1		
20 Ready D / 2 Brosius 5	W				1B			5-0	5-0							
6 Wilson 8	2B		5-0		L-4	53		W		6-3		6			3	3
12 Blankenship 4	3		6-4	5-3		6	8			7						
14 Burdick 6			W SB	5-3		6		6		1B						
16 Hemond 2 / Quirk 2		W SB				6-3				5-0				1		
TOTALS																
TOTALS																

S.P. DARLING — PARRETT P.S. GOSSAGE P.10

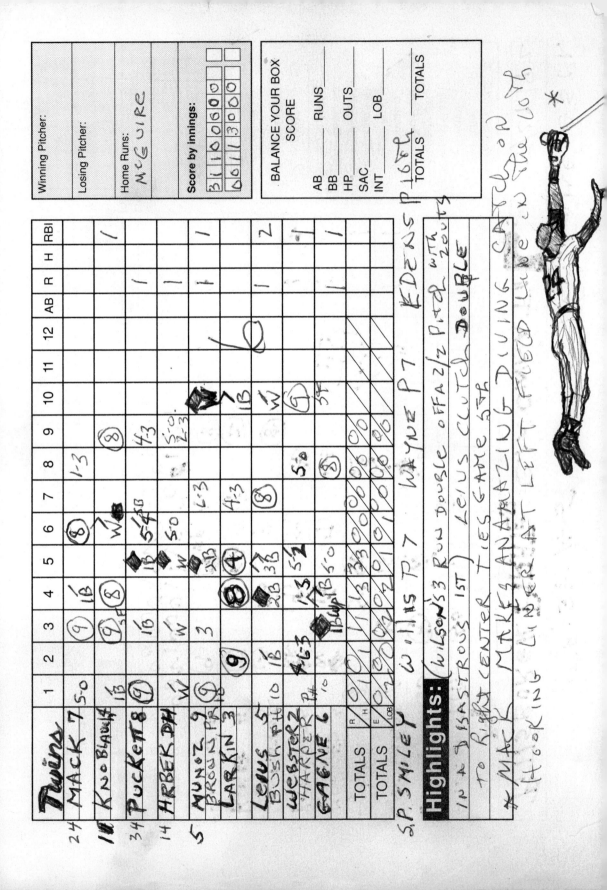

Winning Pitcher:

Losing Pitcher:

Home Runs: McGuire

Score by innings: 3 1 0 0 0 0 | 0 0 1 3 0 0

BALANCE YOUR BOX SCORE

AB ___	RUNS ___		
BB ___	OUTS ___		
HP ___	LOB ___		
SAC ___			
INT ___			
TOTALS P16FL	TOTALS		

Twins

		1	2	3	4	5	6	7	8	9	10	11	12	AB	R	H	RBI
24	MACK 7	5-0		⑨	1B		⑧		1-3						1	
10	KNOBLAUCH 4	1B		⑨	⑧		W			⑧					1	
34	PUCKETT 8	⑨		1B		1B	5-4	1B		4-3					1	1
14	HARPER DH	W		W		W		5-0		5-0 2-3	1B					
5	MUNOZ 9 / BROWN PR / LARKIN 3	⑨	⑨	3	⑧	2B 3B		4-3			W		⑥	1	1	
	LEIUS 5	1B		1B	2B	W 3B		⑧			3U			1	2	
	BUSH PH			4-6-3	1-3	5-2			5-0							
	WEBSTER 2	1B														
	HARPER P	1B							⑧					1	1	
	GAGNE C															

	R	0	0	1	1	3 3	0 0	0 0	0 0
TOTALS	H	0	1	1	1	1	0	0	0
TOTALS	E	0	2	0	2	1	0	0	0
	LOB								

S.P. SMILEY   WILLIS P7   WAYNE P7   EDENS P16FL

Highlights:

(WILSON'S 3 RUN DOUBLE OFF A 2/2 PITCH WITH 2 OUTS
IN A DISASTROUS 1ST) LEIUS CLUTCH DOUBLE
TO RIGHT CENTER TIES GAME 5TH
*MACK MAKES AN AMAZING DIVING CATCH ON
HOOKING LINER AT LEFT FIELD LINE IN THE 6TH *

T.V. GAME ESPN

1ST BY 3½ 14-5

PITTSBURGH PIRATES vs. CINCINNATI ~~RED~~ REDS L

DATE: 5/29/92

VISITOR	1	2	3	4	5	6	7	8	9	10	11	12	AB	R	H	RBI
GIBSON 7	①	4-0	4-0				⑤									
BELL L SD		W	K		W			5-0								
VANSLYKE 8 W		HR	K		1B			W 2B						1		1
BONDS 7 ③		(-3		5-0	SD			4-3	⑧							
MERCED 3		W		1B		⑦								1		1
BUECHELE 5		HR		⑨		5-0		④	②					1		
LAVALLIERE 2		(-3		4-3		3	①									
KING 4		⑤			5-3		4-3		⑧						1	2
SMITH P		⑨			HP											

	R	H	E										
TOTALS	0	0	1	0	0	0	0	0	0	0			
TOTALS	0	0	0	0	0	0	0	1	0				

PLAYER'S NUMBERS

1—Pitcher
2—Catcher
3—First Base
4—Second Base
5—Third Base
6—Shortstop
7—Left Field
8—Center Field
9—Right Field
DH—Designated Hitter

BALANCE YOUR BOX SCORE

AB ____		RUNS ____
BB ____		OUTS ____
HP ____		
SAC ____		
INT ____		LOB ____
	TOTALS ____	TOTALS ____

K = Strikeout	DP = Double Play	⅄ = Called 3rd Strike	# of Fielder plus "–" = Unassisted Groundout
W = Walk	SB = Stolen Base	IW = Intentional Walk	# of Fielder "–" # of 2nd Fielder = Assisted Groundout
FC = Fielder's Choice	PB = Passed Ball	SAC = Sacrifice	
CS = Caught Stealing	FO = Foul Out	SF = Sacrifice Fly	
WP = Wild Pitch	HP = Hit by Pitch	# of Fielder = Flyout	

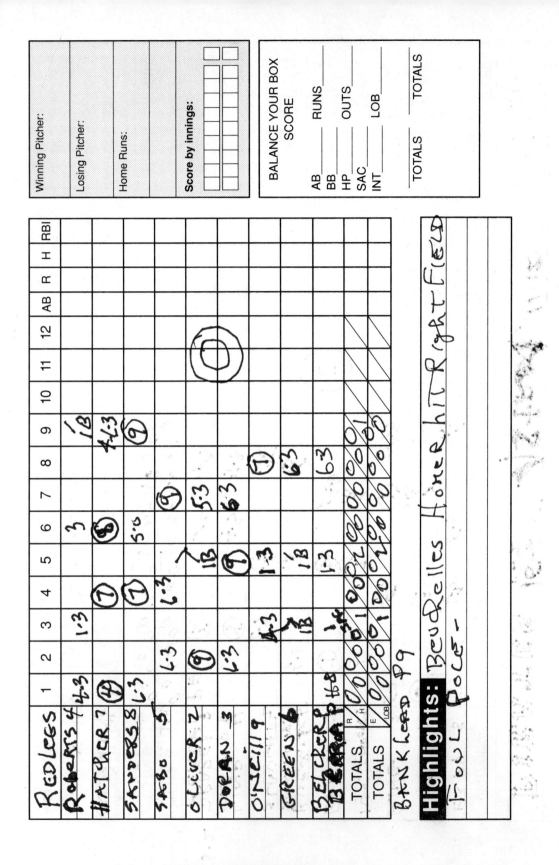

ESPN —

PIRATES 16-6 1ST vs. Astro 11-12   DATE: 5/3/72

VISITOR	1	2	3	4	5	6	7	8	9	10	11	12	AB	R	H	RBI
ESPY 8	③			4-3		6-3			W							
BELL 6	⑥			⑦			1B		5-0							
KING 3	5-3			⑤			⑨	5-3	5-3							
McCLENDON 9		3			⑦		1B									
BONDS 7		⑦			③		L-4-3				Ø					
BUECHELE 5 / VARSHO PR8		4-0			1B			2B								
SLAUGHT 2			2-3					1-3								
LIND 4			⑧		④	4-3		5-3								
MASON P8																
DRABEK P / MERCER P#8		⑤				5-0		4-3								
TOTALS	R	00000	00	0	0	0	0	0	0							
	H	00000	00	0	0	0	0	0	0							
TOTALS	E	LOB														

3-2

PLAYER'S NUMBERS

1—Pitcher
2—Catcher
3—First Base
4—Second Base
5—Third Base
6—Shortstop
7—Left Field
8—Center Field
9—Right Field
DH—Designated Hitter

BALANCE YOUR BOX SCORE

AB ___	RUNS ___
BB ___	OUTS ___
HP ___	
SAC ___	LOB ___
INT ___	

| TOTALS ___ | TOTALS ___ |

SCORING KEY

K = Strikeout	DP = Double Play	⃟ = Called 3rd Strike	# of Fielder plus "—" = Unassisted Groundout
W = Walk	SB = Stolen Base	IW = Intentional Walk	# of Fielder "—" # of 2nd
FC = Fielder's Choice	PB = Passed Ball	SAC = Sacrifice	Fielder = Assisted Groundout
CS = Caught Stealing	FO = Foul Out	SF = Sacrifice Fly	
WP = Wild Pitch	HP = Hit by Pitch	# of Fielder = Flyout	Fielder = Flyout Groundout

∴ ⬦ ⬦(HR)

Single   Double   Triple   Home Run   Run Scored

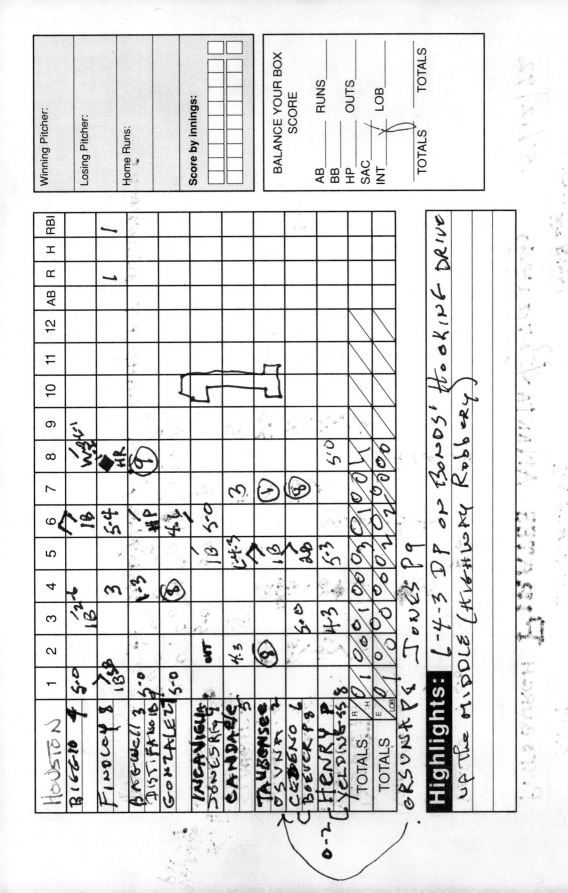

A1-9   1ST PLACE 3½   15MB -3   T.B.S.

PITTSBURGH PIRATES vs. Atlanta Braves   DATE: 5/12/92

VISITOR	1	2	3	4	5	6	7	8	9	10	11	12	AB	R	H	RBI
Redus 9	5-0		8		5-0			9								
Bell 6	4-5-0			8		4		8								
Van Slyke 8	3-1	5-0		1B		1B		8								
McClendon 3 / Espey P9				4		1B	2B		3							
Bonds 7	1B SB			2B		8	6-3	W								
Buechele 5				1				W								1
King 4		6-4		KR6S	6-3		6-3	5-0								
Slaught 2 / Prince PH5			8	8	5-0		5-3	5								
Tomlin P / Miller P?			5-0				3									

	R	1	2	3	4	5	6	7	8	9	10	11	12
TOTALS	H	0	0	1	0	0	2	0	1	0	0		
TOTALS	E	0	0	0	1	0	0	0	0	0			
LOB													

Palacios P5 Naegle P6 Lamp P7 Belinda P8

Varsho PH-7

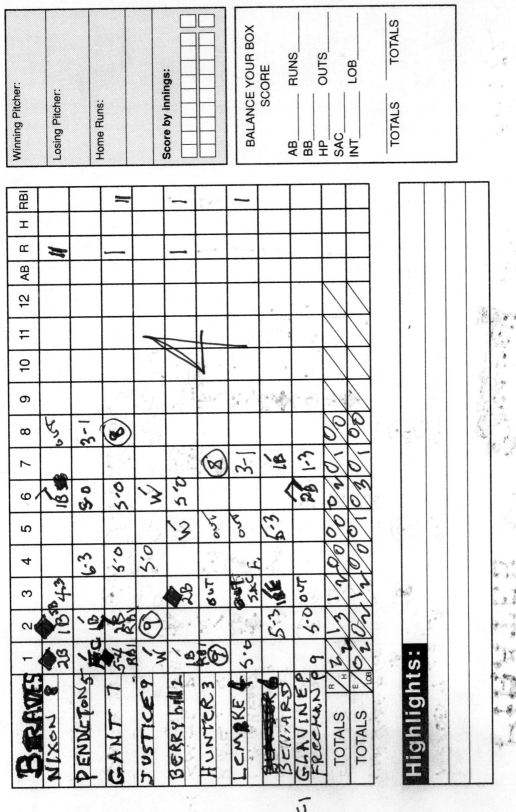

Winning Pitcher:

Losing Pitcher:

Home Runs:

Score by innings:

BALANCE YOUR BOX
SCORE

AB _____ RUNS _____
BB _____ OUTS _____
HP _____
SAC _____ LOB _____
INT _____

TOTALS _____ TOTALS _____

Highlights:

PiRATES vs. Braves   DATE: 5/4/92

1ST +3   Bucs 11 — Braves 10 5/13

VISITOR	1	2	3	4	5	6	7	8	9	10	11	12	AB	R	H	RBI
Merced 7	4-3				3-1			6-0	6-0							
Bell 6	1B		8		3	8		1								
Van Slyke 8	9		4-3 / 1B			1-3		5-0	W					1		
Bonds 7	5-0		7 / 1B			5-0			9 / 2B							
Varsho 9 / Lind 4th		2B	8				8		2B					1		1
Bedecki 5 / Reds P.R. 9		7		8	8		5		7					1		3
L. Avancez		W		1-3		5-0	#R / R6 / 4-3		1B RBI					1		
King 5 4th		7 / 1B							W							1
Smith P / Espe P #9									5-0							

TOTALS	R	0	1	0	0	0	0	1	0	6			
	H	1	4	0	1	0	0	1	0	6			
	E	0	1	0	0	0	0	0	0	0			
LOB													

Palacios 5th / Mason 9

5-1

PLAYER'S NUMBERS

1—Pitcher
2—Catcher
3—First Base
4—Second Base
5—Third Base
6—Shortstop
7—Left Field
8—Center Field
9—Right Field
DH—Designated Hitter

BALANCE YOUR BOX SCORE

AB _____ RUNS _____
BB _____ OUTS _____
HP _____ LOB _____
SAC _____
INT _____

TOTALS _____   TOTALS _____

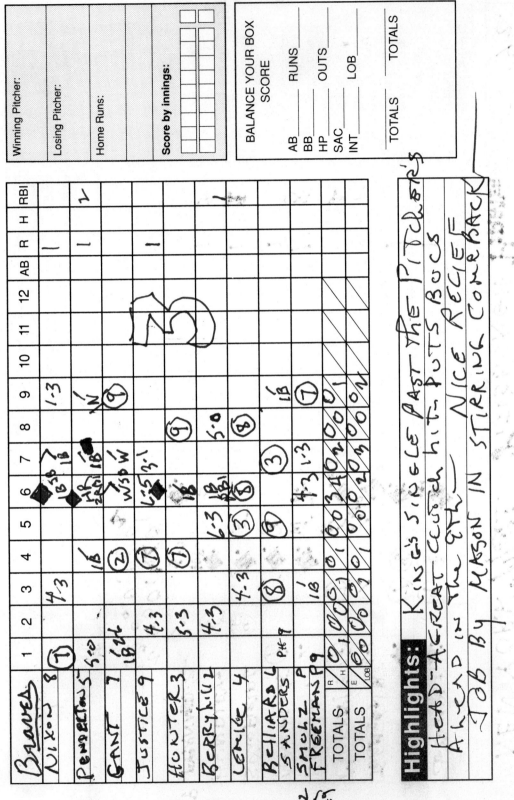

Winning Pitcher:

Losing Pitcher:

Home Runs:

Score by innings:

BALANCE YOUR BOX
SCORE

AB ____ RUNS ____
BB ____ OUTS ____
HP ____
SAC ____ LOB ____
INT ____

TOTALS ____ TOTALS ____

Highlights: King's single past the pitcher's head — A great clutch hit. Puts Bucs ahead in the 9th. Nice relief job by Mason in stirring comeback.

3-2
Brett
P.H.

3RD 27-26 -3

30-23 1ST 2½

NEW YORK Mets vs. PITTSBURGH Pirate DATE: 6-6-92

VISITOR	1	2	3	4	5	6	7	8	9	10	11	12	AB	R	H	RBI
COLEMAN 7			9	8										1		
RANDOLPH 4		9	7	8										1		1
JOHNSON 8 3-1			6													1
MURRAY 3	7		7			7-E7									1	2
BONILLA 9					W	7							1	1		3
MAGADAN 5	9				8											
SCHOFIELD 6		9			5								1	1		
HUNDLEY 2 6-0		5		5-0		3								1		
FERNANDEZ P 5-4		6-0		5-0									1	1		3

	R	H		1	2	0	0	4	0	1	0	2
TOTALS												
TOTALS	E	LOB		0	3	0	0	1	0	0	0	2

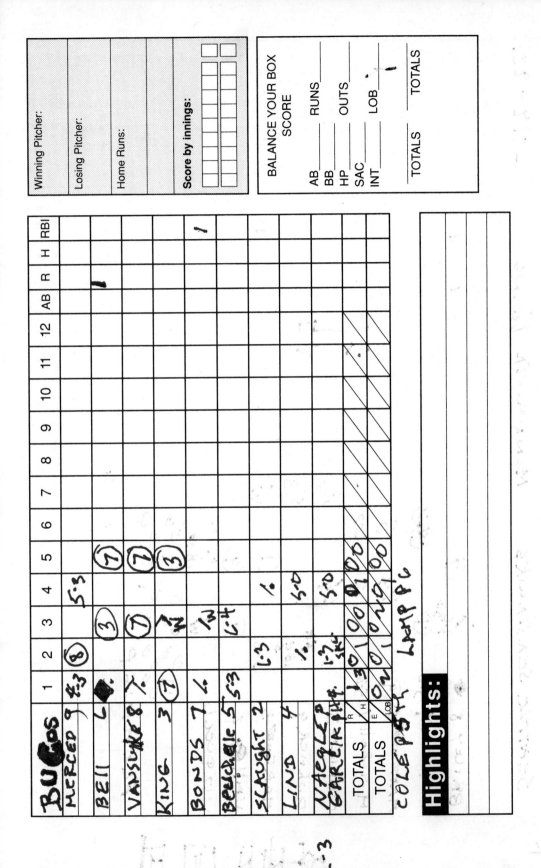

BALANCE YOUR BOX SCORE

AB ___ RUNS ___
BB ___ OUTS ___
HP ___ LOB ___
SAC ___
INT ___

TOTALS ___   TOTALS ___

Winning Pitcher:

Losing Pitcher:

Home Runs:

Score by innings:

BUCOS	1	2	3	4	5	6	7	8	9	10	11	12	AB	R	H	RBI
MERCED 9 4-3		8		5-3										1		
BELL 6			3		1											
VANSLYKE 8 7			1		1											
KING 3 7			2		3											
BONDS 7 6			13	6												1
BEUCHELE 5 5-3			6-4													
SLAUGHT 2		L-3		6												
LIND 4		6		6-0												
NAEGLE P GARCIA P INF.	1-3 SAC			6-0												
TOTALS	R	1	00	01	00											
TOTALS	E	0	00	00	00											

COLE P 5th   LAMP P 6

SEATTLE SEAHAWKS vs. MINNESOTA TWINS   DATE: 6-19-92

PLAYER'S NUMBERS
1—Pitcher
2—Catcher
3—First Base
4—Second Base
5—Third Base
6—Shortstop
7—Left Field
8—Center Field
9—Right Field
DH—Designated Hitter

BALANCE YOUR BOX SCORE

AB ____ RUNS ____
BB ____ OUTS ____
HP ____
SAC ____ LOB ____
INT ____

TOTALS ____ TOTALS ____

# of Fielder plus "−" = Unassisted Groundout
# of Fielder "−" # of 2nd Fielder = Assisted Groundout

VISITOR	1	2	3	4	5	6	7	8	9	10	11	12	AB	R	H	RBI
BRILEY 8	HR		7		⑦								1	1		1
REYNOLDS 4	5-0	3-4·5·0	⑦			⑧·3										
MARTINEZ 5	⑨		⑦	4-3		3										
MITCHELL 7	5-3			18		6-3										
O'BRIEN D		5-0		6-4			5-3									
BJXNCR 9		1BB		5-0			5-3									
MARTINEZ 3		5-0			⑦		W									
VAN H 2			⑨		⑨											
VIZQUEL			W		1B 30											
TOTALS R	1	0	0	0	0	0	0									
H	0	0	0	0	0	0	0									
E	0	0	0	0	1	0	0									

FLEMING

SCORING KEY

K = Strikeout
W = Walk
FC = Fielder's Choice
CS = Caught Stealing
WP = Wild Pitch

DP = Double Play
SB = Stolen Base
PB = Passed Ball
FO = Foul Out
HP = Hit by Pitch

⋊ = Called 3rd Strike
IW = Intentional Walk
SAC = Sacrifice
SF = Sacrifice Fly
# of Fielder = Flyout

Single   Double   Triple   Home Run   Run Scored

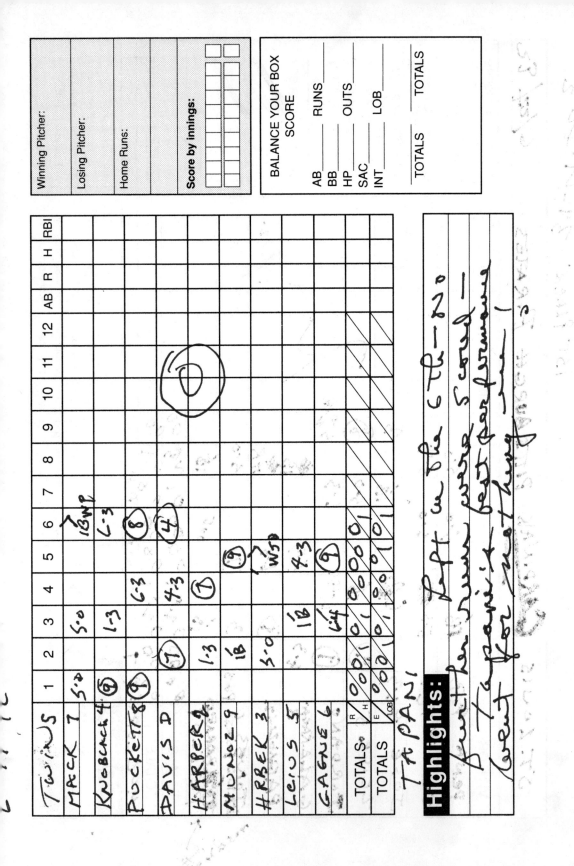

Winning Pitcher:

Losing Pitcher:

Home Runs:

Score by innings:

BALANCE YOUR BOX
SCORE

AB _____ RUNS _____
BB _____ OUTS _____
HP _____ LOB _____
SAC _____
INT _____

TOTALS _____ TOTALS _____

Twins	1	2	3	4	5	6	7	8	9	10	11	12	AB	R	H	RBI
MACK 7	5-0	5-0	5-0			13wp										
Knoblauch 4	⑥		1-3			6-3										
Puckett 8	⑨			6-3		⑧										
Davis D		⑦		4-3		④			⑩							
Harper 2		1-3		①	⑨											
Muñoz 9		1B	1B													
# Rbek 3	5-0	5-0			wp											
Lewis 5			1B		4-3											
Gagne 6			44		⑥											
TOTALS R	0	0	0	1	0	0	0	0	0							
TOTALS H	0	0	1	0	1	0	0	0	0							
E LOB	0	0	1	0	0	1	0	0	0							

TAPANI

Highlights:

Left in the 6th — 2-0

further runners scored —

Tapani's best performance
went for nothing!

ST. LOUIS **CARDINALS** vs. PITTSBURGH PIRATES DATE: 6/22/23

1ST PLACE 39-29 +5½

VISITOR	1	2	3	4	5	6	7	8	9	10	11	12	AB	R	H	RBI
PENA #7	(7)		#B			5·0		6·0								
EDLEY 7L·3			5·3			5·0		6·4								
JOSE 9L·3				6·3			1B		3							
ZL·C·E 5		(9)		1B			5·0		(8)							
JORDAN 9		(1)		6·4F·3	5·3		6·3		5·0·M 5·0·M					1		
GALARAGA 3		4·3			6·3			1B 1B								
PAGNOZZI 2			(5)		(7)			#R	5·0					1		2
TRAVES 6 / CRAWFORD	Pch8		3			6·0 out		1 1B								
OF BORNER PEREZ PH			1B													

TOTALS	R	0	0	0	0	0	0	0	0	0
TOTALS	H	0	0	0	0	0	0	1	0	0
	E	0	0	0	0	0	0	0	0	0

McCLURE P7 DESCEN P8

PLAYER'S NUMBERS
1—Pitcher
2—Catcher
3—First Base
4—Second Base
5—Third Base
6—Shortstop
7—Left Field
8—Center Field
9—Right Field
DH—Designated Hitter

BALANCE YOUR BOX SCORE

AB _____		RUNS _____	
BB _____		OUTS _____	
HP _____			
SAC _____			
INT _____		LOB _____	
TOTALS _____		TOTALS _____	

SCORING KEY

K = Strikeout	DP = Double Play
W = Walk	SB = Stolen Base
FC = Fielder's Choice	PB = Passed Ball
CS = Caught Stealing	FO = Foul Out
WP = Wild Pitch	HP = Hit by Pitch

⅄ = Called 3rd Strike	# of Fielder plus "—" =
IW = Intentional Walk	Unassisted Groundout
SAC = Sacrifice	# of Fielder "—" # of 2nd
SF = Sacrifice Fly	Fielder = Assisted
# of Fielder = Flyout	Groundout

Single · Double ◇ Triple   ⬦ Home Run   ◇ Run Scored

Rosemson Holt

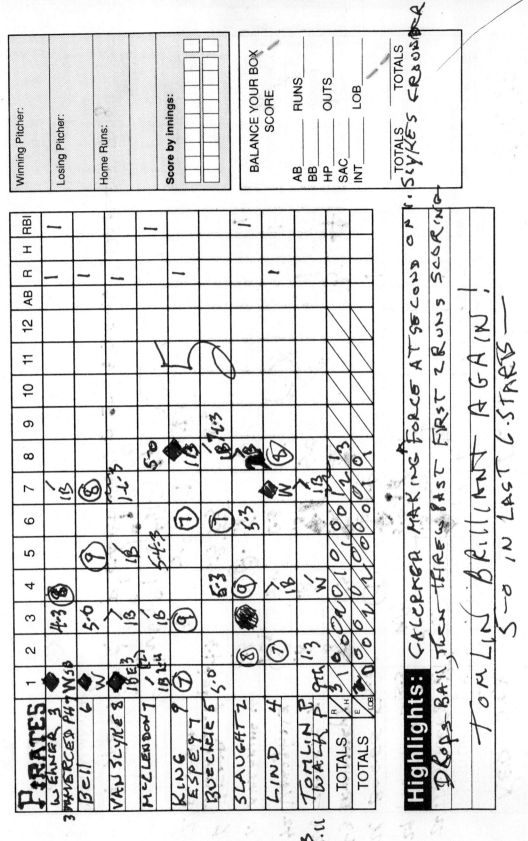

Winning Pitcher:

Losing Pitcher:

Home Runs:

Score by innings:

BALANCE YOUR BOX SCORE

AB _____ RUNS _____
BB _____ OUTS _____
HP _____
SAC _____ LOB _____
INT _____

TOTALS _____   TOTALS _____

SLYKES CROSSER? Mr.

PIRATES

	1	2	3	4	5	6	7	8	9	10	11	12	AB	R	H	RBI
WEHNER 3 3 WALTERSED P47-W3B			4-3				1B						1	1	1	1
BELL 6		W	5-0				8						1	1	1	
VAN SLYKE 8	1B(E3)		7 1B		1B		1-3	5-0					1	1	1	
McLENDON 7	1B 1-4		1B		5-4-3	7		1-3 1B								
KING 9	7		9			7		1B 7-8					1			
ESPEY 7				9	6-4-3	7										
BUECKLE 5	5-0					5-3	W 7	1B 13								
SLAUGHT 2		8						8					1	1		1
LIND 4		7		1B W												
TOMLIN P 9th WALK P	1-3															
TOTALS	R 3	H 1	0	0	0	0	0	0	3							
TOTALS	E 0 0	0	0	0	0	0	0	0	0							
	LOB															

9-3
3-11

Highlights: CALDERER MAKING FORCE AT SECOND ON MR. SLYKES CROSSER

DROP3 BALL THEN THREW PAST FIRST 2 RUNS SCORING

TOMLIN BRILLIANT AGAIN!

5-0 IN LAST 6 STARTS—

DATE: 7/16/92

With Joe, Alice + Nick

RED SOX 2-9 in the Twins R

		1	2	3	4	5	6	7	8	9	10	11	12	AB	R	H	RBI
VISITOR																	
22	HATCHER 8	1B	5-0	4-3			1B	4-3	HR	G					1		4
29	PLANTIER D	5-3		4-3	4-3		1B	5-0									
26	BOGGS 5	4-3			4-3	B.	4B	L-f	5-0					1			
23	BRUNANSKY 9	1B		L-3	1	L-3	HR	1	HR					5	1		1
28	ZUPCIC 7	1B		5-0	1B	L-3	1B		5-5					1	1		
42	VAUGHN 3	RBI			5-0	L-3	L-3	5-5	5-0								1
11	RAMERINE 4	L-3		9		B.	1B		9	7							
6	PENA 2	4-3			1	L-3	5-3			5-0							
	LIVINGHAM	4-3						1									
2	RIVERA 6			9		5-0		1									
TOTALS	R	0	1	0	0	0	1	0	0								
	H	0	0	0	0	0	1	0	0	0							
TOTALS	E	0	1	0	0	0	1	0	0	0							

P. HESKETH   P. GARDINER   P.5   P. iRVINE   DARWIN P. 8

SCORING KEY

K = Strikeout	DP = Double Play	ϰ = Called 3rd Strike	# of Fielder plus "." = Unassisted Groundout
W = Walk	SB = Stolen Base	IW = Intentional Walk	# of Fielder "." # of 2nd
FC = Fielder's Choice	PB = Passed Ball	SAC = Sacrifice	Fielder = Assisted Groundout
CS = Caught Stealing	FO = Foul Out	SF = Sacrifice Fly	
WP = Wild Pitch	HP = Hit by Pitch	# of Fielder = Flyout	

Single   Double   Triple   Home Run   Run Scored

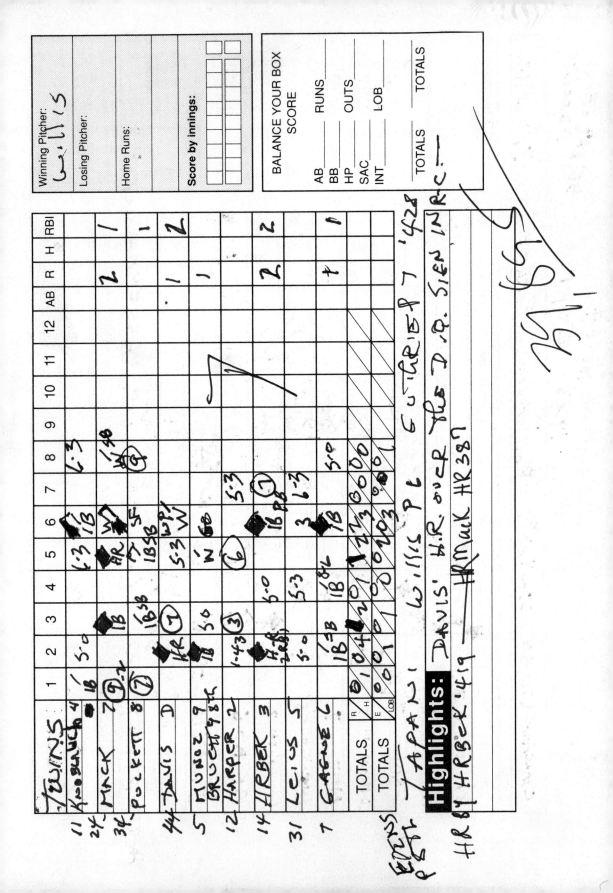

BALANCE YOUR BOX SCORE

AB	RUNS	
BB	OUTS	
HP	LOB	
SAC		
INT		
TOTALS	TOTALS	TOTALS

TWINS	1	2	3	4	5	6	7	8	9	10	11	12	AB	R	H	RBI
11 Knoblauch 4	1B	5-0			6-3	1B		6-3								
24 Mack 7	(4-3)		1B		HR	W		1.4B						2		1
34 Puckett 8	(7)		1Bsb	1Bsb	7 SF	SF	(4)									1
44 Davis D	HR		(7)		5-3	W/P								1		2
5 Munoz 9 / Bruckt 985	1B 50		5-0		W	6B	5-3							1		
12 Harper 2	1-43		(3)		(6)		(7)									
14 Hrbek 3	HR 2RBI			6-0		1B 2B	(1)							2	2	2
31 Leius 5	5-0			5-3		3	6-3									
7 Gagne 6	1=B		1B	18Fc		1B		5-0						4		1
TOTALS R	0	1	0	1	0	1	2	0								
TOTALS H	0	0	1	0	1	3	0	0								
E	0	0	1	0	0	2	0	1								
LOB																

Highlights: Davis' H.R. over the D.Q. Sign NRC

HR 8T HRBek '419 — HRMack #R38T

CHICAGO CUBS 69-67 92½ vs. PITTSBURGH PIRATES DATE: 9/8/92

PLAYER'S NUMBERS

1—Pitcher
2—Catcher
3—First Base
4—Second Base
5—Third Base
6—Shortstop
7—Left Field
8—Center Field
9—Right Field
DH—Designated Hitter

BALANCE YOUR BOX SCORE

AB	____	RUNS	____
BB	____	SCORE	
HP	____	OUTS	____
SAC	____		
INT	____	LOB	____
TOTALS	____	TOTALS	____

VISITOR	1	2	3	4	5	6	7	8	9	10	11	12	AB	R	H	RBI
SMITH 8	3-1				6-0			Ⓚ								1
RYNE SANDBERG 4	⑥		③	5-4-3	6-3	⑤3	6-3	6-3	3-1					1		
GRACE 3	3-1-9			2B	6-3	6-3										
DAWSON 9		5-0		1-B-F	4-3	4-3	6-3	6-3	6-3							
MAY 7		⑥		④	7	4-3	6-3							0		
BUECHELE 5		⑨			7		①		LINE 5							
WILKINS 2					W		5-0		4-6							
ARIAS 6			HR					3-1								
BOSKIE P			W		SAC											
DANIELS P																
TOTALS R H	0 0 0 0 1 1 0 0 0															
TOTALS E LOB	0 0 0 0 0 0 0 0 0															

PATTERSON P 3RD 8LO GYMB 6TH ASS EMBLER P 8

SCORING KEY

◇ Run Scored   ⬦ HR Home Run

⁖ Single   ⁘ Double   ⁙ Triple

K = Strikeout	DP = Double Play	Ӿ = Called 3rd Strike	# of Fielder plus "–"
W = Walk	SB = Stolen Base	IW = Intentional Walk	Unassisted Groundout
FC = Fielder's Choice	PB = Passed Ball	SAC = Sacrifice	# of Fielder "–" # of 2nd
CS = Caught Stealing	FO = Foul Out	SF = Sacrifice Fly	Fielder = Assisted
WP = Wild Pitch	HP = Hit by Pitch	# of Fielder = Flyout	Groundout

PIRATES	1	2	3	4	5	6	7	8	9	10	11	12	AB	R	H	RBI
COLE 9	out		4-3		8		out									
BELL 6	2		2B		7		1-3	5-0						1		
VAN DYKE 8	1B		5-0		1-3	2B		2B						1		
BONDS 7	HR	HR	W			9		2B						2	2	2
KING 5	B	out	1			4-3		1B								2
MERCED 3			8	1-3		HP		5-3								
LaVALLIERE		out		5		6-4		7						1	1	1
GARCIA 4		6		4-3			1-3									
DRABEK 1		1-3														
TOTALS R / H	2 / 1	0 / 0	1 / 2	0 / 0	0 / 0	0 / 0	0 / 0	0 / 1								
TOTALS E / LOB	0 / 0	0 / 0	0 / 1	0 / 0	0 / 0	0 / 0	0 / 0	0 / 0								

Winning Pitcher:

Losing Pitcher:

Home Runs:

Score by innings:

BALANCE YOUR BOX
SCORE

AB ___   RUNS ___
BB ___
HP ___   OUTS ___
SAC ___
INT ___   LOB ___

TOTALS ___   TOTALS ___

Highlights:

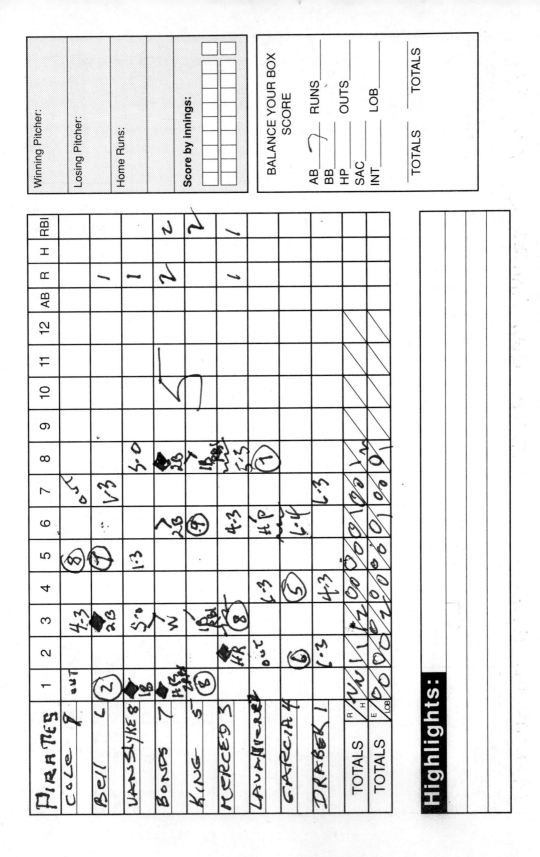

MONTREAL EXPOS vs. PITTSBURGH PIRATES   DATE: 9-16-92

Not shown 80-64
Expos 5-1
84-60 + 4 / 14
Climactic Series of the Season
Boog Buck Clinch

WHITE SOX

VISITOR	1	2	3	4	5	6	7	8	9	10	11	12	AB	R	H	RBI
SAX	4-3		4-3		4-3		4-3									
RAINES	1B			1B		W	L-3									
THOMAS	1			16		8										
BELL	7			7		8										
VENTURA		4-3		3-6		1B										
RASPUT		5-0		1		1										
JOHNSON		4-3		6-4		1B										
FISK			5-0		5-0 6-0											
BELTRE			3-0		6-8		4-3									

	R	1	2	3	4	5	6	7	8	9	10	11	12			
TOTALS	H	0	0	0	1	0	0	0								
TOTALS	E	0	0	0	0	0	0	0								
	LOB															

McDoWell

LEAGUE CHAMPIONSHIPS

National League Championship Series: Game 1

N.L. West Champs	1	2	3	4	5	6	7	8	9	10	11	12	AB	R	H	RBI

TOTALS R H

TOTALS E LOB

1990 Box Score

PITTSBURGH	ab	r	h	rbi
Backman, 3b	2	0	0	0
King, 3b	2	0	0	0
Bell, ss	3	0	0	0
Van Slyke, cf	4	0	0	1
Bonilla, rf	4	0	1	0
Bonds, lf	3	1	1	2
Bream, 1b	3	1	2	0
La Valliere, c	3	0	1	1
Lind, 2b	4	0	0	1
Walk, p	2	0	0	0
Redus, ph	1	0	1	0
Belinda, p	0	0	0	0
Reynolds, ph	1	0	0	0
Patterson, p	0	0	0	0
Power, p	0	0	0	0

CINCINNATI	ab	r	h	rbi
Larkin, ss	2	1	0	0
Hatcher, cf	3	0	1	0
Morris, 1b	3	0	1	1
Benzinger, ph	1	0	1	0
Davis, lf	3	0	1	1
O'Neill, rf	3	0	1	0
Oester, ph	1	0	1	0
Sabo, 3b	4	0	0	0
Reed, c	3	0	0	0
Duncan, 2b	3	0	0	0
Rijo, p	2	0	0	0
Charlton, p	0	0	0	0
Winningham, ph	1	0	0	0
Dibble, p	0	0	0	0

PITTSBURGH	IP	H	R	ER	BB	SO
Walk W, 1-0	6	4	3	3	2	5
Belinda	2	0	0	0	0	3
Patterson	1/3	1	0	0	1	0
Power S, 1	2/3	0	0	0	0	1

CINCINNATI	IP	H	R	ER	BB	SO
Rijo	5 1/3	4	3	1	2	8
Charlton L, 0-1	2 2/3	3	1	1	2	1
Dibble	1	0	0	0	0	3

E—Bonilla. DP—Cincinnati 1. LOB—Pittsburgh 6, Cincinnati 3. 2B—Van Slyke, Davis, O'Neill. 3B—Lind. HR—Bream (1). SB—Redus (1), Larkin (1). CS—Bates. S—Hatcher.

Pittsburgh	001 200 100—4
Cincinnati	300 000 000—3

BALANCE YOUR BOX SCORE

AB	_____	RUNS	_____
BB	_____	OUTS	_____
HP	_____		
SAC	_____	LOB	_____
INT	_____		

TOTALS _____   TOTALS _____

SCORING KEY

Single	Double	Triple	Home Run	Run Scored

K = Strikeout	DP = Double Play	⋉ = Called 3rd Strike	# of Fielder plus "·" = Unassisted Groundout
W = Walk	SB = Stolen Base	IW = Intentional Walk	# of Fielder "·" # of 2nd Fielder = Assisted Groundout
FC = Fielder's Choice	PB = Passed Ball	SAC = Sacrifice	
CS = Caught Stealing	FO = Foul Out	SF = Sacrifice Fly	
WP = Wild Pitch	HP = Hit by Pitch	# of Fielder = Flyout	

Winning Pitcher:

Losing Pitcher:

Home Runs:

Score by innings:

SINCE 1876
NATIONAL LEAGUE
OF PROFESSIONAL BASEBALL CLUBS
™

N.L. East Champs	1	2	3	4	5	6	7	8	9	10	11	12	AB	R	H	RBI
TOTALS	R															
	H															
TOTALS	E															
	LOB															

Highlights:

National League Championship Series: Game 2

1990 Box Score

PITTSBURGH	ab	r	h	rbi
Redus, 1b	2	0	1	0
Bream, 1b	1	0	0	0
Bell, ss	3	0	2	0
Van Slyke, cf	4	0	1	0
Bonilla, rf	4	0	0	0
Bonds, lf	0	0	0	0
King, 3b	3	0	0	0
Reynolds, rf	2	0	0	0
Slaught, c	3	0	0	0
Backman, ph	1	0	0	1
La Valliere, c	3	0	1	0
Lind, 2b	3	1	0	1
Drabek, p	3	0	0	0

CINCINNATI	ab	r	h	rbi
Larkin, ss	3	1	1	0
Winningham, cf	4	1	2	2
O'Neill, rf	4	0	2	0
Davis, lf	4	0	0	0
Morris, 1b	1	0	0	0
Sabo, 3b	3	0	0	0
Oliver, c	3	0	0	0
Duncan, 2b	3	0	0	0
Browning, p	2	0	0	0
Dibble, p	1	0	0	0
Myers, o	0	0	0	0

PITTSBURGH	IP	H	R	ER	BB	SO
Drabek L, 0-1	8	5	2	2	2	8

CINCINNATI	IP	H	R	ER	BB	SO
Browning W, 1–0	6	6	1	1	3	2
Dibble	1⅔	0	0	0	1	2
Myers S, 1	1⅓	0	0	0	1	0

DP—Cincinnati 1. LOB—Pittsburgh 7, Cincinnati 5. 2B—Winningham, O'Neill. HR—Lind (1). SB—Larkin (2), O'Neill (1), Winningham (1). CS—Redus.

Pittsburgh	000 010 000—1
Cincinnati	100 010 00x—2

N.L. West Champs

	1	2	3	4	5	6	7	8	9	10	11	12	AB	R	H	RBI

TOTALS — R / H

TOTALS — E / LOB

SCORING KEY

✓ Single   ⁝⁝ Double   ⟨⟩ Triple   ◇ Home Run   ◇ Run Scored

K = Strikeout	DP = Double Play	X = Called 3rd Strike	# of Fielder plus "·" = Unassisted Groundout
W = Walk	SB = Stolen Base	IW = Intentional Walk	# of Fielder "." # of 2nd Fielder = Assisted Groundout
FC = Fielder's Choice	PB = Passed Ball	SAC = Sacrifice	
CS = Caught Stealing	FO = Foul Out	SF = Sacrifice Fly	
WP = Wild Pitch	HP = Hit by Pitch	# of Fielder = Flyout	

BALANCE YOUR BOX SCORE

AB ___	RUNS ___
BB ___	OUTS ___
HP ___	LOB ___
SAC ___	
INT ___	
TOTALS ___	TOTALS ___

Winning Pitcher:

Losing Pitcher:

Home Runs:

Score by innings:

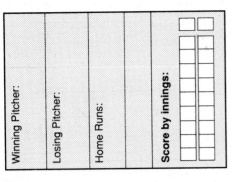

SINCE 1876
NATIONAL
LEAGUE
OF PROFESSIONAL BASEBALL CLUBS
™

N.L. East Champs	1	2	3	4	5	6	7	8	9	10	11	12	AB	R	H	RBI
TOTALS R / H																
TOTALS E / LOB																

Highlights:

National League Championship Series: Game 3

N.L. East Champs	1	2	3	4	5	6	7	8	9	10	11	12	AB	R	H	RBI
TOTALS R / H																
TOTALS E / LOB																

1990 Box Score

CINCINNATI

	ab	r	h	rbi
Larkin, ss	5	1	1	0
Duncan, 2b	5	1	3	4
Sabo, 3b	5	0	1	0
Davis, lf	4	0	1	0
Braggs, rf	4	0	1	0
Benzinger, 1b	4	1	2	0
Oliver, c	0	0	0	0
Bates, pr	0	0	0	0
Reed, c	4	0	3	0
Hatcher, cf	4	2	2	2
Jackson, p	1	0	0	0
Dibble, p	0	0	0	0
Charlton, p	1	0	1	0
Morris, ph	1	0	0	0
Myers, p	0	0	0	0

PITTSBURGH

	ab	r	h	rbi
King, 3b	5	0	2	0
Bell, ss	5	1	2	0
Van Slyke, cf	4	0	1	1
Bonilla, rf	3	0	1	0
Bonds, lf	4	1	1	1
Martinez, 1b	4	0	1	0
Slaught, c	2	0	1	0
Lind, 2b	4	0	0	0
Smith, p	2	0	0	0
Landrum, p	0	0	0	0
Redus, ph	1	0	0	0
Smiley, p	0	0	0	0
Reynolds, ph	1	0	0	0
Belinda, p	0	0	0	0

CINCINNATI

	IP	H	R	ER	BB	SO
Jackson W, 1–0	5⅓	7	2	2	3	4
Dibble	1⅓	1	0	0	1	1
Myers S, 2	1	0	1	0	0	3

PITTSBURGH

	IP	H	R	ER	BB	SO
Smith L, 0–1	5	8	5	0	0	5
Landrum	1	0	0	0	0	1
Smiley	2	2	0	0	0	0
Belinda	1	3	1	1	0	1

E—Duncan. DP—Pittsburgh 1. LOB—Cincinnati 6, Pittsburgh 9. 2B—Hatcher, Bell, Martinez, Slaught, Lind. HR—Hatcher (1), Duncan (1). S—Jackson.

Cincinnati	020 030 001	—6
Pittsburgh	000 200 010	—3

BALANCE YOUR BOX SCORE

AB ____	RUNS ____	
BB ____	OUTS ____	
HP ____	LOB ____	
SAC ____		
INT ____		
TOTALS ____	TOTALS ____	

SCORING KEY

Single	Double	Triple	Home Run	Run Scored

K = Strikeout	DP = Double Play	⅄ = Called 3rd Strike	# of Fielder plus "-" = Unassisted Groundout
W = Walk	SB = Stolen Base	IW = Intentional Walk	# of Fielder "·" # of 2nd
FC = Fielder's Choice	PB = Passed Ball	SAC = Sacrifice	Fielder "·" # of 2nd Fielder = Assisted Groundout
CS = Caught Stealing	FO = Foul Out	SF = Sacrifice Fly	
WP = Wild Pitch	HP = Hit by Pitch	# of Fielder = Flyout	

Winning Pitcher:

Losing Pitcher:

Home Runs:

Score by innings:

BALANCE YOUR BOX SCORE

AB ___ RUNS ___
BB ___ OUTS ___
HP ___ LOB ___
SAC ___
INT ___

TOTALS ___ TOTALS ___

SINCE 1876
NATIONAL
LEAGUE
OF PROFESSIONAL BASEBALL CLUBS
TM

N.L. West Champs	1	2	3	4	5	6	7	8	9	10	11	12	AB	R	H	RBI
TOTALS	R															
	H															
TOTALS	E															
	LOB															

Highlights:

National League Championship Series: Game 4

N.L. East Champs	1	2	3	4	5	6	7	8	9	10	11	12	AB	R	H	RBI

TOTALS R / H

TOTALS E / LOB

1990 Box Score

CINCINNATI	ab	r	h	rbi
Larkin, ss	5	0	0	0
Hatcher, cf	4	0	0	0
O'Neill, rf	4	1	3	1
Davis, lf	4	1	1	0
Morris, 1b	4	2	3	3
Sabo, 3b	3	1	2	0
Reed, c	3	0	0	0
Oliver, c	1	0	0	0
Duncan, 2b	3	0	1	0
Benzinger, ph	0	0	0	0
Oester, 2b	0	0	0	0
Rijo, p	3	0	0	0
Myers, p	0	0	0	0
Quinones, ph	0	0	0	1
Dibble, p	0	0	0	0

PITTSBURGH	ab	r	h	rbi
Backman, 3b	4	1	1	1
Bell, ss	4	1	1	1
Van Slyke, cf	3	0	1	0
Bonilla, rf	4	0	1	1
Bonds, lf	3	0	0	0
Bream, 1b	3	0	1	0
La Valliere, c	3	0	0	0
Lind, 2b	4	0	2	0
Walk, p	2	0	0	0
Reynolds, ph	0	0	0	0
Power, p	0	0	0	0
King, ph	1	0	0	0

CINCINNATI	IP	H	R	ER	BB	SO
Rijo W, 1–0	7	6	3	3	4	7
Myers	1	2	0	0	0	2
Dibble S, 1	1	0	0	0	0	2

PITTSBURGH	IP	H	R	ER	BB	SO
Walk L, 1–1	7	7	4	4	0	3
Power	2	3	1	1	1	2

E—Larkin. DP—Cincinnati 1, Pittsburgh 1. LOB—Cincinnati 5, Pittsburgh 6. 2B—O'Neill, Morris, Backman, Bonilla, Bream. HR—O'Neill (1), Sabo (1), Bell (1). SB—Backman (1), Van Slyke (1), Bonds (1). CS—Bonilla. SF—Sabo, Quinones.

Cincinnati	000 200 201—5
Pittsburgh	100 100 010—3

SCORING KEY

Single · Double · Triple · Home Run · Run Scored

K = Strikeout	DP = Double Play	Ӿ = Called 3rd Strike	# of Fielder plus "-" = Unassisted Groundout
W = Walk	SB = Stolen Base	IW = Intentional Walk	# of Fielder "-" # of 2nd Fielder = Assisted Groundout
FC = Fielder's Choice	PB = Passed Ball	SAC = Sacrifice	
CS = Caught Stealing	FO = Foul Out	SF = Sacrifice Fly	
WP = Wild Pitch	HP = Hit by Pitch	# of Fielder = Flyout	

BALANCE YOUR BOX SCORE

AB ____	RUNS ____
BB ____	OUTS ____
HP ____	LOB ____
SAC ____	
INT ____	
TOTALS ____	TOTALS ____

Winning Pitcher:

Losing Pitcher:

Home Runs:

Score by innings:

BALANCE YOUR BOX SCORE

AB	RUNS
BB	OUTS
HP	LOB
SAC	
INT	TOTALS
TOTALS	

SINCE 1876
NATIONAL
LEAGUE
OF PROFESSIONAL BASEBALL CLUBS
™

N.L. West Champs	1	2	3	4	5	6	7	8	9	10	11	12	AB	R	H	RBI
TOTALS	R												H			
TOTALS	E												LOB			

Highlights:

National League Championship Series: Game 5

N.L. East Champs	1	2	3	4	5	6	7	8	9	10	11	12	AB	R	H	RBI

TOTALS — R / H
TOTALS — E / LOB

1990 Box Score

CINCINNATI

CINCINNATI	ab	r	h	rbi
Larkin, ss	4	1	2	1
Winningham, cf	2	0	1	1
O'Neill, rf	4	0	1	0
Davis, lf	3	0	0	0
Morris, 1b	3	0	0	0
Sabo, 3b	2	0	1	0
Oliver, c	1	1	0	0
Oester, ph	1	0	1	0
Reed, c	1	0	0	0
Duncan, 2b	3	0	1	0
Browning, p	1	0	0	0
Benzinger, ph	1	0	0	1
Mahler, p	0	0	0	0
Charlton, p	0	0	0	0
Quinones, ph	1	0	0	0
Scudder, p	0	0	0	0

PITTSBURGH

PITTSBURGH	ab	r	h	rbi
Redus, 1b	3	0	0	0
Bream, 1b	1	0	1	0
Bell, ss	2	1	1	0
Van Slyke, cf	4	1	2	1
Bonilla, 3b	3	0	1	0
Bonds, lf	3	1	0	0
Reynolds, rf	4	0	2	1
Slaught, c	3	0	0	0
Lind, 2b	3	0	1	0
Drabek, p	3	0	0	0
Patterson, p	0	0	0	0

CINCINNATI	IP	H	R	ER	BB	SO
Browning L, 1–1	5	3	3	3	3	2
Mahler	1⅓	2	0	0	0	1
Charlton	⅓	1	0	0	0	0
Scudder	⅓	1	0	0	0	1

PITTSBURGH	IP	H	R	ER	BB	SO
Drabek W, 1–1	8⅓	7	2	1	1	5
Patterson S,1	⅔	0	0	1	1	0

E—Drabek. DP—Pittsburgh 2. LOB—Cincinnati 5, Pittsburgh 7. 2B—Larkin 2. 3B—Van Slyke. SB—Bonds (2), Reynolds (1). S—Morris. SF—Winningham, Slaught.

Cincinnati	100 000 010—2
Pittsburgh	200 100 00x—3

BALANCE YOUR BOX SCORE

AB ___		RUNS ___	
BB ___		OUTS ___	
HP ___		LOB ___	
SAC ___			
INT ___			
TOTALS ___		TOTALS ___	

SCORING KEY

Single / Double / Triple / Home Run / Run Scored

K = Strikeout	DP = Double Play	✕ = Called 3rd Strike
W = Walk	SB = Stolen Base	IW = Intentional Walk
FC = Fielder's Choice	PB = Passed Ball	SAC = Sacrifice
CS = Caught Stealing	FO = Foul Out	SF = Sacrifice Fly
WP = Wild Pitch	HP = Hit by Pitch	# of Fielder = Flyout

# of Fielder plus "-" = Unassisted Groundout
# of Fielder "-" # of 2nd Fielder = Assisted Groundout

Winning Pitcher:

Losing Pitcher:

Home Runs:

Score by innings:

BALANCE YOUR BOX SCORE

AB	RUNS
BB	OUTS
HP	LOB
SAC	
INT	
TOTALS	TOTALS

SINCE 1876
NATIONAL LEAGUE
OF PROFESSIONAL BASEBALL CLUBS
™

N.L. West Champs	1	2	3	4	5	6	7	8	9	10	11	12	AB	R	H	RBI
TOTALS	R												H			
TOTALS	E												LOB			

Highlights:

TUES. OCTOBER 13, 1992   BRAVES 3 BUCS 2 GAME

THE HOME TEAM

BRAVES 3 BUCS 2 GAME LEAD 1

National League Championship Series: Game 6

1990 Box Score

PITTSBURGH	ab	r	h	rbi
King, 3b	2	0	0	0
Reynolds, rf	1	0	0	0
Bell, ss	3	0	0	0
Van Slyke, cf	4	0	0	0
Bonilla, rf	3	1	1	0
Bonds, lf	4	0	0	0
Martinez, 1b	4	0	0	0
Slaught, c	3	0	0	0
Lind, 2b	1	0	0	0
Power, p	0	0	0	0
Smith, p	1	0	0	0
Belinda, p	1	0	0	0
Redus, ph	1	0	0	0
Landrum, p	0	0	0	0

CINCINNATI	ab	r	h	rbi
Larkin, ss	4	1	2	0
Hatcher, cf	4	0	2	0
O'Neill, rf	2	1	0	1
Quinones, ph	1	0	0	0
Myers, p	0	0	0	0
Davis, lf	4	0	1	0
Sabo, 3b	4	0	1	0
Benzinger, 1b	3	0	0	0
Duncan, 2b	3	0	0	0
Charlton, p	0	0	0	0
Braggs, rf	1	0	0	0
Oliver, c	2	0	1	0
Jackson, p	2	0	0	0
Oester, 2b	1	1	1	0

PITTSBURGH	IP	H	R	ER	BB	SO
Power	2⅓	3	1	1	1	0
Smith L,0-2	4	6	1	1	0	3
Belinda	⅓	1	0	0	0	0
Landrum	⅓	0	0	0	0	0

CINCINNATI	IP	H	R	ER	BB	SO
Jackson	6	1	1	1	4	4
Charlton W, 1-1	1	0	0	0	0	0
Myers S, 3	2	0	0	0	2	3

E—Slaught, Bell, Reynolds. LOB—Pittsburgh 6, Cincinnati 9. 2B—Martinez. SB—Larkin (3), Quinones (1), Davis. CS—Davis.

Pittsburgh	000 010 000—1	
Cincinnati	100 000 10x—2	

ATLANTA N.L. West Champs	1	2	3	4	5	6	7	8	9	10	11	12	AB	R	H	RBI
8 NIXON																
4 BLAUSER																
5 PENDLETON																
9 JUSTICE																
3 BREAM																
7 GANT																
2 BERRYHILL																
6 LEMKE																
1 GLAVINE																

TOTALS: R 0 0 0 0 1 0 0 0 0 — 1
H 0 0 0 1 2 0 0 1 0 — 3
E 0 0 0 0 0 0 0 0 0 — 0

LECRANDT PINCH FREEMAN P.H. MERCER P.8

SCORING KEY

K = Strikeout	✗ = Called 3rd Strike
W = Walk	IW = Intentional Walk
FC = Fielder's Choice	SAC = Sacrifice
CS = Caught Stealing	SF = Sacrifice Fly
WP = Wild Pitch	# of Fielder = Flyout

DP = Double Play	# of Fielder plus "." =
SB = Stolen Base	Unassisted Groundout
PB = Passed Ball	# of Fielder "." # of 2nd
FO = Foul Out	Fielder = Assisted
HP = Hit by Pitch	Groundout

◇ Single   Double   Triple   Home Run   Run Scored

BALANCE YOUR BOX SCORE

AB ___	RUNS ___
BB ___	OUTS ___
HP ___	LOB ___
SAC ___	
INT ___	

TOTALS ___   TOTALS ___   TOTALS ___

Winning Pitcher:

Losing Pitcher:

Home Runs:

Score by innings:

PIRATES

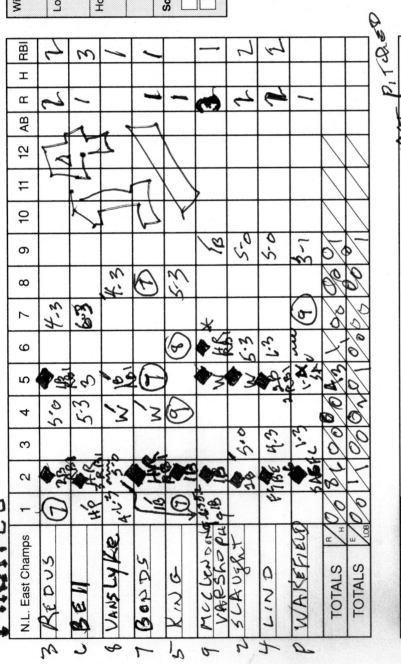

N.L. East Champs	1	2	3	4	5	6	7	8	9	10	11	12	AB	R	H	RBI
3 REDUS	⑦			5-0			4-3							2	2	2
6 BELL				5-3	3		6-3	4-3						1	1	3
8 VAN SLYKE	HR			W												1
7 BONDS	①			W	⑦	⑧	⑦								1	1
5 KING	⑦		5-0	⑨		6-3	5-3		1B					3		
9 McCLENDON / VARSHO PH /						HR			5-0					2	2	
2 SLAUGHT			4-3			1-3			5-0					1	1	2
4 LIND			1-3				⑨		3-1						1	1
P WAKEFIELD																
TOTALS	R 0 0	8	0 0	0 0	3	1	0 0	0 0	0 1							
TOTALS	E 0 0	1	0 0	0 0	0	0	0 5	0 0	0 1							

National League Championship Series: Game 7

N.L. West Champs	1	2	3	4	5	6	7	8	9	10	11	12	AB	R	H	RBI

TOTALS	R															
	H															
TOTALS	E															
	LOB															

SCORING KEY

Single   Double   Triple   Home Run   Run Scored

K = Strikeout	DP = Double Play	X = Called 3rd Strike	# of Fielder plus "•" =
W = Walk	SB = Stolen Base	IW = Intentional Walk	Unassisted Groundout
FC = Fielder's Choice	PB = Passed Ball	SAC = Sacrifice	# of Fielder "-" # of 2nd
CS = Caught Stealing	FO = Foul Out	SF = Sacrifice Fly	Fielder = Assisted
WP = Wild Pitch	HP = Hit by Pitch	# of Fielder = Flyout	Groundout

BALANCE YOUR BOX SCORE

AB	_____	RUNS	_____
BBs	_____	OUTS	_____
HP	_____	LOB	_____
SAC	_____		
INT	_____		
	TOTALS	_____	TOTALS	_____

Winning Pitcher:

Losing Pitcher:

Home Runs:

Score by innings:

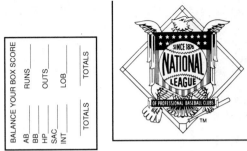

N.L. East Champs	1	2	3	4	5	6	7	8	9	10	11	12	AB	R	H	RBI
TOTALS (R/H)																
TOTALS (E/LOB)																

Highlights:

American League Championship Series: Game 1

A.L. East Champs

A.L. East Champs	1	2	3	4	5	6	7	8	9	10	11	12	AB	R	H	RBI

TOTALS — R / H / E / LOB

1990 Box Score

OAKLAND

OAKLAND	ab	r	h	rbi
Henderson, lf	5	1	1	3
McGee, cf	4	1	2	0
Canseco, rf	2	0	1	0
Baines, dh	3	0	1	0
Blankenship, dh	0	1	0	0
Lansford, 3b	5	1	3	2
Steinbach, c	3	1	3	1
McGwire, 1b	3	2	0	0
Weiss, ss	3	0	1	0
Gallego, 2b	1	0	1	1
Quirk, ph	0	0	0	0
Randolph, 2b	2	0	1	1

BOSTON

BOSTON	ab	r	h	rbi
Reed, 2b	3	0	0	0
Quintana, 1b	4	0	1	0
Boggs, 3b	4	0	1	1
Burks, cf	4	0	0	0
Greenwell, lf	4	0	1	0
Evans, dh	2	0	0	0
Brunansky, rf	3	0	1	0
Pena, c	3	0	0	0
Rivera, ss	2	1	1	0
Marshall, ph	1	0	0	0
Barrett, 2b	0	0	0	0

OAKLAND Pitching

OAKLAND	IP	H	R	ER	BB	SO
Stewart W, 1–0	8	4	1	1	1	3
Eckersley	1	1	0	0	0	0

BOSTON Pitching

BOSTON	IP	H	R	ER	BB	SO
Clemens	6	4	0	0	4	4
Andersen L, 0–1	1	2	2	1	0	0
Bolton	⅔	3	2	1	0	0
Gray	⅓	2	4	4	1	0
Lamp	⅓	4	4	2	0	0
Murphy	⅓	4	2	4	2	0

Oakland	000 000 117—9
Boston	000 100 000—1

E—Gray. DP—Oakland 1, Boston 1. Lob—Oakland 11, Boston 4. 2B—Lansford, Burks. HR—Boggs (1). SB—Canseco (1), Henderson (1), McGee (1). CS—Gallego. SF—Henderson, Canseco.

BALANCE YOUR BOX SCORE

AB ____	RUNS ____
BB ____	OUTS ____
HP ____	
SAC ____	LOB ____
INT ____	
TOTALS ____	TOTALS ____

SCORING KEY

Single · Double · Triple · Home Run · Run Scored

K = Strikeout	DP = Double Play
W = Walk	SB = Stolen Base
FC = Fielder's Choice	PB = Passed Ball
CS = Caught Stealing	FO = Foul Out
WP = Wild Pitch	HP = Hit by Pitch

X = Called 3rd Strike	# of Fielder = Flyout
IW = Intentional Walk	# of Fielder plus "–" = Unassisted Groundout
SAC = Sacrifice	# of Fielder "–" # of 2nd Fielder = Assisted Groundout
SF = Sacrifice Fly	

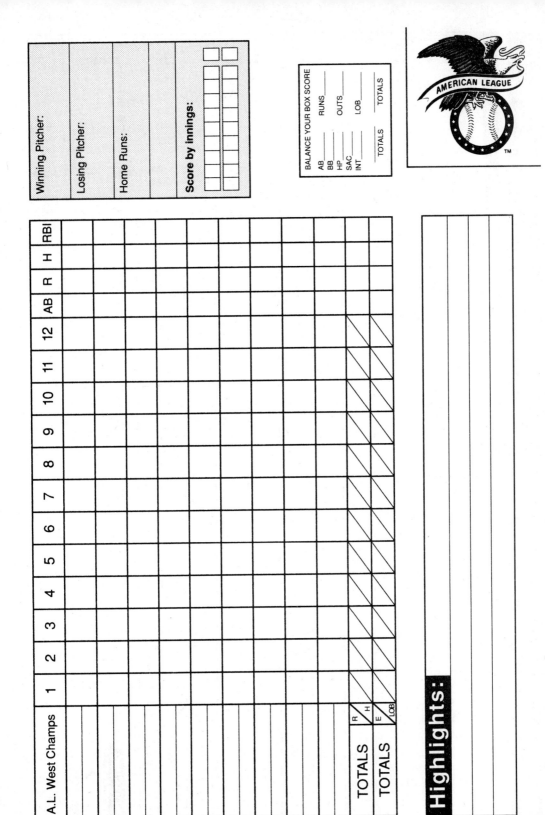

AMERICAN LEAGUE ™

Winning Pitcher:

Losing Pitcher:

Home Runs:

Score by innings:

BALANCE YOUR BOX SCORE

AB ___	RUNS ___
BB ___	OUTS ___
HP ___	LOB ___
SAC ___	
INT ___	
TOTALS ___	TOTALS ___

A.L. West Champs	1	2	3	4	5	6	7	8	9	10	11	12	AB	R	H	RBI
TOTALS													R	H	
TOTALS													E	LOB	

Highlights:

American League Championship Series: Game 2

1990 Box Score

OAKLAND	ab	r	h	rbi
Henderson, lf	5	1	1	0
McGee, cf	5	0	2	0
Canseco, rf	3	2	1	1
Baines, dh	5	1	2	3
Blankenship, dh	0	0	0	0
McGwire, 1b	5	0	2	1
Lansford, 3b	5	0	3	0
Hassey, c	4	0	1	0
Weiss, ss	4	0	0	0
Randolph, 2b	0	0	0	0
Gallego, 2b	3	0	1	0

BOSTON	ab	r	h	rbi
Reed, 2b	4	0	1	0
Quintana, 1b	3	0	1	0
Boggs, 3b	4	0	2	0
Burks, cf	3	0	1	0
Greenwell, lf	3	0	0	0
Evans, dh	4	0	1	0
Brunansky, rf	4	0	0	0
Pena, c	4	0	2	0
Rivera, ss	2	1	0	0
Marshall, ph	1	0	0	0
Barrett, 2b	1	0	0	0
Heep, ph	1	0	0	0

OAKLAND	IP	H	R	ER	BB	SO
Welch W, 1–0	7⅓	6	1	1	3	4
Honeycutt	⅓	0	0	0	0	0
Eckersley S, 1	1⅓	2	0	0	0	2

BOSTON	IP	H	R	ER	BB	SO
Kiecker	5⅔	6	1	1	1	2
Harris L, 0–1	⅓	3	1	1	0	0
Andersen	1	1	0	0	0	1
Reardon	2	3	2	2	1	0

E—Weiss. DP—Oakland 1; Boston 2. LOB—
Oakland 12, Boston 8. 2b—McGee, Baines,
Evans, Rivera. SB—McGee (2); Burks (1). SF—
Quintana.

Oakland	000 100 102—	4
Boston	001 000 000—	1

A.L. East Champs	1	2	3	4	5	6	7	8	9	10	11	12	AB	R	H	RBI

TOTALS	R														
	H														
TOTALS	E														LOB

AMERICAN LEAGUE

Winning Pitcher:

Losing Pitcher:

Home Runs:

Score by innings:

BALANCE YOUR BOX SCORE

AB	RUNS
BB	OUTS
HP	LOB
SAC	
INT	TOTALS
TOTALS	

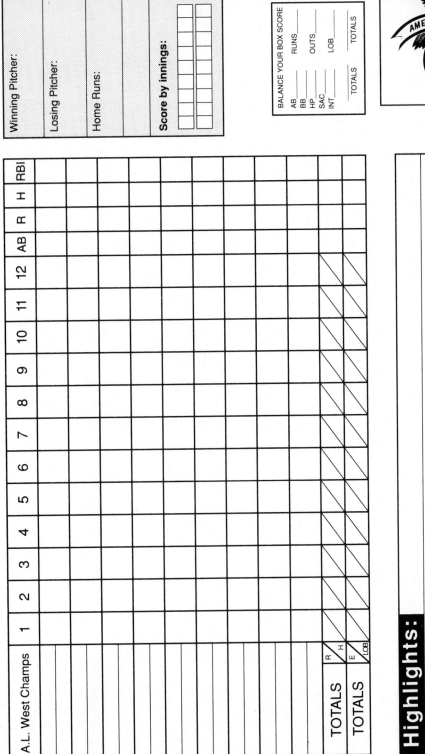

A.L. West Champs	1	2	3	4	5	6	7	8	9	10	11	12	AB	R	H	RBI

TOTALS R H

TOTALS E LOB

Highlights:

American League Championship Series: Game 3

A.L. West Champs	1	2	3	4	5	6	7	8	9	10	11	12	AB	R	H	RBI
TOTALS	R															
	H															
TOTALS	E															
	LOB															

1990 Box Score

BOSTON

	ab	r	h	rbi
Reed, 2b	4	0	0	0
Quintana, 1b	4	0	0	0
Boggs, 3b	4	0	2	0
Burks, cf	4	0	1	0
Greenwell, lf	4	1	1	0
Evans, dh	4	0	2	1
Brunansky, rf	4	0	3	0
Pena, c	4	0	0	0
Rivera, ss	2	0	0	0
Marshall, ph	1	0	0	0
Barrett, 2b	0	0	0	0
Heep, ph	1	0	0	0

OAKLAND

	ab	r	h	rbi
RHenderson, lf	4	1	1	0
Lansford, 3b	3	0	0	0
Canseco, rf	3	0	0	0
Baines, dh	3	0	1	1
McGwire, 1b	3	0	0	0
DHenderson, cf	2	1	0	1
Steinbach, c	3	1	0	0
Randolph, 2b	4	1	2	2
Gallego, ss	3	0	1	0

BOSTON	IP	H	R	ER	BB	SO
Boddicker L, 0-1	8	6	4	2	3	7

OAKLAND	IP	H	R	ER	BB	SO
Moore W, 1-0	6	4	1	1	1	5
Nelson	1⅔	3	0	0	0	0
Honeycutt	⅓	1	0	0	0	0
Eckersley S, 2	1	0	0	0	0	1

E—Boddicker, Rivera, Pena. DP—Boston 1. LOB—Boston 8, Oakland 7. 2B—Boggs. SB—Canseco (2), Baines (1), DHenderson (1). CS—Steinbach, RHenderson. S—Lansford. SF—Brunansky; DHenderson.

Boston	010 000 000—1
Oakland	000 202 00x—4

BALANCE YOUR BOX SCORE

AB ___		RUNS ___	
BB ___		OUTS ___	
HP ___		LOB ___	
SAC ___			
INT ___			
TOTALS ___		TOTALS ___	

SCORING KEY

Single	Double	Triple	Home Run	Run Scored

K = Strikeout	DP = Double Play	Ӿ = Called 3rd Strike	# of Fielder plus "-" =
W = Walk	SB = Stolen Base	IW = Intentional Walk	Unassisted Groundout
FC = Fielder's Choice	PB = Passed Ball	SAC = Sacrifice	# of Fielder "-" # of 2nd
CS = Caught Stealing	FO = Foul Out	SF = Sacrifice Fly	Fielder = Assisted
WP = Wild Pitch	HP = Hit by Pitch	# of Fielder = Flyout	Groundout

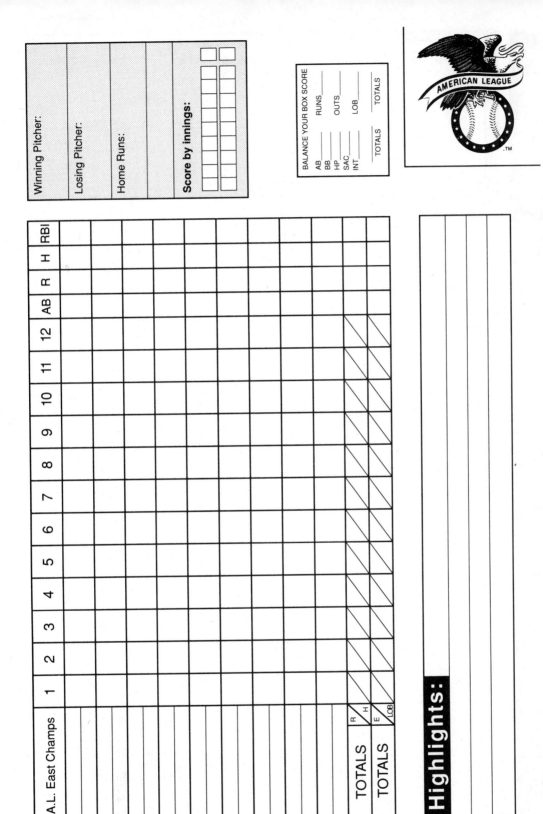

Winning Pitcher:

Losing Pitcher:

Home Runs:

Score by innings:

BALANCE YOUR BOX SCORE

AB		RUNS	
BB		OUTS	
HP		LOB	
SAC			
INT			
	TOTALS		TOTALS

AMERICAN LEAGUE .TM

A.L. East Champs	1	2	3	4	5	6	7	8	9	10	11	12	AB	R	H	RBI
TOTALS													R		H	
TOTALS													E		LOB	

Highlights:

American League Championship Series: Game 4

1990 Box Score

BOSTON

	ab	r	h	rbi
Burks, cf	4	0	1	0
Reed, 2b	4	0	1	0
Boggs, 3b	4	0	2	0
Greenwell, lf	4	0	0	0
Pena, c	3	0	0	0
Evans, dh	3	0	0	0
Brunansky, rf	2	0	0	0
Quintana, 1b	3	0	0	0
Rivera, ss	3	0	0	0

OAKLAND

	ab	r	h	rbi
RHenderson, lf	3	0	1	0
DHenderson, cf	4	0	0	0
Canseco, rf	1	0	0	0
Jennings, rf	1	0	0	0
Baines, dh	3	0	1	0
McGee, dh	0	0	0	0
Hassey, dh	0	0	0	0
Blankenship, dh	3	1	1	0
Lansford, 3b	3	0	1	1
Steinbach, c	2	1	1	0
McGwire, 1b	2	1	0	0
Randolph, 2b	3	0	2	1
Gallego, ss	2	0	1	2

BOSTON

	IP	H	R	ER	BB	SO
Clemens L,0-1	1⅔	3	3	3	1	0
Bolton	2⅔	2	0	0	2	3
Gray	2⅔	1	0	0	2	2
Andersen	1	0	0	0	1	2

OAKLAND

	IP	H	R	ER	BB	SO
Stewart W, 2-0	8	4	1	1	1	0
Honeycutt S, 1	1	0	0	0	1	0

E—Greenwell. DP—Boston 2, Oakland 1. LOB—
Boston 3, Oakland 5. 2B—Burks, Gallego. SB—
RHenderson (2), Blankenship (1). S—Lansford.

Boston	000	000	001—1
Oakland	030	000	00x—3

A.L. West Champs	1	2	3	4	5	6	7	8	9	10	11	12	AB	R	H	RBI

TOTALS — R / H
TOTALS — E / LOB

SCORING KEY

∕ Single ∕∕ Double ∕∕∕ Triple ◇ Home Run ◆ Run Scored

K = Strikeout	DP = Double Play
W = Walk	SB = Stolen Base
FC = Fielder's Choice	PB = Passed Ball
CS = Caught Stealing	FO = Foul Out
WP = Wild Pitch	HP = Hit by Pitch

⅄ = Called 3rd Strike	# of Fielder plus "·" =
IW = Intentional Walk	Unassisted Groundout
SAC = Sacrifice	# of Fielder "·" # of 2nd
SF = Sacrifice Fly	Fielder = Assisted
# of Fielder = Flyout	Groundout

BALANCE YOUR BOX SCORE

AB ____	RUNS ____
BB ____	OUTS ____
HP ____	
SAC ____	LOB ____
INT ____	
TOTALS ____	TOTALS ____

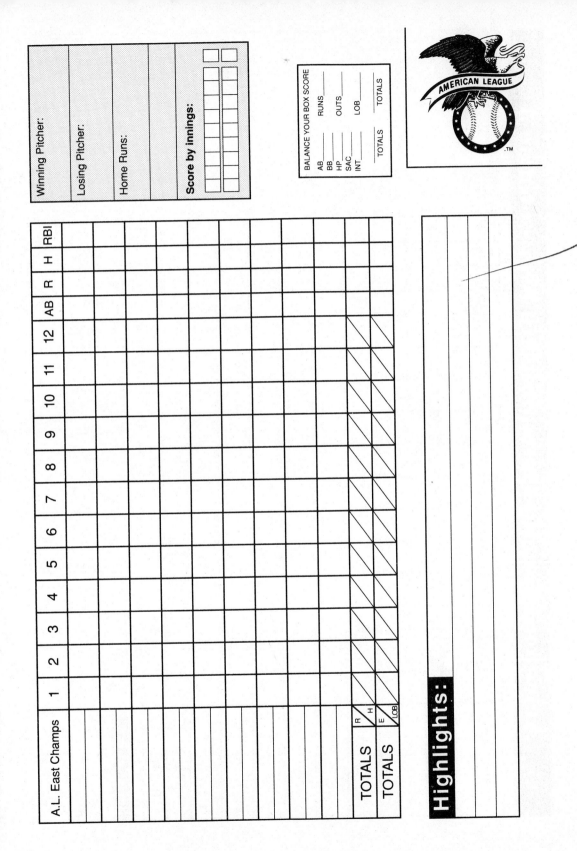

Winning Pitcher:

Losing Pitcher:

Home Runs:

Score by innings:

BALANCE YOUR BOX SCORE

AB _____   RUNS _____
BB _____   OUTS _____
HP _____   LOB _____
SAC _____
INT _____   TOTALS _____
TOTALS _____

AMERICAN LEAGUE .TM

A.L. East Champs	1	2	3	4	5	6	7	8	9	10	11	12	AB	R	H	RBI

TOTALS R H
TOTALS E LOB

Highlights:

American League Championship Series: Game 5

A.L. West Champs	1	2	3	4	5	6	7	8	9	10	11	12	AB	R	H	RBI
TOTALS	R															
	H															
TOTALS	E															
	LOB															

SCORING KEY

╱	Single
⟋⟍	Double
⟋⟍	Triple
◇ (HR)	Home Run
◇	Run Scored

K = Strikeout	DP = Double Play	Ӿ = Called 3rd Strike	# of Fielder plus "." =
W = Walk	SB = Stolen Base	IW = Intentional Walk	Unassisted Groundout
FC = Fielder's Choice	PB = Passed Ball	SAC = Sacrifice	# of Fielder "." # of 2nd
CS = Caught Stealing	FO = Foul Out	SF = Sacrifice Fly	Fielder = Assisted
WP = Wild Pitch	HP = Hit by Pitch	# of Fielder = Flyout	Groundout

BALANCE YOUR BOX SCORE

AB ____		RUNS ____	
BB ____		OUTS ____	
HP ____		SAC ____	
INT ____		LOB ____	
	TOTALS ____		TOTALS ____

AMERICAN LEAGUE ™

Score Sheet

| Winning Pitcher: |
| Losing Pitcher: |
| Home Runs: |
| Score by innings: |

BALANCE YOUR BOX SCORE

AB		RUNS	
BB		OUTS	
HP		LOB	
SAC			
INT			
	TOTALS		TOTALS

A.L. East Champs	1	2	3	4	5	6	7	8	9	10	11	12	AB	R	H	RBI
TOTALS	R															
	H															
TOTALS	E															
	LOB															

Highlights:

American League Championship Series: Game 6

A.L. East Champs	1	2	3	4	5	6	7	8	9	10	11	12	AB	R	H	RBI

| TOTALS | R | H |
| TOTALS | E | LOB |

SCORING KEY

⟋ Single ⟍ Double ⟋⟍ Triple ◇HR Home Run ◇ Run Scored

K = Strikeout	DP = Double Play	⊁ = Called 3rd Strike	# of Fielder plus "-" =
W = Walk	SB = Stolen Base	IW = Intentional Walk	Unassisted Groundout
FC = Fielder's Choice	PB = Passed Ball	SAC = Sacrifice	# of Fielder "-" # of 2nd
CS = Caught Stealing	FO = Foul Out	SF = Sacrifice Fly	Fielder = Assisted
WP = Wild Pitch	HP = Hit by Pitch	# of Fielder = Flyout	Groundout

BALANCE YOUR BOX SCORE

AB ____	RUNS ____
BB ____	
HP ____	OUTS ____
SAC ____	LOB ____
INT ____	
TOTALS ____	TOTALS ____

AMERICAN LEAGUE

Winning Pitcher:

Losing Pitcher:

Home Runs:

Score by innings:

BALANCE YOUR BOX SCORE

AB		RUNS	
BB		OUTS	
HP			
SAC		LOB	
INT			
TOTALS		TOTALS	

A.L. West Champs	1	2	3	4	5	6	7	8	9	10	11	12	AB	R	H	RBI
TOTALS													R	H		
TOTALS													E	LOB		

Highlights:

American League Championship Series: Game 7

A.L. East Champs	1	2	3	4	5	6	7	8	9	10	11	12	AB	R	H	RBI

TOTALS		R
TOTALS		H
		E
		LOB

SCORING KEY

Single ⟋ Double ⟍⟍ Triple ⟍⟍⟍ Home Run ◇HR Run Scored ◇

K = Strikeout	DP = Double Play	K = Called 3rd Strike	# of Fielder plus "." =
W = Walk	SB = Stolen Base	IW = Intentional Walk	Unassisted Groundout
FC = Fielder's Choice	PB = Passed Ball	SAC = Sacrifice	# of Fielder "." # of 2nd
CS = Caught Stealing	FO = Foul Out	SF = Sacrifice Fly	Fielder = Assisted
WP = Wild Pitch	HP = Hit by Pitch	# of Fielder = Flyout	Groundout

BALANCE YOUR BOX SCORE

AB _____   RUNS _____
BB _____   OUTS _____
HP _____   LOB _____
SAC _____
INT _____

TOTALS _____   TOTALS _____

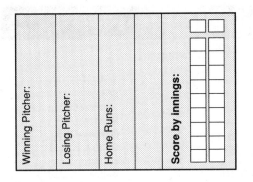

Winning Pitcher:

Losing Pitcher:

Home Runs:

Score by innings:

BALANCE YOUR BOX SCORE

AB	RUNS
BB	OUTS
HP	LOB
SAC	
INT	TOTALS
TOTALS	

AMERICAN LEAGUE

™

A.L. West Champs	1	2	3	4	5	6	7	8	9	10	11	12	AB	R	H	RBI
TOTALS	R															
	H															
TOTALS	E															
	LOB															

Highlights:

League Championship Series

COMPLETE RESULTS BY YEAR

NATIONAL LEAGUE

YEAR	WINNER	LOSER
1969	New York, East 3	Atlanta, West 0
1970	Cincinnati, West 3	Pittsburgh, East 0
1971	Pittsburgh, East, 3	San Francisco, West, 1
1972	Cincinnati, West, 3	Philadelphia, East, 2
1973	New York, East, 3	Cincinnati, West, 2
1974	Los Angeles, West, 3	Philadelphia, East, 1
1975	Cincinnati, West, 3	Philadelphia, East, 0
1976	Cincinnati, West, 3	Philadelphia, East, 0
1977	Los Angeles, West, 3	Philadelphia, East, 1
1978	Los Angeles, West, 3	Philadelphia, East, 1
1979	Philadelphia, East, 3	Cincinnati, West, 0
1980	Philadelphia, East, 3	Houston, West, 2
1981	Los Angeles, West, 3	Montreal, East, 2*
1982	St. Louis, East, 3	Atlanta, West, 0
1983	Philadelphia, East, 3	Los Angeles, West, 1
1984	San Diego, West, 3	Chicago, East, 2
1985	St. Louis, East, 4	Los Angeles, West, 2
1986	New York, East, 4	Houston, West, 2
1987	St. Louis, East, 4	San Francisco, West, 3
1988	Los Angeles, West, 4	New York, East, 3
1989	San Francisco, West,4	Chicago, East, 2
1990	Cincinnati, West, 4	Pittsburgh, East 2

AMERICAN LEAGUE

YEAR	WINNER	LOSER
1969	Baltimore, East, 3	Minnesota, West, 0
1970	Baltimore, East, 3	Minnesota, West, 0
1971	Baltimore, East, 3	Oakland, West, 3
1972	Oakland, West, 3	Detroit, East, 2
1973	Oakland, West, 3	Baltimore, East, 2
1974	Oakland, West, 3	Baltimore, East, 1
1975	Boston, East, 3	Oakland, West, 0
1976	New York, East, 3	Kansas City, West, 2
1977	New York, East, 3	Kansas City, West, 2
1978	New York, East, 3	Kansas City, West, 1
1979	Baltimore, East, 3	California, West, 1
1980	Kansas City, West, 3	New York, East, 0
1981	New York, East, 3	Oakland, West, 0*
1982	Milwaukee, East, 3	California, West, 2
1983	Baltimore, East, 3	Chicago, West, 1
1984	Detroit, East, 3	Kansas City, West, 0
1985	Kansas City, West, 4	Toronto, East, 3
1986	Boston, East, 4	California, West, 3
1987	Minnesota, West, 4	Detroit, East, 1
1988	Oakland, West, 4	Boston, East, 0
1989	Oakland, West, 4	Toronto, East, 1
1990	Oakland, West, 4	Boston, East, 0

*Eastern Division Series: Montreal 3; Philadelphia 2
Western Division Series: Los Angeles 3: Houston 2

Eastern Division Series: New York 3; Milwaukee 2
Western Division Series: Oakland 3, Kansas City 0

WORLD SERIES

World Series: Game 1

N.L. Champs	1	2	3	4	5	6	7	8	9	10	11	12	AB	R	H	RBI
TOTALS	R															
	H															
TOTALS	E															
	LOB															

1990 Box Score

OAKLAND	ab	r	h	rbi
RHenderson, lf	5	0	3	0
McGee, cf	5	0	1	0
Canseco, rf	2	0	0	0
McGwire, 1b	3	0	0	0
Lansford, 3b	4	0	2	0
Steinbach, c	4	0	1	0
Randolph, 2b	4	0	0	0
Gallego, ss	4	0	1	0
Stewart, p	1	0	0	1
Jennings, ph	1	0	1	0
Burns, p	0	0	0	0
Nelson, p	0	0	0	0
Hassey, ph	1	0	1	0
Sanderson, p	0	0	0	0
Eckersley, p	0	0	0	0
DHenderson, ph	1	0	0	0

CINCINNATI	ab	r	h	rbi
Larkin, ss	4	1	3	0
Hatcher, cf	3	3	3	1
O'Neill, rf	2	1	2	1
Davis, lf	4	1	2	3
Morris, 1b	3	0	0	0
Sabo, 3b	3	0	1	2
Oliver, c	4	0	0	0
Duncan, 2b	3	0	0	0
Rijo, p	3	0	0	0
Diblé, p	0	0	0	0
Benzinger, ph	1	0	1	0
Myers, p	0	0	0	0

OAKLAND	IP	H	R	ER	BB	SO
Stewart L, 0–1	4	3	4	4	4	3
Burns	⅔	3	3	3	1	0
Nelson	1⅓	2	0	0	1	0
Sanderson	1	1	0	0	0	0
Eckersley	1	0	1	0	0	1

CINCINNATI	IP	H	R	ER	BB	SO
Rijo W, 1–0	7	7	0	0	2	5
Diblé	1	0	0	0	1	0
MYERS	1	1	0	0	0	2

E—Gallego. DP—Oakland 2, Cincinnati 1. LOB—Oakland 11, Cincinnati 6. 2B—RHenderson 2, Hatcher 2. HR—Davis (1). SB—McGee (1), Lansford (1). CS—Sabo.

Oakland	000 000 000—0
Cincinnati	202 030 00x—7

BALANCE YOUR BOX SCORE

AB	____	RUNS	____
BB	____	OUTS	____
HP	____	LOB	____
SAC	____		
INT	____		
TOTALS	____	TOTALS	____

SCORING KEY

◇ Single   ◇ Double   ◇ Triple   ◇ Home Run   Run Scored

K = Strikeout	DP = Double Play	Ӿ = Called 3rd Strike
W = Walk	SB = Stolen Base	IW = Intentional Walk
FC = Fielder's Choice	PB = Passed Ball	SAC = Sacrifice
CS = Caught Stealing	FO = Foul Out	SF = Sacrifice Fly
WP = Wild Pitch	HP = Hit by Pitch	# of Fielder = Flyout

# of Fielder plus "·" = Unassisted Groundout
# of Fielder "·" # of 2nd Fielder = Assisted Groundout

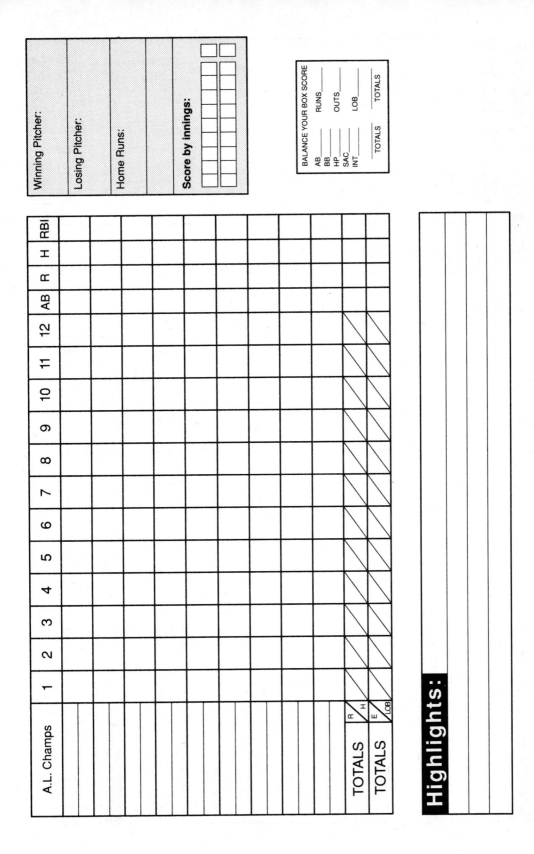

Winning Pitcher:

Losing Pitcher:

Home Runs:

Score by innings:

BALANCE YOUR BOX SCORE

AB _____	RUNS _____
BB _____	OUTS _____
HP _____	
SAC _____	LOB _____
INT _____	
_____ TOTALS	_____ TOTALS

A.L. Champs	1	2	3	4	5	6	7	8	9	10	11	12	AB	R	H	RBI
TOTALS	R															
	H															
TOTALS	E															
	LOB															

Highlights:

World Series: Game 2

N.L. Champs	1	2	3	4	5	6	7	8	9	10	11	12	AB	R	H	RBI

| TOTALS | R | H |
| TOTALS | E | LOB |

SCORING KEY

◇ Single ◇ Double ◇ Triple ◇ Home Run ● Run Scored

K = Strikeout	DP = Double Play	Ӿ = Called 3rd Strike	# of Fielder plus "." =
W = Walk	SB = Stolen Base	IW = Intentional Walk	Unassisted Groundout
FC = Fielder's Choice	PB = Passed Ball	SAC = Sacrifice	# of Fielder "." # of 2nd
CS = Caught Stealing	FO = Foul Out	SF = Sacrifice Fly	Fielder = Assisted
WP = Wild Pitch	HP = Hit by Pitch	# of Fielder = Flyout	Groundout

1990 Box Score

OAKLAND	ab	r	h	rbi
RHenderson, lf	4	0	1	0
Lansford, 3b	4	0	1	0
Canseco, rf	5	0	1	2
McGwire, 1b	4	0	1	0
DHenderson, cf	4	0	2	0
Steinbach, c	4	0	0	0
Randolph, 2b	4	0	2	0
Hassey, c	4	0	0	1
Bordick, ss	0	0	0	0
Gallego, ss	4	0	1	0
Baines, ph	1	0	0	0
Eckersley, p	0	0	0	0
Welch, p	3	0	0	0
Honeycutt, p	0	0	0	0
McGee, cf	0	0	0	0

CINCINNATI	ab	r	h	rbi
Larkin, ss	5	1	3	0
Hatcher, cf	4	2	4	1
O'Neill, rf	4	0	0	0
Davis, lf	3	0	0	1
Morris, 1b	3	1	0	0
Braggs, ph	0	0	0	1
Dibble, p	0	0	0	0
Bates, ph	1	1	1	0
Sabo, 3b	5	0	3	1
Oliver, 2b	3	1	2	0
Duncan, 2b	1	0	0	0
Jackson, p	2	0	1	0
Scudder, p	0	0	0	0
Oester, ph	1	0	0	0
Armstrong, p	0	0	0	0
Winningham, ph	1	0	1	0
Charlton, p	0	0	0	0
Benzinger, 1b	1	0	0	0

OAKLAND	IP	H	R	ER	BB	SO
Welch	7⅓	9	4	4	2	2
Honeycutt	1⅓	3	1	1	0	0
Eckersley L, 0–1	⅓	0	0	0	0	0

CINCINNATI	IP	H	R	ER	BB	SO
Jackson	2⅔	6	4	3	2	0
Scudder	1⅓	1	0	0	0	3
Armstrong	3	1	0	0	0	3
Charlton	1	0	0	0	0	0
Dibble W, 1–0	2	2	0	0	2	2

E—Hassey, McGwire; Jackson, Oliver. DP—Cincinnati 1. LOB—Oakland 10, Cincinnati 10. 2B—Larkin, Hatcher 2, Oliver. 3B—Hatcher. HR—Canseco (1). SB—RHenderson (1). S—Lansford, Welch. SF—Hassey.

| Oakland | 103 000 000 0—4 |
| Cincinnati | 200 100 010 1—5 |

BALANCE YOUR BOX SCORE

AB _____	RUNS _____
BB _____	
HP _____	OUTS _____
SAC _____	
INT _____	LOB _____
TOTALS _____	TOTALS _____

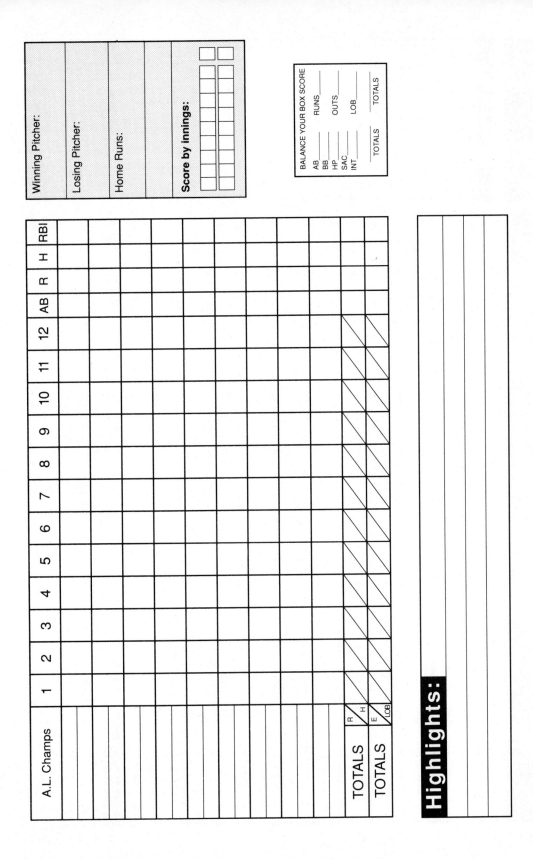

Winning Pitcher:

Losing Pitcher:

Home Runs:

Score by innings:

BALANCE YOUR BOX SCORE

AB _____ RUNS _____
BB _____ OUTS _____
HP _____ LOB _____
SAC _____
INT _____ TOTALS _____

TOTALS _____ TOTALS _____

A.L. Champs	1	2	3	4	5	6	7	8	9	10	11	12	AB	R	H	RBI
TOTALS R H																
TOTALS E LOB																

Highlights:

World Series: Game 3

A.L. Champs

A.L. Champs	1	2	3	4	5	6	7	8	9	10	11	12	AB	R	H	RBI

TOTALS: R __ H __
TOTALS: E __ LOB __

SCORING KEY

, Single ,, Double ,,, Triple ◇ Home Run Run Scored

K = Strikeout	DP = Double Play	☓ = Called 3rd Strike	# of Fielder plus "-" =
W = Walk	SB = Stolen Base	IW = Intentional Walk	Unassisted Groundout
FC = Fielder's Choice	PB = Passed Ball	SAC = Sacrifice	# of Fielder "-" # of 2nd
CS = Caught Stealing	FO = Foul Out	SF = Sacrifice Fly	Fielder = Assisted
WP = Wild Pitch	HP = Hit by Pitch	# of Fielder = Flyout	Groundout

1990 Box Score

CINCINNATI

	ab	r	h	rbi
Larkin, ss	5	0	2	1
Hatcher, cf	5	1	2	1
O'Neill, rf	3	1	1	0
Davis, lf	5	1	1	1
Morris, dh	4	0	2	0
Sabo, 3b	4	2	2	3
Benzinger, 1b	5	1	2	1
Oliver, c	5	1	2	1
Duncan, 2b	4	1	1	0
Browning, p	0	0	0	0
Dibble, p	0	0	0	0
Myers, p	0	0	0	0

OAKLAND

	ab	r	h	rbi
RHenderson, lf	3	1	1	1
Lansford, 3b	3	0	0	0
Canseco, rf	4	0	0	0
DHenderson, cf	4	1	1	2
Baines, dh	4	1	1	1
McGwire, 1b	4	0	1	0
Steinbach, c	4	0	3	0
Randolph	2	0	0	0
Gallego, ss	4	0	0	0
McGee, ph	1	0	0	0
Bordick, ss	0	0	0	0
Blankenship, ph	1	0	0	0
Moore, p	0	0	0	0
Sanderson, p	0	0	0	0
Klink, p	0	0	0	0
Nelson, p	0	0	0	0
Burns, p	0	0	0	0
Young, p	0	0	0	0

CINCINNATI	IP	H	R	ER	BB	SO
Browning W, 1-0	6	6	3	3	2	2
Dibble	$1\frac{2}{3}$	1	0	0	0	2
Myers	$1\frac{1}{3}$	1	0	0	0	1

OAKLAND	IP	H	R	ER	BB	SO
Moore L, 0-1	$2\frac{2}{3}$	8	6	2	2	1
Sanderson	$\frac{2}{3}$	3	2	2	1	0
Klink	0	1	0	0	1	0
Nelson	$3\frac{1}{3}$	0	0	0	1	0
Burns	1	1	0	0	0	0
Young	1	1	0	0	0	0

E—Oliver, McGwire. DP—Oakland 2. LOB—Cincinnati 9, Oakland 6. 2B—Oliver, DHenderson. 3B—Larkin. HR—Sabo 2 (2), Baines (1), RHenderson (1). SB—Duncan (1), O'Neill (1). RHenderson (2), Randolph (1).

Cincinnati	017 000 000—8
Oakland	021 000 000—3

BALANCE YOUR BOX SCORE

AB ___		RUNS ___	
BB ___		OUTS ___	
HP ___			
SAC ___		LOB ___	
INT ___			
TOTALS ___		TOTALS ___	

N.L. Champs	1	2	3	4	5	6	7	8	9	10	11	12	AB	R	H	RBI
TOTALS													R			
													H			
TOTALS													E			
													LOB			

Winning Pitcher:

Losing Pitcher:

Home Runs:

Score by innings:

BALANCE YOUR BOX SCORE

AB _____	RUNS _____
BB _____	OUTS _____
HP _____	
SAC _____	LOB _____
INT _____	
TOTALS	TOTALS

Highlights:

World Series: Game 4

1990 Box Score

CINCINNATI	ab	r	h	rbi
Larkin, ss	3	0	1	0
Hatcher, cf	3	1	2	0
Winningham, cf	3	0	0	0
O'Neill, rf	3	0	0	1
Davis, lf	0	0	0	0
Braggs, lf	3	0	0	1
Morris, dh	3	0	3	0
Sabo, 3b	4	0	0	0
Benzinger, 1b	4	0	1	0
Oliver, c	4	0	0	0
Duncan, 2b	4	0	0	0
Rijo, p	0	0	0	0
Myers, p	0	0	0	0

OAKLAND	ab	r	h	rbi
RHenderson, lf	4	1	1	0
McGee, rf	4	0	0	0
DHenderson, cf	2	0	1	0
Baines, dh	1	0	0	0
Canseco, dh	4	0	1	0
Lanford, 3b	4	0	0	0
Quirk, c	3	0	0	0
McGwire, 1b	3	0	0	0
Randolph, 2b	3	0	0	0
Gallego, ss	1	0	0	0
Hassey, ph	1	0	0	0
Bordick, ss	0	0	0	0
Stewart, p	0	0	0	0

CINCINNATI	IP	H	R	ER	BB	SO
Rijo W, 2–0	8⅓	2	1	1	3	9
Myers S, 1	⅔	0	0	0	0	0

OAKLAND	IP	H	R	ER	BB	SO
Stewart L, 0–2	9	7	2	1	2	2

E—Oliver; Stewart. DP—Oakland 1. LOB—Cincinnati 7, Oakland 4. 2B—Sabo, Oliver, McGee. SB—Gallego (1), RHenderson (3). CS—Hatcher. S—O'Neill. SF—Morris.

Cincinnati	000 000 020	—2
Oakland	100 000 000	—1

A.L. Champs

A.L. Champs	1	2	3	4	5	6	7	8	9	10	11	12	AB	R	H	RBI
TOTALS																
TOTALS																

R | H | E | LOB

SCORING KEY

Single ╱ Double ╲ Triple ⟩⟩ Home Run ◇ Run Scored ◇

K = Strikeout	DP = Double Play
W = Walk	SB = Stolen Base
FC = Fielder's Choice	PB = Passed Ball
CS = Caught Stealing	FO = Foul Out
WP = Wild Pitch	HP = Hit by Pitch

⋊ = Called 3rd Strike	# of Fielder plus "–" Unassisted Groundout
IW = Intentional Walk	# of Fielder "." # of 2nd
SAC = Sacrifice	Fielder = Assisted
SF = Sacrifice Fly	Groundout
# of Fielder = Flyout	

BALANCE YOUR BOX SCORE

AB ____		RUNS ____
BB ____		OUTS ____
HP ____		LOB ____
SAC ____		
INT ____		
TOTALS ____		TOTALS ____

| Winning Pitcher: |
| Losing Pitcher: |
| Home Runs: |
| **Score by innings:** |

BALANCE YOUR BOX SCORE

AB ___	RUNS ___
BB ___	OUTS ___
HP ___	
SAC ___	LOB ___
INT ___	
TOTALS ___	TOTALS ___

N.L. Champs	1	2	3	4	5	6	7	8	9	10	11	12	AB	R	H	RBI
TOTALS	R															
	H															
TOTALS	E															
	LOB															

Highlights:

World Series: Game 5

A.L. Champs	1	2	3	4	5	6	7	8	9	10	11	12	AB	R	H	RBI
TOTALS													R			
													H			
TOTALS													E			
													LOB			

SCORING KEY

Single   Double   Triple   Home Run   Run Scored

K = Strikeout	DP = Double Play
W = Walk	SB = Stolen Base
FC = Fielder's Choice	PB = Passed Ball
CS = Caught Stealing	FO = Foul Out
WP = Wild Pitch	HP = Hit by Pitch

Ʞ = Called 3rd Strike	# of Fielder plus "-" =
IW = Intentional Walk	Unassisted Groundout
SAC = Sacrifice	# of Fielder "-" # of 2nd
SF = Sacrifice Fly	Fielder = Assisted
# of Fielder = Flyout	Groundout

BALANCE YOUR BOX SCORE

AB _____		RUNS _____	
BB _____		OUTS _____	
HP _____		LOB _____	
SAC _____			
INT _____			
	TOTALS _____		TOTALS _____

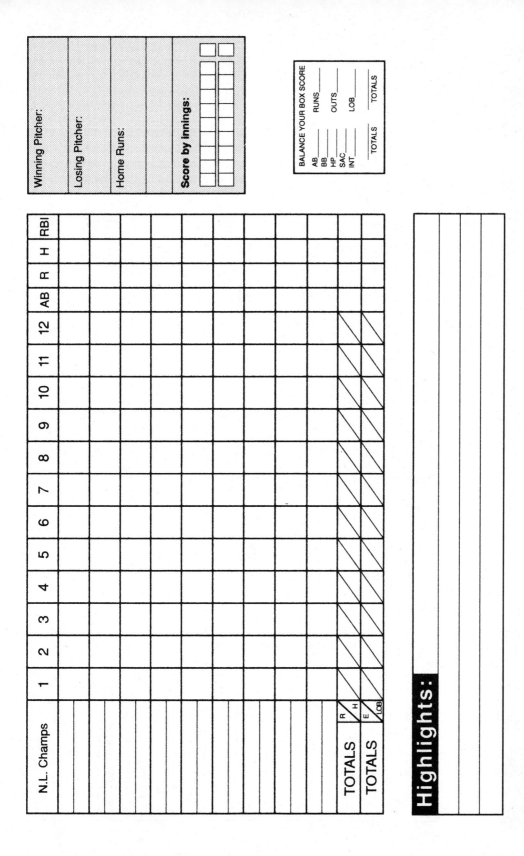

Winning Pitcher:

Losing Pitcher:

Home Runs:

Score by innings:

BALANCE YOUR BOX SCORE

AB _____ RUNS _____
BB _____ OUTS _____
HP _____
SAC _____ LOB _____
INT _____

_____ TOTALS _____ TOTALS
TOTALS TOTALS

N.L. Champs	1	2	3	4	5	6	7	8	9	10	11	12	AB	R	H	RBI
TOTALS	R															
	H															
TOTALS	E															
	LOB															

Highlights:

World Series: Game 6

N.L. Champs	1	2	3	4	5	6	7	8	9	10	11	12	AB	R	H	RBI

TOTALS	R															
	H															
TOTALS	E															
	LOB															

SCORING KEY

✓ Single	◇ Double	◇ Triple	◇ Home Run / Run Scored

K = Strikeout	DP = Double Play	Ϟ = Called 3rd Strike	# of Fielder plus "–" = Unassisted Groundout
W = Walk	SB = Stolen Base	IW = Intentional Walk	# of Fielder "–" # of 2nd Fielder = Assisted Groundout
FC = Fielder's Choice	PB = Passed Ball	SAC = Sacrifice	
CS = Caught Stealing	FO = Foul Out	SF = Sacrifice Fly	
WP = Wild Pitch	HP = Hit by Pitch	# of Fielder = Flyout	

BALANCE YOUR BOX SCORE

AB _____		RUNS _____	
BB _____		OUTS _____	
HP _____		LOB _____	
SAC _____			
INT _____			
	TOTALS		TOTALS

BALANCE YOUR BOX SCORE

AB		RUNS	
BB		OUTS	
HP			
SAC		LOB	
INT			
	TOTALS		TOTALS

A.L. Champs	1	2	3	4	5	6	7	8	9	10	11	12	AB	R	H	RBI
TOTALS	R															
	H															
TOTALS	E															
	LOB															

Highlights:

OCT 27 — 1991 —

PUCKETT HOMER IN 11th.
GIVES TWINS GAME SIX
4-3

World Series: Game 7

ATLANTA NL Champs BRAVES	1	2	3	4	5	6	7	8	9	10	11	12	AB	R	H	RBI
SMITH 2①	①		W 1		1B			1B		5-0						
PENDLETON 5 3		1B	⑦		⑥			2B		L-3						
GANT 8 5-0	5-0	5-0	6-4	6-0	5-0	3-1		3								
JUSTICE 9		1B		6-0		3-1		W								
BREAM 3		4-3		⑦		3		3-2-3	5-3							
HUNTER 7		5-0		2B	⑧		5-0		L-3							
OLSON 2		④		⑨												
LEMKE 4			4-3		1B		⑧		5-0							
BELLIARD 6 BLAUSER 0	1B HP	1B HP	1B HP	2-3AC.			5-0		②							
TOTALS	R	0	0	0	0	0	0	0	0	0	0					
TOTALS	H	0	0	0	0	0	0	0	0	0	0					
	E	0	0	6	0	2	1	2	0	3	0					
	LOB															

SMOLTZ P. 7⅓ 6H 4SO 1W
STANTON P 8 ⅔
PENA P 9

MINNESOTA

TWINS
A.L. Champs

Winning Pitcher:

Losing Pitcher:

Home Runs:

Score by innings:

BALANCE YOUR BOX SCORE

AB ___	RUNS ___
BB ___	OUTS ___
HP ___	
SAC ___	LOB ___
INT ___	
___ TOTALS	___ TOTALS

	1	2	3	4	5	6	7	8	9	10	11	12	AB	R	H	RBI
GLADDEN 7	5·0		2B					⑧		2B						
KNOBLAUCH 4	⑨	⑨	⑨		⑧			1B		SAC 5-3						
PUCKETT 6	1-3		5·0			W		W		W						
HERBEK 3		⑨		HP		⑧		④	DP-7	W						
LARKIN PH 10									1B							
DAVIS D		5·0		⑦	④	3U-7	5-3		1B	1B RBI						
BROWN PKG									1B							
HARPER 2		1B		⑨					1!							
MACK 9		1B		④			5-3		4U-3							
PAGLIARULO 5		3-1			④		5-3	7	W							
SORRENTO PH 9																
GAGNE 6			5-3		5·0			1B	5·0							
NEWMAN BUSH PH 8																
TOTALS	R 0	0	0	0	0	0	0	0	0	0	0	0				
	H 0	0	0	1	0	0	0	0	2	0	0	2				
TOTALS	E 0	0	0	0	0	0	0	0	0	0	0					

PR NEWMAN 5 5 GT
LOB
5 5 10

Highlights:

MORRIS P.

World Series

COMPLETE RESULTS BY YEAR

YEAR	WINNER	LOSER	YEAR	WINNER	LOSER
1903	Boston A.L., 5	Pittsburgh N.L., 3	1948	Cleveland A.L., 4	Boston N.L., 2
1905	New York N.L., 4	Philadelphia A.L., 1	1949	New York A.L., 4	Brooklyn N.L., 1
1906	Chicago A.L., 4	Chicago N.L., 2	1950	New York A.L., 4	Philadelphia N.L., 0
1907	Chicago N.L., 4	Detroit A.L., 1 tie	1951	New York A.L., 4	New York N.L., 2
1908	Chicago N.L., 4	Detroit A.L., 1	1952	New York A.L., 4	Brooklyn N.L., 3
1909	Pittsburgh A.L., 4	Detroit A.L., 3	1953	New York A.L., 4	Brooklyn N.L., 2
1910	Philadelphia A.L., 4	Chicago N.L., 1	1954	New York N.L., 4	Cleveland A.L., 0
1911	Philadelphia A.L., 4	New York N.L., 2	1955	Brooklyn N.L., 4	New York A.L., 3
1912	Boston A.L., 4	New York N.L., 3,1 tie	1956	New York A.L., 4	Brooklyn N.L., 3
1913	Philadelphia A.L., 4	New York N.L., 1	1957	Milwaukee N.L., 4	New York A.L., 3
1914	Boston New York 4	Philadelphia A.L., 0	1958	New York A.L., 4	Milwaukee N.L., 3
1915	Boston A.L., 4	Philadelphia N.L., 1	1959	Los Angeles N.L., 4	Chicago A.L., 2
1916	Boston A.L., 4	Brooklyn N.L., 1	1960	Pittsburgh N.L., 4	New York A.L., 3
1917	Chicago A.L., 4	New York N.L., 2	1961	New York A.L., 4	Cincinnati N.L., 1
1918	Boston A.L., 4	Chicago N.L., 2	1962	New York A.L., 4	San Francisco N.L., 3
1919	Cincinnati N.L., 5	Chicago A.L., 3	1963	Los Angeles N.L., 4	New York A.L., 0
1920	Cleveland A.L., 5	Brooklyn N.L., 2	1964	St. Louis N.L., 4	New York A.L., 3
1921	New York N.L., 5	New York A.L., 3	1965	Los Angeles N.L., 4	Minnesota A.L., 3
1922	New York N.L., 4	New York A.L., 1 tie	1966	Baltimore A.L., 4	Los Angeles N.L., 0
1923	New York A.L., 4	New York N.L., 2	1967	St. Louis N.L., 4	Boston A.L., 3
1924	Washington A.L., 4	New York N.L., 3	1968	Detroit A.L., 4	St. Louis N.L., 3
1925	Pittsburgh N.L., 4	Washington A.L., 3	1969	New York N.L., 4	Baltimore A.L., 1
1926	St. Louis N.L., 4	New York A.L., 3	1970	Baltimore A.L., 4	Cincinnati N.L., 1
1927	New York A.L., 4	Pittsburgh N.L., 0	1971	Pittsburgh N.L., 4	Baltimore A.L., 3
1928	New York A.L., 4	St. Louis N.L., 0	1972	Oakland A.L., 4	Cincinnati N.L., 3
1929	Philadelphia A.L., 4	Chicago N.L., 1	1973	Oakland A.L., 4	New York N.L., 3
1930	Philadelphia A.L., 4	St. Louis N.L., 2	1974	Oakland A.L., 4	Los Angeles N.L., 1
1931	St. Louis N.L., 4	Philadelphia A.L., 3	1975	Cincinnati N.L., 4	Boston A.L., 3
1932	New York A.L., 4	Chicago N.L., 0	1976	Cincinnati N.L., 4	New York A.L., 0
1933	New York N.L., 4	Washington A.L., 1	1977	New York A.L., 4	Los Angeles N.L., 2
1934	St. Louis N.L., 4	Detroit A.L., 3	1978	New York A.L., 4	Los Angeles N.L., 2
1935	Detroit A.L., 4	Chicago N.L., 2	1979	Pittsburgh N.L., 4	Baltimore A.L., 3
1936	New York A.L., 4	New York N.L., 2	1980	Philadelphia N.L., 4	Kansas City A.L., 2
1937	New York A.L., 4	New York N.L., 1	1981	Los Angeles N.L., 4	New York A.L., 2
1938	New York A.L., 4	Chicago N.L., 0	1982	St. Louis N.L., 4	Milwaukee A.L., 3
1939	New York A.L., 4	Cincinnati N.L., 0	1983	Baltimore A.L., 4	Philadelphia N.L., 1
1940	Cincinnati N.L., 4	Detroit A.L., 3	1984	Detroit A.L., 4	San Diego N.L., 1
1941	New York A.L., 4	Brooklyn N.L., 1	1985	Kansas City A.L., 4	St. Louis N.L., 3
1942	St. Louis N.L., 4	New York A.L., 1	1986	New York N.L., 4	Boston A.L., 3
1943	New York A.L., 4	St. Louis N.L., 1	1987	Minnesota A.L., 4	St. Louis N.L., 3
1944	St. Louis N.L., 4	St. Louis A.L., 2	1988	Los Angeles N.L., 4	Oakland A.L., 1
1945	Detroit A.L., 4	Chicago N.L., 3	1989	Oakland A.L., 4	San Francisco N.L., 0
1946	St. Louis N.L., 4	Boston A.L., 3	1990	Cincinnati, N.L., 4	Oakland, A.L. 0
1947	New York A.L., 4	Brooklyn N.L., 3			

Awards

MOST VALUABLE PLAYER

	AMERICAN LEAGUE	NATIONAL LEAGUE
Year	**Winner**	**Winner**
1980	George Brett, Kansas City, 3B	Mike Schmidt, Philadelphia, 3B
1981	Rollie Fingers, Milwaukee, P	Mike Schmidt, Philadelphia, 3B
1982	Robin Yount, Milwaukee, SS	Dale Murphy, Atlanta, OF
1983	Cal Ripken, Baltimore, SS	Dale Murphy, Atlanta, OF
1984	Willie Hernandez, Detroit, P	Ryne Sandberg, Chicago, 2B
1985	Don Mattingly, New York, 1B	Willie McGee, St. Louis, OF
1986	Roger Clemens, Boston, P	Mike Schmidt, Philadelphia, 3B
1987	George Bell, Toronto, OF	Andre Dawson, Chicago, OF
1988	Jose Canseco, Oakland, OF	Kirk Gibson, Los Angeles, OF
1989	Robin Yount, Milwaukee, OF	Kevin Mitchell, San Francisco, OF
1990	Rickey Henderson, Oakland, OF	Barry Bonds, Pittsburgh, OF
1991		

CY YOUNG

1980	Steve Stone, Baltimore	Steve Carlton, Philadelphia
1981	Rollie Fingers, Milwaukee	Fernando Valenzuela, Los Angeles
1982	Pete Vuckovich, Milwaukee	Steve Carlton, Philadelphia
1983	LaMarr Hoyt, Chicago	John Denny, Philadelphia
1984	Willie Hernandez, Detroit	Rick Sutcliffe, Chicago
1985	Bret Saberhagen, Kansas City	Dwight Gooden, New York
1986	Roger Clemens, Boston	Mike Scott, Houston
1987	Roger Clemens, Boston	Steve Bedrosian, Philadelphia
1988	Frank Viola, Minnesota	Orel Hershiser, Los Angeles
1989	Bret Saberhagen, Kansas City	Mark Davis, San Diego
1990	Bob Welch, Oakland	Doug Drabek, Pittsburgh
1991		

BASEBALL WRITERS' ASSOCIATION ROOKIE AWARDS

1980	Joe Charboneau, Cleveland, OF	Steve Howe, Los Angeles, P
1981	Dave Righetti, New York, P	Fernando Valenzuela, Los Angeles, P
1982	Cal Ripken, Baltimore, SS-3B	Steve Sax, Los Angeles, 2B
1983	Ron Kittle, Chicago, OF	Darryl Strawberry, New York, OF
1984	Alvin Davis, Seattle, 1B	Dwight Gooden, New York, P
1985	Ozzie Guillen, Chicago, OF	Vince Coleman, St. Louis, OF
1986	Jose Canseco, Oakland, OF	Todd Worrell, St. Louis, P
1987	Mark McGwire, Oakland, 1B	Benito Santiago, San Diego, C
1988	Walt Weiss, Oakland, SS	Chris Sabo, Cincinnati, 3B
1989	Gregg Olson, Baltimore, P	Jerome Walton, Chicago, OF
1990	Sandy Alomar, Cleveland, C	Dave Justice, Atlanta, OF
1991		

MANAGER OF THE YEAR

1983	Tony LaRussa, Chicago	Tommy Lasorda, Los Angeles
1984	Sparky Anderson, Detroit	Jim Frey, Chicago
1985	Bobby Cox, Toronto	Whitey Herzog, St. Louis
1986	John McNamara, Boston	Hal Lanier, Houston
1987	Sparky Anderson, Detroit	Buck Rogers, Montreal
1988	Tony LaRussa, Oakland	Tommy Lasorda, Los Angeles
1989	Frank Robinson, Baltimore	Don Zimmer, Chicago
1990	Jeff Torborg, Chicago	Jim Leyland, Pittsburgh
1991		